SOLID SEASONS

Solid Seasons

THE FRIENDSHIP OF
HENRY DAVID THOREAU AND
RALPH WALDO EMERSON

Jeffrey S. Cramer

COUNTERPOINT
Berkeley, California

Solid Seasons

Images courtesy of the Walden Woods Project

Library of Congress Cataloging-in-Publication Data
Names: Cramer, Jeffrey S., 1955– author.
Title: Solid seasons : the friendship of Henry David Thoreau and
    Ralph Waldo Emerson / Jeffrey S. Cramer.
Description: First hardcover edition. | Berkeley, California :
    Counterpoint, 2019. | Includes bibliographical references.
Identifiers: LCCN 2018045435 | ISBN 9781640091313
Subjects: LCSH: Thoreau, Henry David, 1817–1862—Friends and
    associates. | Emerson, Ralph Waldo, 1803–1882—Friends and
    associates. | Authors, American—19th century—Biography. |
    Friendship—United States—History—19th century.
Classification: LCC PS3053 .C83 2019 | DDC 818/.309 [B]—dc23
LC record available at https://lccn.loc.gov/2018045435

Jacket design by Sarah Brody
Book design by Jordan Koluch

COUNTERPOINT
2560 Ninth Street, Suite 318
Berkeley, CA 94710
www.counterpointpress.com

Printed in the United States of America
Distributed by Publishers Group West

10 9 8 7 6 5 4 3 2 1

To friends—
past, present, and future

Every man passes his life in the search after friendship.

—RALPH WALDO EMERSON,
Journal, February 3, 1840

No word is oftener on the lips of men than Friendship.

—HENRY DAVID THOREAU,
A Week on the Concord and Merrimack Rivers

Contents

Foreword

I read John Lehmann's *Three Literary Friendships* in 1984. It explores the relationships of Lord Byron and Percy Bysshe Shelley, Arthur Rimbaud and Paul Verlaine, and, the reason I bought the book at the time, Robert Frost and Edward Thomas. Literary friendships have always intrigued me. Public lives as expressed through their shared writings give us one portrait; personal lives through their private writings give another. The questions for me are how may the two be reconciled, and how does the theme of friendship inform their writings?

To begin work on this book, I placed contemporary accounts—journal passages, letters, documents, etc.—of both subjects together, making visible some relational patterns that might otherwise have been overlooked. Combining public and private records allowed me to trace the intricacies and intimacies of their friendship. It was a relationship not only deeply integral to both men on a personal level but also important to the history of American thought and letters. Any biography that concentrates on either Thoreau *or* Emerson tends to diminish the other figure because that person is, by the nature of biography, secondary. In this book, both men remain central and equal.

It is my hope that their friendship may be seen in a new light and that I did not become the "great inquisitor" Emerson described in "The Method of Nature" who merely attempts to bore an Artesian well through our conventions and theories, and pierce to the core of things. But as soon as he probes the crust, behold gimlet, plumb-line, and philosopher take a lateral direction, in spite of all resistance, as if some strong wind took everything off its feet, and if you come month after month to see what progress our reformer has made,—not an inch has he pierced,—you still find him with new words in the old place, floating about in new parts of the same old vein or crust.

It was essential to find the truth of their friendship and not simply present the "same old vein or crust" by relying on myths that have been perpetuated or stories that have remained incomplete because they appeared more dramatic that way. In order to do that, I did not rely on any story told in previous biographies or critical works. I traced stories back, whenever possible, in an attempt to find out if there was a reliable source, and to not merely repeat what had been told before.

Part I of *Solid Seasons* tells the story of their friendship; Parts II and III let the two friends speak for themselves about friendship generally and about each other specifically; the book concludes with Emerson's biographical sketch of Thoreau, an expanded version of the eulogy he delivered at Thoreau's funeral.

No biography is definitive; no examination of a life is complete. "I know better than to claim any completeness for my picture," Emerson wrote in "Experience." I have chosen to concentrate on decisive moments and events—and not detail every walk, every conversation these friends shared together—to offer, in *Solid Seasons*, a new view of an old story: the meaning of friendship. The essence of friendship,

Emerson said, was "entireness, a total magnanimity and trust." Thoreau defined it as the "unspeakable joy and blessing that results to two or more individuals who from constitution sympathize."

PART I

Solid Seasons

A Biography of the Friendship
of Henry David Thoreau
and Ralph Waldo Emerson

I . . . have had what the Quakers call "a solid season," once or twice.

—RALPH WALDO EMERSON,
to Henry David Thoreau, February 1843

There was one other with whom I had "solid seasons," long to be remembered, at his house in the village . . .

—HENRY DAVID THOREAU,
Walden

When Ralph Waldo Emerson moved to Concord, Massachusetts, in October 1834, he was thirty-one years old and boarding with his step-grandfather in the Old Manse. His first wife had died from tuberculosis. He had travelled to Europe where he met Thomas Carlyle, William Wordsworth, and Samuel Taylor Coleridge. He had begun to give public lectures. When he moved into his own home, Bush, the following year, he was remarried, financially independent, and about to have his first book, *Nature*, published. That same year the seventeen-year-old Concord-born Henry David Thoreau was attending Harvard College.

Stories vary as to how and when they met, but one story Emerson told is this:

> My first intimacy with Henry began after his graduation in 1837. Mrs. Brown, Mrs. Emerson's sister from Plymouth, then boarded with Mrs. Thoreau and her children in the Parkman house, where the Library now stands, and saw the young people every day. She would bring me verses of Henry's,—the "Sic Vita," for instance, which he had thrown into Mrs. Brown's window, tied round a bunch of violets gathered in his walk,—and once a passage out of his Journal, which he had read to Sophia Thoreau, who spoke of it to Mrs. Brown as resembling a passage in one of my Concord lectures.[1]

Emerson was generous with both time and money, and his assistance to the young Thoreau was no exception. Emerson loaned Thoreau money in May to travel to Maine to look for a teaching position, accompanied by his personal recommendation: "I cordially recommend Mr. Henry D. Thoreau, a graduate of Harvard University in August, 1837, to the confidence of such parents or guardians as may propose to employ him as an instructor. I have the highest confidence in Mr. Thoreau's moral, character and in his intellectual ability. He is an excellent scholar, a man of energy and kindness, and I shall esteem the town fortunate that secures his services."[2] He also wrote to Josiah Quincy, president of Harvard College, trying to secure some financial aid for Thoreau by attributing his lower academic standing to illness rather than any other cause.

Thoreau's interest in Emerson was also increasing. Having borrowed and read Emerson's *Nature* from the college library twice while attending Harvard, he purchased a copy to give to his classmate William Allen, calling it, in an echo of Robert Burns's "Epistle to a Young Friend," "neither a sang nor a sermon."[3] He sang Emerson's "Concord Hymn" in the choir at the dedication of the Obelisk at Concord's North Bridge in July 1837. And then on August 31 Emerson delivered the Phi Beta Kappa address to Thoreau's graduating class at Harvard. "The American Scholar" was hailed by Oliver Wendell Holmes as America's "intellectual Declaration of Independence."[4] It spoke of and to "Man Thinking," not an intellectual and academic cerebration, but a thinking with the entirety of soul and self-trust, culminating in the triad, "We will walk on our own feet; we will work with our own hands; we will speak our own minds."[5]

At the time of his graduation, Thoreau was not yet keeping a journal, so his immediate reaction to his Harvard commencement is not known, but when he gave his first public lecture the following spring in Concord, he revisited the memory: "One goes to a cattle-show expecting to find many men and women assembled, and beholds only working oxen and neat cattle. He goes to a commencement thinking that there at least he may find the men of the country; but such, if there were any, are completely merged in the day, and have become so many walking commencements, so that he is fain to take himself out of sight and hearing of the orator, lest he lose his own identity in the nonentities around him."[6]

Whether he felt himself losing his identity at his commencement, or whether this was in reaction to or in fear of his falling into the pull of Emerson's orbit, it was something with which Emerson would agree, and which he made explicit in his address: "I had better never see a book than to be warped by its attraction clean out of my own orbit, and made a satellite instead of a system. The one thing in the world, of value, is the active soul."[7]

Friends and followers came to Concord to meet with Emerson, often commenting on Thoreau as an Emerson wannabe. Among those present in July 1838 was James Russell Lowell, briefly suspended from Harvard, who found it "exquisitely amusing" to see how Thoreau "imitates Emerson's tone and manner. With my eyes shut I shouldn't know them apart."[8] A decade later Lowell was even more stringently satirical in *A Fable for Critics*, in which he wrote,

> There comes ——, for instance; to see him's rare sport,
> Tread in Emerson's tracks with legs painfully short;
> How he jumps, how he strains, and gets red in the face,
> To keep step with the mystagogue's natural pace!

He follows as close as a stick to a rocket,

His fingers exploring the prophet's each pocket.

Fie, for shame, brother bard; with good fruit of your
own,

Can't you let neighbor Emerson's orchards alone?[9]

But Lowell wasn't alone in seeing Thoreau adopting Emersonian characteristics. David Haskins Greene, Thoreau's Harvard classmate, was

quite startled by the transformation that had taken place in him. His short figure and general caste of countenance were, of course, unchanged; but in his manners, in the tones and inflections of his voice, in his modes of expression, even in the hesitations and pauses of his speech, he had become the counterpart of Mr. Emerson. Mr. Thoreau's college voice bore no resemblance to Mr. Emerson's, and was so familiar to my ear that I could readily have identified him by it in the dark. I was so much struck with the change, and with the resemblance in the respects referred to between Mr. Emerson and Mr. Thoreau, that I remember to have taken the opportunity as they sat near together, talking, of listening to their conversation with closed eyes, and to have been unable to determine with certainty which was speaking. It was a notable instance of unconscious imitation.[10]

Frank Sanborn, educator, reformer, and journalist, shortly after his move to Concord in 1853 dismissed Thoreau as "a sort of pocket edition of Mr. Emerson, as far as outward appearance goes, in coarser binding and with woodcuts instead of the fine steel-engravings of Mr. Emerson. He is a little under size, with a huge Emersonian nose . . . He dresses very plainly, wears his collar turned over like Mr. Emerson. . . . He talks like Mr. Emerson and so spoils the good things which he says; for what in Mr. Emerson is charming, becomes ludicrous in Thoreau, because an imitation."[11] One journalist, on hearing his talk on "White Beans and Walden Pond," thought Thoreau "might very probably attain to a more respectable rank, if he were satisfied to be himself, Henry D. Thoreau, and not aim to be Ralph Waldo Emerson or any body else."[12]

If this was something Emerson himself recognized in the early days of their friendship—"I am very familiar with all his thoughts,—they are my own quite originally drest."[13]—he soon became exasperated by the comparison which would persist long after Thoreau's death. Emerson defended his friend: "I am sure he is entitled to stand quite alone on his proper merits. There might easily have been a little influence from his neighbors on his first writings: He was not quite out of college, I believe, when I first saw him: but it is long since I, and I think all who knew him, felt that he was the most independent of men in thought and in action."[14] Emerson had no patience for narrow views of Thoreau. "Now and then I come across a man that scoffs at Thoreau," he told Pendleton King in 1870, "and thinks him affected. For example, Mr. James Russell Lowell is constantly making flings at him. I have tried to show him that Thoreau did things that no one could have done without high powers; but to no purpose."[15]

Thoreau's mother also saw a resemblance, although with a more maternal reference—"How much Mr. Emerson does talk like my Henry."[16]

Emerson and Thoreau would take long walks together, boat on the river, have discussions alone or with others in Emerson's circle in Emerson's study or around the dinner table with family. On October 22, 1837, during one of their many exchanges, Emerson tried to think of people who kept journals. He could only name the French essayist Michel de Montaigne, his neighbor Amos Bronson Alcott, his aunt Mary Moody Emerson, and himself. "Beside these," he wrote the next day, "I did not last night think of another."[17] It was at this time that he asked Thoreau the question that became the first entry in Thoreau's two-million-word journal: "'What are you doing now?' he asked. 'Do you keep a journal?' So I make my first entry to-day."[18]

The journal, for both writers, was an integral part of their process. Thoreau's journal contains around two million words, Emerson's over three million. For both men, journals were the work of a lifetime but not their life's work. They laid the groundwork for the lectures and essays and books that were to follow. When Thoreau and Emerson combed their journals for material, it mattered little when, where, or even what circumstance had prompted an entry, as long as the text reflected the theme of what they were currently writing. "It is surely foolish," Emerson expressed in his journal, "to adhere rigidly to the order of time in putting down one's thoughts, and to neglect the order of thought. I put like things together."[19]

Emerson considered his journal his "Savings Bank. I grow richer because I have somewhere to deposit my earnings; and fractions are worth more to me because corresponding fractions are waiting here that shall be made integers by their addition."[20] It was similar for Thoreau. "Each thought that is welcomed and recorded is a nest egg," he wrote, "by the side of which more will be laid. Thoughts accidentally thrown together become a frame in which more may be developed and exhibited. Perhaps this is the main value of a habit of writing, of keeping a journal,—that so we remember our best hours and stimulate ourselves."[21]

Their work habits, however, were quite different.

Emerson wrote that Thoreau "knew but one secret, which was to do one thing at a time, and though he has his evenings for study, if he was in the day inventing machines for sawing his plumbago, he invents wheels all the evening and night also; and if this week he has some good reading and thoughts before him, his brain runs on that all day, whilst pencils pass through his hands." Emerson found in himself "an opposite facility or perversity, that I never seem well to do a particular work until another is due. I cannot write the poem, though you give me a week, but if I promise to read a lecture the day after to-morrow, at once the poem comes into my head and now the rhymes will flow. And let the proofs of the *Dial* be crowding on me from the printer, and I am full of faculty how to make the lecture."[22]

At the end of 1837 Lidian Emerson wrote that her husband had "taken to Henry with great interest," finding him uncommon "in mind and character."[23] It was these moments of uncommonness and originality, mixed with Thoreau's contrariness, that often interested Emerson.

At the "teacher's meeting" last night, my good Edmund Hosmer, after disclaiming any wish to difference Jesus from a human mind, suddenly seemed to alter his tone, and said that Jesus made the world and was the Eternal God. Henry Thoreau merely remarked that "Mr. Hosmer had kicked the pail over." I delight much in my young friend, who seems to have as free and erect a mind as any I have ever met. He told as we walked this afternoon a good story about a boy who went to school with him, Wentworth, who resisted the school mistress's command that the children should bow to Dr. Heywood and other gentlemen as they went by, and when Dr. Heywood stood waiting and cleared his throat with a Hem, Wentworth said, "You need n't hem, Doctor. I shan't bow."[24]

In December 1837 Emerson shared a discovery with Thoreau. The previous year he had "found a new musical instrument which I call the ice-harp. A thin coat of ice covered a part of the pond, but melted around the edge of the shore. I threw a stone upon the ice which rebounded with a shrill sound, and falling again and again, repeated the note with pleasing modulation. I thought at first it was the 'peep, peep' of a bird I had scared. I was so taken with the music that I threw down my stick and spent twenty minutes in throwing stones single or in handfuls on this crystal drum."[25] "My friend tells me," Thoreau wrote, "he has discovered a new note in nature, which he calls the Ice-Harp."[26]

In the following spring Thoreau described their friendship.

> Two sturdy oaks I mean, which side by side
>   Withstand the winter's storm,
>   And, spite of wind and tide,
>   Grow up the meadow's pride,
>   For both are strong.

> Above they barely touch, but, undermined
>   Down to their deepest source,
>   Admiring you shall find
>   Their roots are intertwined
>   Insep'rably.[27]

Comments *about* Emerson began to appear in Thoreau's journal, but Emerson's journal began to hold statements and stories *by* Thoreau, some of which Thoreau would include later in his own writings, such as the "good story" Emerson noted in September 1838 about Deacon Parkman "who lived in the house he now occupies, and kept a store close by. He hung out a salt fish for a sign, and it hung so long and grew so hard, black and deformed, that the deacon forgot what thing it was, and nobody in town knew, but being examined chemically it proved to be salt fish. But duly every morning the deacon hung it on its peg."[28] A decade later this story would be incorporated into *Walden*.

Even in the early years of the friendship, there were times when the assumed roles of Emerson as mentor and Thoreau as student were inverted. Their influence was, from the very beginning, mutual. Emerson recognized that "our receptivity is unlimited; and, with the great, our thoughts and manners easily become great."[29] Things Thoreau said or did would impress Emerson to the point that they would find their way into his work, from early essays written shortly after they met to those written after Thoreau's death. As he confessed to his journal, "Have I said it before in these pages? then I will say it again, that it is a curious commentary on society that the expression of a devout sentiment by any young man who lives in society strikes me with surprise and has all the air and effect of genius."[30] One such moment came as he thought of his "brave Henry here who is content to live now, and feels no shame in not studying any profession, for he does not postpone his life, but lives already,—pours contempt on these crybabies of routine and Boston. He has not one chance but a hundred chances."[31] Thoreau's ideas inform the writing of Emerson's seminal essay, "Self-Reliance": "He walks abreast with his days and feels no shame in not 'studying a profession,' for he does not postpone his life, but lives already. He has not one chance, but a hundred chances."[32]

"My good Henry Thoreau made this else solitary afternoon sunny with his simplicity and clear perception," Emerson wrote in 1838, part of which he would later incorporate into his essay on "New England Reformers."

> How comic is simplicity in this double-dealing, quacking world. Everything that boy says makes merry with society, though nothing can be graver than his meaning. I told him he should write out the history of his college life, as Carlyle has his tutoring. We agreed that the seeing the stars through a telescope would be worth all the astronomical lectures. Then he described Mr. Quimby's electrical lecture here, and the experiment of the shock, and added that "college corporations are very blind to the fact that the twinge in the elbow is worth all the lecturing."[33]

"Montaigne is spiced throughout with rebellion," Emerson wrote, "as much as Alcott or my young Henry Thoreau."[34] It was an aspect of Thoreau's personality that intrigued him as much as it at times exasperated him. In a letter to Margaret Fuller in early 1839, Emerson referred to Thoreau as "my protestor,"[35] an idea he'd expressed in a recent lecture, "The Protest," in which he made several direct references to ideas born of their conversations. The young who "alone have dominion of the world, for they walk in it with a free step," and the "impatient youth" who is "galled ... by the first infractions of his right,"[36] came from a walk to Walden Pond the previous November during which Thoreau

> complained of the proprietors who compelled him, to whom, as much as to any, the whole world belonged, to walk in a strip of road and crowded him out of all

the rest of God's earth. He must not get over the fence: but to the building of that fence he was no party. Suppose, he said, some great proprietor, before he was born, had bought up the whole globe. So he had been hustled out of nature. Not having been privy to any of these arrangements, he does not feel called on to consent to them, and so cuts fishpoles in the woods without asking who has a better title to the wood than he.[37]

Thoreau's argument over private ownership versus public use of land was a lifelong one. More than a decade later Emerson recorded in his journal how Thoreau ignored the question of property because he

could go wherever woods and waters were, and no man was asked for leave—once or twice the farmer withstood, but it was to no purpose,—he could as easily prevent the sparrows or tortoises. It was their land before it was his, and their title was precedent. . . .

Moreover the very time at which he used their land and water (for his boat glided like a trout everywhere unseen,) was in hours when they were sound asleep. Long before they were awake he went up and down to survey like a sovereign his possessions, and he passed onward, and left them before the farmer came out of doors.[38]

The right of the citizen to have more land available for public use culminated in Thoreau's 1859 journal statement: "Each town should have a park, or rather a primitive forest, of five hundred or a thousand acres, where a stick should never be cut for fuel, a common possession forever, for instruction and recreation."[39] Emerson "defended . . . the good institution" of private ownership, "as a scheme, not good, but the best that could be hit on for making the woods and waters and fields available to wit and worth, and for restraining the bold, bad man."[40] Their discussions on this topic formed the central dialogue found in Emerson's essay "The Conservative," in which Emerson points out the fundamental differences between the reformer, modeled after Thoreau, and the conservative, a role that Emerson sometimes reluctantly found himself adopting.

> Of course conservatism always has the worst of the argument, is always apologizing, pleading a necessity, pleading that to change would be to deteriorate: it must saddle itself with the mountainous load of the violence and vice of society, must deny the possibility of good, deny ideas, and suspect and stone the prophet; whilst innovation is always in the right, triumphant, attacking, and sure of final success. Conservatism stands on man's confessed limitations, reform on his indisputable infinitude; conservatism on circumstance, liberalism on power; one goes to make an adroit member of the social frame, the other to postpone all things to the man himself; conservatism is debonair and social, reform is individual and imperious. We are reformers in spring and summer, in autumn and winter we stand by the old; reformers in the morning, conservers at night.[41]

Alcott may have captured the essence of this dilemma, as Thoreau noted in his journal: "Alcott spent the day with me yesterday. He spent the day before with Emerson. He observed that he had got his wine and now he had come after his venison. Such was the compliment he paid me."[42] Alcott often compared the two, noting in his journal in 1852 after attending Emerson's lecture "Wealth" that "there are finer things to be said in praise of Poverty, which it takes a person superior to Emerson even to say worthily. Thoreau is the better man, perhaps, to celebrate that estate."[43]

While Emerson found Thoreau's constant aspect of reform and rebellion tedious—"Always some weary captious paradox to fight you with . . ."[44]—Thoreau saw a man he doubted "could trundle a wheelbarrow through the streets, because it would be out of character."[45] Thoreau delighted in the story that Emerson, Louis Agassiz, and a few others

> broke some dozens of ale-bottles, one after another, with their bullets, in the Adirondack country, using them for marks! It sounds rather Cockneyish. He says that he shot a peetweet for Agassiz, and this, I think he said, was the first game he ever bagged. He carried a double-barrelled gun,—rifle and shotgun,—which he bought for the purpose, which he says received much commendation,—all parties thought it a very pretty piece. Think of Emerson shooting a peetweet (with shot) for Agassiz, and cracking an ale-bottle (after emptying it) with his rifle at six rods! They cut several pounds of lead out of the tree.[46]

On the last day of August 1839, Thoreau and his brother, John, made a two-week river excursion from Concord, Massachusetts, to Concord, New Hampshire. Emerson applauded the two brothers with approbation tinged with wistfulness after they returned from their excursion: "Now here are my wise young neighbors who, instead of getting, like the wordmen, into a railroad-car, where they have not even the activity of holding the reins, have got into a boat which they have built with their own hands, with sails which they have contrived to serve as a tent by night, and gone up the Merrimack to live by their wits on the fish of the stream and the berries of the wood."[47]

Later that month Emerson wrote his brother William that George Ripley and others were reviving "at this time the old project of a new journal,"—what would become *The Dial: A Magazine for Literature, Philosophy, and Religion*—"for the exposition of absolute truth, but I doubt a little if it reach the day," insisting, with a sweep of self-deception, that he "will never be editor, though I am counted on as a contributor."[48] As he told Margaret Fuller, "I believe we all feel much alike in regard to this Journal; we all wish it to be, but do not wish to be in any way personally responsible for it."[49]

The Dial would also serve as a receptacle for the writings of those Emerson wanted to help and whose work he might want to promote. He knew, however, the limitations of the "fine people" who would write for this journal and whose work would appear "nowhere else," but in Thoreau he saw a different potential: "My Henry Thoreau will be a great poet for such a company, and one of these days for all companies."[50] He saw Thoreau as a contributor, providing him with an outlet for his early writings, and later, when Emerson did become editor, as an apprentice, positioning Thoreau as his assistant.

Margaret Fuller was *The Dial*'s first editor, and Emerson tried to encourage her about Thoreau's work, though eventually needing to concede, "I do not like his piece very well, but I admire this perennial threatening attitude, just as we like to go under an overhanging precipice," he wrote her in early 1842.[51] The majority of Thoreau's *Dial* contributions would not be published until Emerson took on the editorship, at which point his friend's work had some, although a very limited, distribution.

In the spring of 1840 Emerson had been working on pieces that would form his first series of *Essays*. In June he was finishing up his essay on friendship, which he would place in the center of his book, as Thoreau would do when placing his own friendship essay in *A Week on the Concord and Merrimack Rivers*. Emerson's essay contains the realization with which he wrestled his entire life: "Friends such as we desire are dreams and fables."[52]

He was writing so much that he told Fuller he had "become a scrivener."[53] At the end of June, Emerson and Thoreau visited the Cliffs at Fair Haven for what Emerson called their "villeggiatura," a country holiday, perhaps a well-deserved break from his book. Emerson's journal entry for that date started with a view of his surroundings—"I saw nothing better than the passage of the river by the dark clump of trees that line the bank in one spot for a short distance"—before commenting on friendship.

> We chide the citizen because, with all his honest merits, he does not conceive the delicacies and nobility of friendship, but we cannot forgive the poet if he does not substantiate his fine romance by the municipal virtues of justice, fidelity and pity. . . .
>
> I think we must give up this superstition of company to spend weeks and fortnights. Let my friend come and say that he has to say, and go his way. Otherwise we live for show. That happens continually in my house, that I am expected to play tame lion by readings and talkings to the friends. The rich live for show: I will not.[54]

Thoreau's journal at this same time shows a yearning combined with disappointment. Entries leading up to their holiday were anticipative and sanguine. "We will warm us at each other's fire," he wrote,[55] followed two days later by "Our friend's is as holy a shrine as any God's, to be approached with sacred love and awe. Veneration is the measure of Love."[56] But subsequently he wrote, "Of all phenomena, my own race are the most mysterious and undiscoverable. For how many years have I striven to meet one, even on common manly ground, and have not succeeded!"[57] He had begun to see, as he would say in a different context, "the interval between our hopes and their fulfillment."[58]

Feeling out of step with Emerson, Thoreau wrote the first version of what would evolve into his most renowned quotation about the different drummer.

> A man's life should be a stately march to a sweet but unheard music, and when to his fellows it shall seem irregular and inharmonious, he will only be stepping to a livelier measure, or his nicer ear hurry him into a thousand symphonies and concordant variations. There will be no halt ever, but at most a marching on his post, or such a pause as is richer than any sound, when the melody runs into such depth and wildness as to be no longer heard, but implicitly consented to with the whole life and being. He will take a false step never, even in the most arduous times, for then the music will not fail to swell into greater sweetness and volume, and itself rule the movement it inspired.[59]

In February of 1841 he wrote,

> Wait not till I invite thee, but observe
> I'm glad to see thee when thou com'st.[60]

Emerson's poem "The Sphinx" was published in the first issue of *The Dial*. In March Thoreau began a long journal entry analyzing Emerson's poem stanza by stanza, sometimes using the poem as a starting point for a more personal inquiry. Emerson wrote in his poem,

Have I a lover
    Who is noble and free?—
I would he were nobler
    Than to love me.

Eterne alternation
    Now follows, now flies;
And under pain, pleasure,—
    Under pleasure, pain lies.
Love works at the centre,
    Heart-heaving alway;
Forth speed the strong pulses
    To the borders of day.[61]

After reading these lines Thoreau wrote, "In friendship each will be nobler than the other, and so avoid the cheapness of a level and idle harmony. Love will have its chromatic strains,—discordant yearnings for higher chords,—as well as symphonies. Let us expect no finite satisfaction."[62]

In mid-March 1841 Emerson gave copies of *Essays* to family and friends, including Thoreau, likely prompting Thoreau's poem "Friendship"—one of several given that title—written that month.

Now we are partners in such legal trade,
We'll look to the beginnings, not the ends,
Nor to pay-day, knowing true wealth is made
For current stock and not for dividends.[63]

There was consideration in early 1841 of the Alcotts moving in with the Emersons, but such plans were dropped—much to Abigail "Abba" Alcott's relief—when Samuel May, Abba's brother, promised to provide for the family. With this prospect out of the way, Emerson invited

Thoreau to move in with them and Thoreau agreed. In exchange for room and board, Thoreau would provide a few hours of "what labor he chooses to do."[64] Emerson's cook at the time did not understand or appreciate the arrangement, saying that Thoreau wasn't "worth his porridge to do the chores."[65] For Emerson, however, he was "a very skilful laborer and I work with him as I should not without him."[66] Such an arrangement—one Thoreau instead of six Alcotts— must have seemed fortuitous to both the Emersons.

In addition to physical labor, though, Thoreau was given opportunities that would be beneficial to a young writer, and these would have been part of Emerson's plan from the first in inviting Thoreau into his household: working on *The Dial*, proofing Emerson's texts, being fully integrated into Emerson's intellectual and literary circle. Shortly after his move, Thoreau wrote in his journal,

> At R.W.Es.
>
> The charm of the Indian to me is that he stands free and unconstrained in Nature, is her inhabitant and not her guest, and wears her easily and gracefully. But the civilized man has the habits of the house. His house is a prison, in which he finds himself oppressed and confined, not sheltered and protected. He walks as if he sustained the roof; he carries his arms as if the walls would fall in and crush him, and his feet remember the cellar beneath. His muscles are never relaxed. It is rare that he overcomes the house, and learns to sit at home in it, and roof and floor and walls support themselves, as the sky and trees and earth.
>
> It is a great art to saunter.[67]

From Emerson's description, "Henry Thoreau is coming to live with me and work with me in the garden and teach me to graft apples,"[68] Margaret Fuller reduced Thoreau to simply Emerson's "working-man this year."[69] Emerson, however, thought of him in broader terms, describing him to Thomas Carlyle as "a poet whom you may one day be proud of;—a noble, manly youth, full of melodies and inventions,"[70] and to *his* brother as "a scholar and a poet and as full of buds of promise as a young apple tree."[71]

Emerson suffered from periods of unidentified complaints. "We have all been feebler folk,"[72] he wrote of his family, and more specifically about himself, that he had "been such a hypochondriac lately with my indispositions."[73] Although he looked forward to when "the South Wind returns,—the woods and fields and my garden will heal me,"[74] he saw Thoreau as a "great benefactor and physician to me," and expected "now to be suddenly well and strong though I have been a skeleton all the spring until I am ashamed."[75]

When the two friends boated on the Concord River that summer, Emerson described "my valiant Thoreau" as "the good river-god" who

> introduced me to the riches of his shadowy, starlit, moonlit stream, a lovely new world lying as close and yet as unknown to this vulgar trite one of the streets and shops as death to life, or poetry to prose. Through one field only we went to the boat and then left all time, all science, all history, behind us, and entered into Nature with one stroke of a paddle. Take care, good friend! I said, as I looked west into the sunset overhead and underneath, and he with his face toward me rowed towards it,—take care; you know not what you do, dipping your wooden oar into this enchanted liquid, painted with all reds and purples and yellows, which glows under and behind you. Presently this glory faded, and the stars

came and said, "Here we are"; began to cast such private and ineffable beams as to stop all conversation.[76]

Thoreau eagerly awaited correspondence when the friends were apart. Lidian wrote to her husband and emphasized that "Henry seems joyful when there is news from you."[77]

As their friendship progressed, Emerson became ever more anticipatory of what Thoreau would accomplish, and although he recognized that "all the fine souls have a flaw which defeats every expectation they excite," he also found that "to have awakened a great hope in another, is already some fruit is it not?"[78] Even in the early days Emerson exacted high expectations of what he had hoped to discover in Thoreau, telling him "that his freedom is in the form, but he does not disclose new matter. . . . But if the question be, what new ideas has he thrown into circulation, he has not yet told what that is which he was created to say."[79]

By October Emerson was indicating a nascent strain in their relationship, admiring Thoreau as "a person of extraordinary health and vigor, of unerring perception, and equal expression," but acknowledging that "yet he is impracticable, and does not flow through his pen or (in any of our legitimate aqueducts) through his tongue."[80] Thoreau felt a hindrance in the progress of their friendship, writing a poem that winter titled "Delay in Friendship," which asks,

Wilt thou not wait for me my friend,
Or give a longer lease?[81]

Thoreau understood Emerson's position and intent in his kindnesses and help, but at times he also may have misconstrued them.

> But he goes unappeased
> Who is on kindness bent.[82]

He may have felt that Emerson demanded something greater, had an expectation that could not be fulfilled. Thoreau was trying to establish his own voice, a voice of defiant self-reliance that asked, "If I am not I, who will be?"[83]

Whatever temporary impasse these friends may have been experiencing, something unexpected brought them a shared and overpowering grief when the beginning of 1842 saw tragedy strike both the Thoreau and Emerson families. "I begin my letter," Lidian wrote her sister, "with the strange sad news that John Thoreau has this afternoon left this world."[84] John had cut his left-hand thumb while stropping his razor on New Year's Day. Not thinking it serious, he replaced the missing skin and bandaged it. Although within a few days it began to cause him pain, not until January 8 did he actually remove the bandage. The flesh was foul smelling, discolored, and darkened. Gangrene had set in.

The skin had already begun to mortify when John visited Dr. Josiah Bartlett that Saturday evening. The Concord physician examined and redressed the wound. Although his father, also Dr. Josiah Bartlett, had written a pamphlet in 1808 on tetanus and the use of amputation as a cure, Bartlett did not find any reason for concern. There are no medical records to explain why he was not alarmed. On his way home John began to experience pain in various parts of his body. He was barely able to complete the one-third-mile walk. By morning his jaw was stiff. Excruciating spasms that evening confirmed the onset of lockjaw. Thoreau was called home from the Emersons'.

On Monday, the doctor told John that it was too late for anything to be done, and that his death would be quick but painful. "Is there no hope?" he asked. The doctor replied simply, "None," to which John said, "The cup that my Father gives me, shall I not drink it?" Lidian reported that John retained "his senses and some power of speech to the last. He said from the first he knew he should die—but was perfectly quiet and trustful—saying that God had always been good to him and he could trust Him now. His words and behavior throughout were what Mr. Emerson calls manly—even *great*."[85]

Later that day John took leave of his family, all but his brother. Henry remained when everyone else had left the room. He sat down and talked, as John had asked him to do, about nature and poetry. "I shall be a good listener," he said with what strength and humor he could muster, "for it is difficult for me to interrupt you." The next day, in his final hour, John looked at his brother with what Thoreau described as a "transcendental smile full of Heaven,"[86] although it was likely the *risus sardonicus* caused by muscle spasms. Henry returned a smile. This was the last that passed between them. John died on Tuesday afternoon at 2:00 in his brother's arms.

In the evening Thoreau walked the half mile to Emerson's house to see his friend, "but no one else," as Lidian wrote. One does not know, one can only imagine, the conversation that took place behind the closed doors of Emerson's study. The death of Thoreau's brother could only have stirred memories of Emerson's own fraternal losses. His brother Edward died in 1834 and, more parallel to Thoreau's loss, Charles in 1836. He had described Charles to Lidian as "my noble friend who was my ornament my wisdom and my pride. . . . How much I saw through his eyes. I feel as if my own were very dim."[87] Passages from Charles's journals were printed in *The Dial*, and Emerson paid tribute to both brothers in his poem "Dirge."

What was said in the privacy of Emerson's study is not recorded in the journals or correspondence of either man, although parts of it may have been conveyed to Lidian, who wrote,

> He says John took leave of all the family on Monday with perfect calmness and more than resignation. It is a beautiful fate that has been granted him and I think he was worthy of it. At first it seemed not beautiful but terrible. Since I have heard particulars and recollected all the good I have heard of him I feel as if a pure spirit had been translated.[88]

When Lidian later asked Thoreau "if this sudden fate gave any shock to John when he first was aware of his danger," he answered, "None at all."[89] It had been John's belief that he would die early.[90]

The following morning Thoreau returned to Bush to get his clothes, unsure when he would return as a member of the Emerson household. Before noon he was back on Main Street with his family. Lidian loved "him for the feeling he showed and the effort he made to be cheerful. He did not give way in the least but his whole demeanour was that of one struggling with sickness of heart."[91] This sickness of heart with which Thoreau struggled would soon surface in a way that caused considerable alarm to his family and friends.

Edward Emerson remembered being told that the "shock, the loss, and the sight of his brother's terrible suffering at the end, for a time overthrew Henry so utterly that . . . he sat still in the house, could do nothing, and his sisters led him out passive to try to help him."[92] Thoreau's depression soon manifested itself physically. On Saturday, January 22, Emerson returned to Concord from Boston, where he had delivered the last lecture of his series "On the Times," only to find his friend "ill and threatened with *lock-jaw!* his brother's disease. It is strange—unaccountable—yet the symptoms seemed precise and on the increase. You may judge we were all alarmed and I not the least who have the highest hopes of this youth."[93]

By Monday Emerson could write that Thoreau's "affection be it what it may, is relieved essentially, and what is best, his own feeling of better health established."[94] It was a slow process. "I must confess," Thoreau wrote in his journal, "there is nothing so strange to me as my own body. I love any other piece of nature, almost, better."[95] A month later Lidian was writing that "Henry is better—nearly well. But his headache or the cause of it, made his eyes so weak that he did not read or write much for two days or more."[96] Good health still wasn't totally restored. In March Thoreau wrote that he had been "confined to my chamber for a month with a prolonged shock of the same disorder—from close attention to, and sympathy with him, which I learn is not without precedent."[97] A year later, on the anniversary of John's death, Thoreau asked in his journal, "What am I at present?" He answered, "A diseased bundle of nerves standing between time and eternity like a withered leaf that still hangs shivering on its stem."[98]

The relief Emerson experienced over his friend's returning health that January was brief. Waldo, Emerson's five-year-old son, showed signs of scarlet fever. It began with a soreness of the throat and a fever. Eruptions on the skin appeared, similar to measles but occurring more rapidly, yet following the eruptions the fever did not begin to subside as with measles. Waldo's skin took on broad patches of the vivid red color that gave the disease its name. Seizures were followed by delirium. His "sweet and wonderful boy," Emerson wrote Carlyle, was "hurried out of my arms in three short days by Scarlatina."[99]

When Alcott sent his daughter, the nine-year-old Louisa, to ask after Waldo's health, it would be one of her earliest remembrances of Emerson and one she would not forget. He came to the door looking "so worn with watching, and changed by sorrow, that I was startled, and could only stammer out my message." He simply answered, "Child, he is dead," and closed the door. Louisa ran home to tell her family the news. She later recollected that it was "my first glimpse of a great grief; but I never have forgotten the anguish that made a familiar face so tragical, and gave those few words more pathos than the sweet lamentation of" Emerson's poetic requiem for his son, "Threnody."[100]

For a period following Waldo's death, Emerson saw the world only in relation to his son. "What he looked upon is better," he wrote on January 30, "what he looked not upon is insignificant." On waking he found that the sun had risen as usual "with all his light, but the landscape was dishonored by this loss. For this boy, in whose remembrance I have both slept and awaked so oft, decorated for me the morning star, the evening cloud, how much more all the particulars of daily economy."[101]

Until this time Emerson had relied on his intellect to carry him through a crisis. Even the death of his first wife, Ellen, and his brother Charles had not brought him to this place. The pretense, based on his previous experiences of death, was shaken; he had once confessed, "if my wife, my child, my mother, should be taken from me, I should still remain whole, with the same capacity of cheap enjoyment from all things. I should not grieve enough, although I love them."[102] Now, however, he admitted simply in his journal, "The wisest knows nothing."[103] The ideas expressed in his essay "Compensation"—"The death of a dear friend, wife, brother, lover, which seemed nothing but privation, somewhat later assumes the aspect of a guide or genius; for it commonly operates revolutions in our way of life, terminates an epoch of infancy or of youth which was waiting to be closed, breaks up a wonted occupation, or a household, or style of living, and allows the formation of new ones more friendly to the growth of character."[104]—did little to assuage the pain he was currently feeling. In an undated, and later cancelled, journal entry from 1843, Emerson wrote down Lidian's wish that she had never been born, followed by her statement with which he must have been in agreement, "I do not see how God can compensate me for the sorrow of existence."[105] He could not anticipate a return to the comfort expressed in his poem "Give All to Love," in which he wrote that

When half-gods go,
The gods arrive.[106]

In an effort to capture what he had lost, Emerson began to collect little bits of Waldo's conversations in his journal. It was his way of dealing with the dead and the dying, and he would do it again when Margaret Fuller drowned, and later when Thoreau was dying. He remembered the fanciful names Waldo gave to the parts of the toy house he was always building, such as the Interspeglium and the Coridaga. Once when Waldo asked if there were other countries besides the United States and his father began to name them, Thoreau commented on the boy's large way of speech that offered questions that "did not admit of an answer; they were the same which you would ask yourself." When it happened to thunder while Waldo was blowing his willow whistle, he said that his music "makes the thunder dance."

One time he asked Lidian, "Mamma, may I have this bell which I have been making, to stand by the side of my bed?"

"Yes," his mother answered, "it may stand there."

"But Mamma," Waldo suggested, "I am afraid it will alarm you. It may sound in the middle of the night, and it will be heard all over the town; it will be louder than ten thousand hawks; it will be heard across the water, and in all the countries. It will be heard all over the world. It will sound like some great glass thing which falls down and breaks all to pieces."[107]

The following month Emerson wrote to his childless friend Carlyle: "You can never sympathize with me; you can never know how much of me such a young child can take away."[108]

Although Emerson wrote in "Experience" that "Grief too will make us idealists. In the death of my son, now more than two years ago, I seem to have lost a beautiful estate,— no more. I cannot get it nearer to me,"[109] Margaret Fuller saw a loneliness that remained. Two years after Waldo's death she wrote Emerson, "I know you are not a 'marker of days' nor do in any way encourage those useless pains which waste the strength needed for our nobler purposes, yet it seems to me this season can never pass without opening anew the deep wound. . . . I miss him when I go to your home, I miss him when I think of you there; you seem to me lonely as if he filled you to a place which no other ever could in any degree." She exhibited an understanding and perspective rare for the mid-nineteenth century. She recognized that "Little Edith has been injured in my affections by being compared with him. . . . I do not like to have her put in his place or likened to him; that only makes me feel that she is not the same and do her injustice." Even more to the point she told her friend, "I hope you will have another son, for I perceive that men do not feel themselves represented to the next generation by *daughters*, but I hope, if you do, there will be no comparisons made . . ."[110]

Emerson's reply reflected none of Fuller's concerns for his other children, living or yet to be born. Instead he wrote of his still-present pain, telling Fuller that when Lidian said, "'It is two years today—' I only heard the bell-stroke again. I have had no experiences no progress to put me into better intelligence with my calamity than when it was new."[111]

When Emerson's house burned thirty years later, friends and neighbors worked hurriedly to save what they could. Emerson collected together the letters of his first wife, Ellen, along with Waldo's clothes that he had kept. He was not making a desperate effort to save those relics of lost loved ones. It was the opposite. His daughter described how her father gathered those personal objects and then "deliberately threw them into the fire."[112] With those gestures Emerson threw the last vestiges of Ellen and Waldo into the burning Bush.

When Emerson was lecturing in New York a few months after Waldo died, Lidian wrote him, including "an extract from a letter Henry sent this week to" her sister, Lucy Jackson Brown. "I did not know it was there till I had written some lines—but will not tear it from the sheet since you may like it as well as I do—and if so it will cheer your loneliness."[113] Thoreau wrote,

> As for Waldo, he died as the mist rises from the brook, which the sun will soon dart his rays through. Do not

the flowers die every autumn? He had not even taken root here. I was not startled to hear that he was dead; it seemed the most natural event that could happen. His fine organization demanded it, and nature gently yielded its request. It would have been strange if he had lived. Neither will nature manifest any sorrow at his death, but soon the note of the lark will be heard down in the meadow, and fresh dandelions will spring from the old stocks where he plucked them last summer.[114]

Lidian asked Thoreau to send Emerson

a letter by this opportunity—and he seems quite ready to do so. He had a sick headache about the time you went away, and has not been quite well since,—has had a cold and weak eyes—and some return of spasmodic affection. But is very bright and interesting and beguiles what time he can do nought else in with playing on the flute. He finds that exercise, which he hoped would be a relief—only increases his ails—so that I have begged him not to feel the care of the wood—and have had Colombe to work one day upon it—as we were in need both of green and dry hard wood.[115]

On March 11 Henry wrote a long letter that contained some thoughts on death.

Nature is not ruffled by the rudest blast—The hurricane only snaps a few twigs in some nook of the forest. The snow attains its average depth each winter, and the chicadee lisps the same notes. The old laws prevail in spite of pestilence and famine. No genius or virtue so rare and revolutionary appears in town or village, that the pine ceases to exude resin in the wood, or beast or bird lays aside its habits.

How plain that death is only the phenomenon of the individual or class. Nature does not recognize it, she finds her own again under new forms without loss. Yet death is beautiful when seen to be a law, and not an accident—It is as common as life. Men die in Tartary, in Ethiopia—in England—in Wisconsin. And after all what portion of this so serene and living nature can be said to be alive? Do this year's grasses and foliage outnumber all the past?

Every blade in the field—every leaf in the forest— lays down its life in its season as beautifully as it was taken up. It is the pastime of a full quarter of the year. Dead trees—sere leaves—dried grass and herbs—are not these a good part of our life? And what is that pride of our autumnal scenery but the hectic flush—the sallow and cadaverous countenance of vegetation—its painted throes—with the November air for canvas—

When we look over the fields are we not saddened because these particular flowers or grasses will wither— for the law of their death is the law of new life. Will not the land be in good heart *because* the crops die down from year to year? The herbage cheerfully consents to bloom, and wither, and give place to a new.

So is it with the human plant. We are partial and selfish when we lament the death of the individual, unless our plaint be a paean to the departed soul, and a sigh as the wind sighs over the fields, which no shrub interprets into its private grief.

One might as well go into mourning for every sere leaf—but the more innocent and wiser soul will snuff a fragrance in the gales of autumn, and congratulate Nature upon her health.

After I have imagined thus much will not the Gods feel under obligations to make me realize something as good?[116]

The naturalness of dying expressed here, in relation to both recent deaths, would resurface when Thoreau was redacting "Autumnal Tints" on his deathbed: "How many flutterings before they rest quietly in their graves! They that soared so loftily, how contentedly they return to dust again, and are laid low, resigned to lie and decay at the foot of the tree, and afford nourishment to new generations of their kind, as well as to flutter on high! They teach us how to die."[117]

Thoreau prefaced his letter with a nod to the impasse they had reached in their relationship, the difficulty of speaking about personal matters face-to-face, by saying that

there seems to be no occasion why I who have so little to say to you here at home should take pains to send you any of my silence in a letter—Yet since no correspondence can hope to rise above the level of those homely speechless hours, as no spring ever bursts above the level of the still mountain tarn whence it issued—I will not delay to send a venture. As if I were to send you a piece of the house-sill—or a loose casement rather. Do not neighbors sometimes halloo with good will across a field, who yet never chat over a fence?[118]

Thoreau thought Emerson's coolness and reserve was "because his love for me is waxing and not waning.... Heaven is to come. I hope this is not it."[119] Emerson was aware of his own coolness, confessing in his journal in 1843, "It is a pathetic thing to meet a friend prepared to love you, to whom yet, from some inaptitude, you cannot communicate yourself with that grace and power which only love will allow."[120] There was an explosion of writing about friendship as Thoreau tried to work it out in his journal. "Words should pass between friends as the lightning passes from cloud to cloud." He didn't want

> friends to feed and clothe our bodies,—neighbors are kind enough for that,—but to do the like offices to ourselves. We wish to spread and publish ourselves, as the sun spreads its rays; and we toss the new thought to the friend, and thus it is dispersed. Friends are those twain who feel their interests to be one. Each knows that the other might as well have said what he said. All beauty, all music, all delight springs from apparent dualism but real unity. My friend is my real brother. I see his nature groping yonder like my own. Does there go one whom I know? then I go there.
>
> The field where friends have met is consecrated forever. Man seeks friendship out of the desire to realize a home here. As the Indian thinks he receives into himself the courage and strength of his conquered enemy, so we add to ourselves all the character and heart of our friends. He is my creation. I can do what I will with him. There is no possibility of being thwarted; the friend is like wax in the rays that fall from our own hearts.
>
> The friend does not take my word for anything, but he takes me. He trusts me as I trust myself. We only need be as true to others as we are to ourselves, that there may be ground enough for friendship.[121]

In April Emerson asked Thoreau to write a review of some scientific surveys of Massachusetts he had been reading. He told Fuller that he had "set Henry Thoreau on the good track of giving an account of them in the Dial, explaining to him the felicity of the subject for him as it admits of the narrative of all his woodcraft, boatcraft and fishcraft." It was his constant wish to bring Thoreau's work to a wider audience, and "as private secretary to the President of the Dial, his works and fame may go out into all lands, and, as happens to great Premiers, quite extinguish the titular Master."[122] Thoreau's "Natural History of Massachusetts" was published in the next issue of *The Dial*.

As 1842 drew to a close, Thoreau, Emerson, and Nathaniel Hawthorne had a skating party on the frozen meadow next to the Old Manse. Sophia Hawthorne described Thoreau's "dithyrambic dances and Bacchic leaps on the ice—very remarkable, but very ugly, methought. Next him followed Mr. Hawthorne who, wrapped in his cloak, moved like a self-impelled Greek statue, stately and grave. Mr. Emerson closed the line, evidently too weary to hold himself erect, pitching headforemost, half lying on the air."[123]

In his "Address Delivered Before the Senior Class in Divinity College, Cambridge," Emerson noted, "It is already beginning to indicate character and religion to withdraw from the religious meetings."[124] Thoreau signed off from the First Parish Church in Concord at the beginning of 1841, writing simply to the clerk, "I do not wish to be considered a member of the First Parish in this town."[125] God was not to be found in the formal tenets of organized religion. God was not to be found confined between the walls of a church with a ministerial mediator. God was not to be found weekly on Sundays with the Sabbatarians.

As Emerson wrote in his Divinity College address, "In how many churches, by how many prophets, tell me, is man made sensible that he is an infinite Soul; that the earth and heavens are passing into his mind; that he is drinking forever the soul of God?"[126] Or as he wrote later in "Politics": "The wise man . . . needs no library, for he has not done thinking; no church, for he is a prophet."[127]

"The strains of a more heroic faith vibrate through the week days and the fields than through the Sabbath and the Church," Thoreau wrote. "To shut the ears to the immediate voice of God, and prefer to know him by report will be the only sin."[128] So when Emerson's mother came home from church in January 1843 to report to Lidian that she had been astonished to see Thoreau, not only sitting in church that Sabbath day, but in Emerson's pew, it was quite a surprise. Lidian then reported the story to her husband, who was away on a lecture tour. It is possible that Thoreau was in some way conciliating Lidian, who "had a conversation with him a few days since on his heresies—but had no expectation of so speedy a result,"[129] but Thoreau also seemed to take some relish in substituting for Emerson when the opportunity arose. Whatever his reasons for sitting in Emerson's pew, a little over a week later he was writing to his friend, "The best way to correct a mistake is to make it right."[130]

Lidian described in a letter to her husband the happy domestic scene he was missing. "It is 'after dinner,'" she wrote,

and your peerless Edith is looking most beautifully as she dances with Henry or lays her innocent head on his music-box that she may drink yet deeper of its sweetness. Now am I interrupted by an exclamation from all present—the cherub face appears above the screen for Uncle Henry takes care that Edie shall take as high flights in Papa's absence as ever—she rides on his shoulder or is held high up in the air—I think he adds to her happiness, and she no less to his. I wish you had seen her this morning.[131]

Lidian went on to recount the popping of the corn: "I brought the warming pan into the dining-room and the corn was quickly shelled into it and held over the fire by Henry who was master of ceremonies—and enjoyed the frolic as well as any child of us all. When the snapping was heard in full chorus I with my napkin lifted the hot cover the pan was taken off and the corn flew over the rug and the children like a snow storm."[132]

In the first week of February Lidian described Thoreau recovering from an unspecified illness, and that he "has so far improved in health as to be quite able, as he thinks, to shovel snow once more, deep though it be. He has made very handsome paths from both doors and the great blocks of snow lie on each side attesting that they were no trifle to dispose of—I don't know that I ever saw the snow deeper on a level." She told Emerson that Thoreau was not going to write him at this time, "has deferred writing with my consent till you have answered his first one."[133]

Emerson had told Lidian how occupied he was, previously saying that he had "received with great contentment Henry's excellent letter but what kept me from writing to you kept me from him."[134] In a letter to Thoreau he wrote, "I think that some letter must have failed for I cannot have let ten days go by without writing home. I have kept no account but am confident that that cannot be."[135] Emerson was lecturing in Philadelphia, then was in New York visiting his brother William. While he was away Thoreau gave one of his earliest lectures in Concord, "The Life and Character of Sir Walter Raleigh," and Emerson enthusiastically urged Lidian to "not fail to tell me every particular concerning Henry's lecture when that comes—and the brightest star of the winter shed its clear beams on that night!"[136] Lidian wrote that

> Henry's Lecture pleased me much—and I have reason to believe others liked it. Henry tells me he is so happy as to have received Mr. *Keye's* suffrage and the Concord paper has spoken well of it. I think you would have been a well pleased listener. I should like to hear it two or three times more. Henry ought to be known as a man who can give a Lecture. You must advertise him to the extent of your power. A few Lyceum fees would satisfy his moderate wants—to say nothing of the improvement and happiness it would give both him and his fellow creatures if he could utter what is "most within him"— and be heard.[137]

When Thoreau did write, possibly without waiting for a letter from Emerson, he told of the family that "it will inform you of the state of all if I only say that I am well and happy in your house here in Concord," and made only a passing mention to his talk, though referencing Emerson's wish for a bright starlit night: "I lectured this week. It was as bright a night as you could wish. I hope there were no stars thrown away on the occasion."[138]

Days passed without further correspondence. "I think you have made Henry wait a reasonable—or *un*reasonable time for an answer to his letter," Lidian wrote.[139] Emerson did write Thoreau on that same day, but only on business matters. Thoreau also wrote that day, with an overt nod to their disrupted correspondence,

> As the packet still tarries, I will send you some thoughts, which I have lately relearned, as the latest public and private news.

How mean are our relations to one another! Let us pause till they are nobler. A little silence, a little rest, is good. It would be sufficient employment only to cultivate true ones.

The richest gifts we can bestow are the least marketable. We hate the kindness which we understand. A noble person confers no such gift as his whole confidence: none so exalts the giver and the receiver; it produces the truest gratitude. Perhaps it is only essential to friendship that some vital trust should have been reposed by the one in the other. I feel addressed and probed even to the remote parts of my being when one nobly shows, even in trivial things, an implicit faith in me. When such divine commodities are so near and cheap, how strange that it should have to be each day's discovery! A threat or a curse may be forgotten, but this mild trust translates me. I am no more of this earth; it acts dynamically; it changes my very substance. I cannot do what before I did. I cannot be what before I was. Other chains may be broken, but in the darkest night, in the remotest place, I trail this thread. Then things cannot *happen*. What if God were to confide in us for a moment! Should we not then be gods?

How subtle a thing is this confidence! Nothing sensible passes between; never any consequences are to be apprehended should it be misplaced. Yet something has transpired. A new behavior springs; the ship carries new ballast in her hold. A sufficiently great and generous trust could never be abused. It should be cause to lay down one's life,—which would not be to lose it. Can there be any mistake up there? Don't the gods know where to invest their wealth? Such confidence, too, would be reciprocal. When one confides greatly in you, he will feel the roots of an equal trust fastening themselves in him. When such trust has been received or reposed, we dare not speak, hardly to see each other; our voices sound harsh and untrustworthy. We are as instruments which the Powers have dealt with. Through what straits would we not carry this little burden of a magnanimous trust! Yet no harm could possibly come, but simply faithlessness. Not a feather, not a straw, is entrusted; that packet is empty. It is only *committed* to us, and, as it were, all things are committed to us.

The kindness I have longest remembered has been of this sort,—the sort unsaid; so far behind the speaker's lips that almost it already lay in my heart. It did not have far to go to be communicated. The gods cannot misunderstand, man cannot explain. We communicate like the burrows of foxes, in silence and darkness, under ground. We are undermined by faith and love. How much more full is Nature where we think the empty space is than where we place the solids!—full of fluid influences. Should we ever communicate but by these? The spirit abhors a vacuum more than Nature. There is a tide which pierces the pores of the air. These aerial rivers, let us not pollute their currents. What meadows do they course through? How many fine mails there are which traverse their routes! He is privileged who gets his letter franked by them.

I believe these things.[140]

When Thoreau did finally receive letters from his friend, he joyously wrote, "My dear Friend,—I got your letters, one yesterday and the other to-day, and they have made me quite happy."[141] Feeling confident again in their friendship, Thoreau could write in all honesty, "Do not think that my letters require as many special answers. I get one as often as you write to Concord," urging Emerson to "make haste home before we have settled all the great questions, for they are fast being disposed of."[142]

When his "A Walk to Wachusett" was published in the January 1843 issue of the *Boston Miscellany of Literature and Fashion*, Thoreau had trouble getting paid by the publisher. "Did I tell you," Lidian wrote her husband, "that Bradbury & Soden have refused to pay Henry more than two thirds of the money they promised for his 'Walk to W,' and that they postpone the payment even of that? Will it not do for you to call on your return through Boston and demand it for him?"[143] Emerson did his best, writing Thoreau, "I am sorry to say that when I called on Bradbury & Soden nearly a month ago, their partner in their absence informed me that they could not pay you at present any part of their debt on account of the *Boston Miscellany*. . . . I shall not fail to refresh their memory at intervals."[144] Thoreau soon told Emerson not to "think of Bradbury & Soden any more. . . . I see that they have given up their shop here."[145]

While Emerson was still in New York, Thoreau wrote to him about his "long kindness" and his own unexpressed gratitude that he had been Emerson's "pensioner for nearly two years, and still left free as under the sky."[146] Realizing his position and the obligations he owed to their friendship, as well as perhaps feeling the weight of such obligations, it was now time to move on, though not without asking Emerson's assistance. Thoreau wrote in early March that he had been "meditating some other method of paying debts than by lectures and writing which will only do to talk about. If anything of that 'other' sort should come to your ears in N.Y. will you remember it for me?"[147]

Emerson suggested to his brother that Thoreau might make an excellent tutor for his three children—the youngest, Charles, still an infant; three-year-old Haven;

but principally seven-year-old Willie. William Emerson agreed. It would give Thoreau not only a paid position for which he was well qualified but also access to the New York publishers and editors. On returning to Concord Emerson discussed the idea with Thoreau. He explained that it was more Willie himself than his grammar and geography that would be subject to Thoreau's influence; he should take the boy to the woods as well as into the city. For that he would get lodging and board, firewood when needed, and one hundred dollars per annum. Thoreau had found a position he wished to sustain, "to be the friend and educator of a boy, and one not yet subdued by schoolmasters."[148]

Perhaps he might be able to perform some clerical work in William Emerson's office, or for someone Emerson knew, to supplement his income until he could obtain some literary work in the city. Such was Thoreau's hope. For all concerned, this was an auspicious and welcome opportunity. Elizabeth Hoar sent him an inkstand as a token; Prudence Ward gave him a small microscope.

Emerson wrote his brother a brief caveat based on his own experiences. Thoreau "is a bold and a profound thinker," he wrote, "though he may easily chance to pester you with some accidental crotchets and perhaps a village exaggeration of the value of facts."[149] Emerson had confessed as much to Hawthorne, who wrote in his journal around this time, "Mr. Emerson appears to have suffered some inconveniency from his experience of Mr. Thoreau as an inmate."[150] But Emerson concluded his warning with the promise that "if you should content each other," Willie would soon come "to value him for his real power to serve and instruct him. I shall eagerly look, though not yet for some time, for tidings how you speed in this new relation."[151]

Thoreau visited Hawthorne before leaving, going out on the river with him in the Musketaquid, the boat

Thoreau had sold him in the fall. Hawthorne was glad on Thoreau's account, as he is "physically out of health, and, morally and intellectually, seems not to have found exactly the guiding clue; and in all these respects, he may be benefitted by his removal." It was on everyone's mind but only Hawthorne expressed it on paper: "Also, it is one step towards a circumstantial position in the world." But on his own account, the introverted and sometimes reclusive Hawthorne would have preferred that Thoreau stay, "he being one of the few persons, I think, with whom to hold intercourse is like hearing the wind among the boughs of a forest-tree."[152]

Elizabeth Hoar told Emerson that "I love Henry, but do not like him."[153] As he struggled with his own relationship with Henry, this may have seemed like a motto to their own friendship. "Young men, like Henry Thoreau, owe us a new world, and they have not acquitted the debt," Emerson wrote in his journal. "For the most part, such die young, and so dodge the fulfilment."[154] Perhaps in New York Thoreau would not be able to dodge what Emerson thought he owed the world.

Emerson was confident about this new episode in his young friend's life, writing to his brother, "And now goes our brave youth into the new house, the new connexion, the new City. I am sure no truer and no purer person lives in wide New York."[155] Henry was missed. Waldo wrote him, "You will not doubt that you are well remembered here, by young, older, and old people and your letter to your mother was borrowed and read with great interest, pending the arrival of direct accounts and of later experiences especially in the city."[156]

Away from home Henry realized not just what he owed to Waldo, but also to Lidian. "I believe a good many conversations with you were left in an unfinished state, and now indeed I don't know where to take them up," he wrote her.

> I think of you as some elder sister of mine, whom I could not have avoided,—a sort of lunar influence,— only of such age as the moon, whose time is measured by her light. You must know that you represent to me woman. . . . I thank you for your influence for two years. I was fortunate to be subjected to it, and am now to remember it. It is the noblest gift we can make; what signify all others that can be bestowed? You have helped to keep my life "on loft," as Chaucer says of Griselda, and in a better sense. You always seemed to look down at me as from some elevation—some of your high humilities—and I was the better for having to look up. I felt taxed not to disappoint your expectation; for could there be any accident so sad as to be respected for something better than we are? It was a pleasure even to go away from you, as it is not to meet some, as it apprised me of my high relations; and such a departure is a sort of further introduction and meeting. Nothing makes the earth seem so spacious as to have friends at a distance; they make the latitudes and longitudes.[157]

Thoreau reminded Lidian to not think

> fate is so dark there, for even here I can see a faint reflected light over Concord. . . .
>
> I have hardly begun to live on Staten Island yet; but, like the man who, when forbidden to tread on English ground, carried Scottish ground in his boots, I carry Concord ground in my boots and in my hat,—and am I not made of Concord dust? I cannot realize that

it is the roar of the sea I hear now, and not the wind in Walden woods. I find more of Concord, after all, in the prospect of the sea, beyond Sandy Hook, than in the fields and woods.[158]

Sometimes his homesickness manifested itself physically. "I have been sick ever since I came here—rather unaccountably, what with a cold, bronchitis, acclimation etc.—still unaccountably."[159] He was disappointed in what little of New York he had seen so far. He tried to write something for *The Dial* but wasn't sure he could "finish an account of a winter's walk in Concord in the midst of a Staten Island summer."[160] When he did finish it, it was too late for immediate publication, but Emerson offered to hold on to it, for which Thoreau was grateful. "As for the 'Winter's Walk,'" Thoreau wrote, "I should be glad to have it printed in the D. if you think it good enough, and will criticise it—otherwise send it to me and I will dispose of it."[161] Emerson found the essay full of Thoreau's "old fault of unlimited contradiction. . . . it makes me nervous and wretched to read it, with all its merits."[162] When the next issue of *The Dial* was being sent to the printer, Emerson wrote to Thoreau that he

had some hesitation about it, notwithstanding its faithful observation and its fine sketches of the pickerel-fisher and of the woodchopper, on account of *mannerism*, an old charge of mine,—as if, by attention, one could get the trick of the rhetoric; for example, to call a cold place sultry, a solitude public, a wilderness *domestic* (a favorite word), and in the woods to insult over cities, whilst the woods, again, are dignified by comparing them to cities, armies, etc. By pretty free omissions, however, I have removed my principal objections.[163]

When James Russell Lowell omitted one sentence from Thoreau's essay "Chesuncook" in 1858, Thoreau was uncompromisingly vehement when he said that the "editor has, in this case, no more right to omit a sentiment than to insert one, or put words into my mouth."[164] In relation to "A Winter's Walk" and Emerson's edits, he was much more forgiving. Whether simply from this happening earlier in his writing career, or out of deference to his friend, he wrote Emerson, "I doubt if you have made more corrections in my manuscript than I should have done ere this, though they may be better; but I am glad you have taken any pains with it."[165]

"I don't like the city better, the more I see it, but worse," Thoreau wrote after months in New York. "I am ashamed of my eyes that behold it. It is a thousand times meaner than I could have imagined. . . . The pigs in the street are the most respectable part of the population."[166] One highlight, however, was the theologian Henry James, about whom Emerson had said "you must not fail to visit."[167] Thoreau found in James someone who

> makes humanity seem more erect and respectable. . . .
> He is a man, and takes his own way, or stands still in his
> own place. I know of no one so patient and determined
> to have the good of you. It is almost friendship, such
> plain and human dealing. I think that he will not write
> or speak inspiringly; but he is a refreshing forward-
> looking and forward-moving man, and he has natu-
> ralized and humanized New York for me. He actually
> reproaches you by his respect for your poor words. I had
> three hours' solid talk with him, and he asks me to make
> free use of his house.[168]

But he was not happy with his situation.

> I do not feel myself especially serviceable to the good people with whom I live, except as inflictions are sanctified to the righteous. And so, too, must I serve the boy. I can look to the Latin and mathematics sharply, and for the rest behave myself. But I cannot be in his neighborhood hereafter as his Educator, of course, but as the hawks fly over my own head. I am not attracted toward him but as to youth generally. He shall frequent me, however, as much as he can, and I'll be I.[169]

When he received a letter from Lidian in June, he started reading it but decided to go

> to the top of the hill at sunset, where I can see the ocean, to prepare to read the rest. It is fitter that it should hear it than the walls of my chamber. . . . I am almost afraid to look at your letter. . . .
>
> You seem to me to speak out of a very clear and high heaven, where any one may be who stands so high. Your voice seems not a voice, but comes as much from the blue heavens as from the paper.[170]

It is clear from his answer to Lidian that they shared an emotional intimacy that each sometimes failed to find in Emerson, and that there was a confidence and trust that, again, they missed in Emerson. "My dear friend," Thoreau wrote her, "it was very noble in you to write me so trustful an answer. It will do as well for another world as for this." They were connected. "I think I know your thoughts without seeing you, and as well here as in Concord. You are not at all strange to me." She confided to him about her "sad hours," the result of some physical ailment. In closing he expressed the "joy your letter gives me," and sent his "love to my other friend and brother, whose nobleness I slowly recognize."[171]

In September, among other local news, Emerson lamented the conditions of the Irish laborers who had come to lay down the tracks for the railroad that would be extending past Walden Pond to Fitchburg.

Now the humanity of the town suffers with the poor Irish, who receives but sixty, or even fifty cents, for working from dark till dark, with a strain and a following up that reminds one of negro-driving. Peter Hutchinson told me he had never seen men perform so much; he should never think it hard again if an employer should keep him at work till after sundown. But what can be done for their relief as long as new applicants for the same labor are coming in every day? These of course reduce the wages to the sum that will suffice a bachelor to live, and must drive out the men with families. The work goes on very fast.[172]

Thoreau may not have felt Emerson's sympathy went far enough. Although he didn't do it, Emerson briefly contemplated selling his home in Concord. Thoreau told his friend, "The sturdy Irish arms that do the work are of more worth than oak or maple. Methinks I could look with equanimity upon a long street of Irish cabins and pigs and children revelling in the genial Concord dirt, and I should still find my Walden wood and Fair Haven in their tanned and happy faces."[173]

In mid-November Thoreau was in Concord to spend Thanksgiving with his family and to give a lecture. He was back in New York the first week of December, but his brief visit home may have been an overwhelming reminder of what he was missing; in two weeks he returned home to Concord for good. He asked Emerson to tie up any loose ends with his brother; Emerson sent William thanks from Thoreau "for the purse and says that the Pindar he will return through me, and says that he left nothing of any value at all in his chamber. You will please use your discretion with any matters found there."[174]

Although the New York adventure did not yield the results everyone had hoped for, Thoreau did have two pieces published outside *The Dial*—"A Walk to Wachusett" in the *Boston Miscellany of Literature and Fashion* and "Paradise (to be) Regained" in the *United States Magazine and Democratic Review*. "I could heartily wish," Emerson wrote his friend while still in New York, "that this country, which seems all opportunity, did actually offer more distinct and just rewards of labor to that unhappy class of men who have more reason and conscience than strength of back and of arm."[175] Soon Thoreau would enter a new phase in his writing career, a prolific period in which he wrote, or began to write, his two most famous works: *Walden* and "Civil Disobedience."

"It matters not how small the beginning may seem to be," Thoreau wrote in "Civil Disobedience."[176] His move to Walden Pond on July 4, 1845, was just such a small beginning. His noting of the event was inauspicious. "Yesterday I came here to live,"[177] he wrote in his journal the next day. That he moved on the anniversary of American independence has been touted as Thoreau's own day of independence, which may be little more than academic mythologizing. A more personal reason may have prompted his timing, and his claim that its falling on Independence Day was an "accident"[178] is more truth than literary device. Thoreau went to Walden Pond to write a book commemorating his brother. By moving in on the fourth of July he would awaken to see the sun rise on his new life at the Pond on the morning of what would have been John's thirtieth birthday.

Walden Woods was marginal land. Not arable, it was good only for woodlots. The land on which Thoreau built his house was one of Emerson's lots, and he was able to live on his friend's land in exchange for the same type of labor and help he gave when living in the Emerson household. The woods were also home to people who, in their own way, were marginal to Concord society: the Irish building the railroad, the formerly enslaved, alcoholics, those simply called lurkers, and now Henry David Thoreau. It was no wonder people made "very particular inquiries" concerning his life there.[179] When people asked what he was doing there, he presented a lecture, "A History of Myself," before the Concord Lyceum. This became the foundation for *Walden*.

Thoreau woke with the sun, and his days might include a morning bath in the pond, a period for reading and writing, hoeing his bean field, a long walk through the woods botanizing and observing, a second bath or afternoon swim. He might row out on the pond or the river, playing his flute, visit friends and family in Concord, or receive visitors at his house by the Pond, take a night walk, and occasionally answer the call of Emerson.

During his first winter at the Pond, out from under Emerson's roof, Thoreau began writing brief assessments of Emerson in his journal, such as: "Emerson does not consider things in respect to their essential utility, but an important partial and relative one, as works of art perhaps. His probes pass one side of their centre of gravity. His exaggeration is of a part, not of the whole."[180]

In a year's time Thoreau completed a draft of his first book, *A Week on the Concord and Merrimack Rivers*, which

Emerson was already touting as "a seven days' voyage in as many chapters, pastoral as Isaak Walton, spicy as flagroot, broad and deep as Menu."[181] Emerson admired what the two Thoreau brothers had done. They were not an example of those "students of words" Emerson criticized in "New England Reformers" who are

> shut up in schools, and colleges, and recitation-rooms, for ten or fifteen years, and come out at last with a bag of wind, a memory of words, and do not know a thing. We cannot use our hands, or our legs, or our eyes, or our arms. We do not know an edible root in the woods, we cannot tell our course by the stars, nor the hour of the day by the sun. It is well if we can swim and skate. We are afraid of a horse, of a cow, of a dog, of a snake, of a spider.[182]

He saw in the Thoreau brothers two who would "read God directly."[183] "Experience," Emerson wrote, "is hands and feet to every enterprise."[184] As he said in "The American Scholar," "So much only of life as I know by experience, so much of the wilderness have I vanquished and planted, or so far have I extended my being, my dominion. I do not see how any man can afford . . . to spare any action in which he can partake."[185]

Thoreau believed in the benefits of old shoes. New shoes were commonly too narrow, but an old shoe that had formed to the idiosyncrasies of your foot, that was synonymous with comfort. As he noted in his journal, "King James loved his old shoes best. Who does not?"[186] After visiting the cobbler in Concord in July of 1846, Thoreau was met by Sam Staples. Edward Emerson described Staples as one who "rose through the grades of bar-tender, clerk, constable and jailer, deputy-sheriff, representative to the General Court, auctioneer, real-estate agent, and gentleman-farmer, to be one of the most valued and respected fathers of the village-family."[187]

Staples was finishing his term as the tax collector that year. Since he needed to either collect any outstanding taxes or, as a consequence for his failure to do so, pay them himself, he attempted to collect from Thoreau. Thoreau refused on principle. Neither a volunteerist nor a no-government man, it was a matter of personal protest in which he refused to pay a tax to a government that allowed for slavery. So Staples arrested him.

Thoreau was introduced to his cellmate. Hugh Connell was an Irishman a few years younger than Thoreau. He was accused of burning Israel Hunt's barn in the neighboring town of Sudbury and was awaiting trial. "As near as I could discover," Thoreau wrote in "Civil Disobedience," "he had probably gone to bed in a barn when drunk, and smoked his pipe there; and so a barn was burnt."[188] Thoreau's sympathy may have partly stemmed from his own accidental burning of hundreds of acres of woodland two years before, for which he escaped any fine or imprisonment, and only occasionally suffered hearing the words "burnt woods" whispered behind his back. Connell, however, poor and foreign, lacking the friends and standing that Thoreau enjoyed, did not get off as lightly.

Staples left. The door was locked. Connell showed Thoreau where to hang his hat, "and how he managed matters there" while Thoreau "pumped my fellow-prisoner as dry as I could, for fear I should never see him again."[189] Word travelled. Soon someone came and paid Thoreau's tax to Staples's daughter, Ellen, while her father was out.[190] Although Thoreau should have been released, Staples had already removed his boots by the time Ellen told him about the paid debt. He decided to let his prisoner remain in jail for the night.

Breakfast came—a pint of chocolate with brown bread. Thoreau ate what he could, leaving some bread, which Connell seized with instructions that he should save it up for lunch or dinner. When Connell was let out to work at haying in a neighboring field, that was the last Thoreau saw of him. It is unlikely he knew that Connell soon served five years in prison for arson. Although Thoreau was angry at the intervention of his anonymous taxpayer, and Staples's insistence that he leave the jail, he and his jailer "were always good friends," Edward Emerson wrote.[191]

The next day Alcott and Emerson had a long discussion about the incarceration. Alcott wrote in his journal about his "earnest talk with Emerson dealing with civil powers and institutions, arising from Thoreau's going to jail for refusing to pay his tax." Alcott said that Emerson "thought it mean and skulking, and in bad taste,"[192] a summation that has unfairly stuck to Emerson. He wrote page after page in his journal of arguments both for and against Alcott's position, and what presumably was Thoreau's.

In one passage Emerson showed a complete understanding and, ultimately, a sense of pride in his friend's stand.

These—rabble—at Washington are really better than the sniveling opposition. They have a sort of genius of a bold and manly cast, though Satanic. They see, against the unanimous expression of the people, how much a little well-directed effrontery can achieve, how much crime the people will bear, and they proceed from step to step, and it seems they have calculated but too justly upon your Excellency, O Governor Briggs. Mr. Webster told them how much the war cost, that was his protest, but voted the war, and sends his son to it. They calculated rightly on Mr. Webster. My friend Mr. Thoreau has gone to jail rather than pay his tax. On him they could not calculate. The Abolitionists denounce the war and give much time to it, but they pay the tax.[193]

"Don't run amuck against the world," Emerson wrote, briefly considering the position that if the state "means you well"—if ninety parts of what it does is for good and "ten parts for mischief"—then you "cannot fight heartily for a fraction." The falsity of this justification was apparent as he continued, "The Abolitionists ought to resist and go to prison in multitudes on their known and described disagreements from the state. . . . I should heartily applaud them."[194]

Ultimately Emerson took issue with those abolitionists who spoke for freeing the enslaved but were not willing to give up a lifestyle that directly supported the institutions they condemned: cotton, rum, shipping. "In the particular," he wrote, "it is worth considering that refusing payment of the state tax does not reach the evil so nearly as many other methods within your reach." It was "your coat, your sugar" that kept people in chains. "Yet these"—and he must have seen he was criticizing himself in this as well—"you do not stick at buying."[195] In another entry he wrote, "Your objection, then, to the State of Massachusetts is deceptive. Your true quarrel is with the state of Man."[196]

On July 26 Thoreau spent two hours talking with Alcott, the one person in Concord most likely to understand. Alcott had gone through a similar arrest in January 1843. His wife wrote the following entry in Alcott's journal: "A day of some excitement, as Mr. Alcott had refused to pay his town tax and they had gone through the form of taking him to jail. After waiting some time to be committed, he was told it was paid by a friend." Alcott later explained it this way:

> Staples, the town collector, called to assure me that he should next week advertize my land to pay for the tax, unless it was paid before that time. Land for land, man for man. I would, were it possible, know nothing of this economy called "the State," but it will force itself upon the freedom of the free-born and the wisest bearing is to over-bear it, let it have its own way, the private person never going out of his way to meet it. It shall put its hand into a person's pocket if it will, but I shall not put mine there on its behalf.[197]

Charles Lane, the British social reformer, voluntarist, and friend of Alcott, was not an easy man to like. His haughty arrogance turned many away from him, both inside the Alcott family, Abba and Louisa May, and outside, Thoreau and Emerson. Emerson wrote that Lane's "nature and influence do not invite mine, but always freeze me."[198] His account of Alcott's arrest for *The Liberator*, however, must have been stimulating to Thoreau. Lane wrote that Alcott, being

> convinced that the payment of the town tax involved principles and practices most degrading and injurious to man, he had long determined not to be a voluntary party to its continuance....
>
> To the county jail, therefore, Mr. Alcott went, or rather was forced by the benignant State and its delicate instrument....
>
> This act of non-resistance, you will perceive, does not rest on the plea of poverty. For Mr. Alcott has always supplied some poor neighbor with food and clothing to

a much higher amount than his tax. Neither is it wholly based on the iniquitous purposes to which the money when collected is applied. For part of it is devoted to education, and education has not a heartier friend in the world than Bronson Alcott. But it is founded on the moral instinct which forbids every moral being to be a party, either actively or permissively, to the destructive principles of power and might over peace and love.[199]

Thoreau gave two lectures in Concord in 1848, possibly two parts of the same lecture. "The Relation of the Individual to the State" and "The Rights and Duties of the Individual in Relation to the State" explained his actions and principles to his curious neighbors. Elizabeth Peabody, planning the first issue of her *Aesthetic Papers* in early 1849, asked Thoreau to contribute a manuscript after hearing about one of the lectures. He wrote Peabody on April 5 that he would send "the article in question before the end of next week." His offering "the paper to your *first volume* only" was moot. The journal folded after its initial issue.

A week after Thoreau's arrest the Concord Female Anti-Slavery Society held their second celebration of West Indian Emancipation at Thoreau's house at Walden Pond. People spoke from his doorway, including Emerson. Previously Emerson had read his address "On the Anniversary of the Emancipation of the Negroes in the British West Indies" at the August 1844 meeting of the Society, where Frederick Douglass was also to speak. Because abolitionists had been outspoken about the clergy, they were denied use of the First Parish, and the weather prevented the use of the meadow next to the Old Manse. The Town Hall was then decided on. The town selectmen, however, would not direct the sexton to ring the meeting-house bell to alert people of the change in venue. Thoreau, "seeing the timidity of one unfortunate youth, who dared not touch the bell rope, took hold of it with a strong arm; and the bell, (though set in its own way,) pealed forth its summons right merrily."[200] Nearly twenty years later Emerson recalled the event. "I have never recorded a fact, which perhaps ought to have gone into my sketch of 'Thoreau,' that . . . when I read my Discourse on Emancipation [in the British West Indies], in the Town Hall, in Concord, and the selectmen would not direct the sexton to ring the meeting-house bell, Henry went himself, and rung the bell at the appointed hour."[201]

In "The Method of Nature" Emerson asked, "Shall we not quit our companions, as if they were thieves and pot-companions, and betake ourselves to some desert cliff of Mount Katahdin, some unvisited recess of Moosehead Lake, to bewail our innocency and to recover it, and with it the power to communicate again with these sharers of a more sacred idea?"[202] So when Thoreau was invited to accompany his cousin George Thatcher, who was in the lumber business in Maine and would be traveling to look at some property, he took the opportunity to make an excursion away from Walden, away from Concord, away from friends. While visiting a lumber camp, Thoreau found a copy of Emerson's address "On the Anniversary of the Emancipation of the Negroes in the British West Indies."[203] Emerson was never far away.

In the summer of 1846 Emerson imagined a retreat of his own. He showed his selected site to both Thoreau and Alcott; Thoreau drew a diagram of a small house to which Alcott added "another story, as a lookout."[204] Although these plans were not brought to fruition, Emerson did not abandon the idea of a personal sanctuary. The following summer he decided to build a small summerhouse in the field next to Bush that could be used as a study. Thoreau, Alcott, and Emerson began cutting hemlocks for posts. Built organically from Alcott's intuition rather than any architectural design, the house was "fashioned from gnarled limbs of pine, oak with knotty excrescences and straight trunks of cedar, a fantastic but pleasing structure. . . . feeling its way up, as it were, dictated at each step by the suggestion of the crooked bough that was used and necessarily often altered. . . . Thoreau drove the nails, and drove them well, but as Mr. Alcott made the eaves curve upward for beauty, and lined the roof with velvet moss and *sphagnum*, Nature soon reclaimed it."[205] While working with Alcott, Thoreau felt "he was nowhere, doing nothing."[206] Emerson's mother called it "The Ruin." Emerson referred to it as "Tumbledown-Hall."[207] In the fall Thoreau wrote to Emerson,

> Alcott has heard that I laughed and so set the people a laughing at his arbor, though I never laughed louder than when on the ridge pole. But now I have not laughed for a long time, it is so serious. He is very grave to look at. . . . As for the building I feel a little oppressed when I come near it, it has so great a disposition to be beautiful. It is certainly a wonderful structure on the whole, and the fame of the architect will endure as long—as it shall stand.[208]

Miraculously completed, it remained standing—another miracle—but was so drafty and visited by mosquitoes from the nearby meadow that Emerson was unable to use it.

As Thoreau re-read Emerson's *Essays* in his house at Walden Pond during his second winter, he felt "that they were not poetry—that they were not written exactly at the right crisis though inconceivably near to it."[209] Thoreau attempted to assess who and what Emerson was.

> Emerson again is a critic, poet, philosopher, with talent not so conspicuous, not so adequate to his task; but his field is still higher, his task more arduous. Lives a far more intense life; seeks to realize a divine life; his affections and intellect equally developed. Has advanced farther, and a new heaven opens to him. Love and Friendship, Religion, Poetry, the Holy are familiar to him. The life of an Artist; more variegated, more observing, finer perception; not so robust, elastic; practical enough in his own field; faithful, a judge of men. There is no such general critic of men and things, no such trustworthy and faithful man. More of the divine realized in him than in any. A poetic critic, reserving the unqualified nouns for the gods.[210]

"Emerson has special talents unequalled," he wrote as he realized what Emerson's true gift was. "His personal influence upon young persons greater than any man's. In his world every man would be a poet, Love would reign, Beauty would take place, Man and Nature would harmonize."[211] In this role Emerson would continue to promote Thoreau's writings to others, writing to Thomas Carlyle in February 1847, "You are yet to read a good American book made by this Thoreau, and which shortly is to be printed, he says."[212] "Mrs. Ripley and other members of the opposition," he wrote to Margaret Fuller, perhaps because he felt she was one of the opposition, "came down the other night to hear Henry's Account of his housekeeping at Walden Pond, which he read as a lecture, and were charmed with the witty wisdom which ran through it all."[213]

When Thoreau's manuscript had been completed,

Emerson enlisted his brother William to use his connections to find a publisher, but more to the purpose he wrote to Evert Duyckinck, one of the leading editors of the day in the New York literary scene, about Thoreau's

book of extraordinary merit, which he wishes to publish. It purports to be the account of "An Excursion on the Concord and Merrimack Rivers," which he made some time ago in company with his brother, in a boat built by themselves. The book contains about the same quantity of matter for printing as Dicken's Pictures of Italy. I have represented to Mr. Thoreau, that his best course would undoubtedly be, to send the book to you, to be printed by Wiley & Putnam, that it may have a good edition and wide publishing.

This book has many merits. It will be as attractive to *lovers of nature*, in every sense, that is, to naturalists, and to poets, as Isaak Walton. It will be attractive to scholars for its excellent literature, and to all thoughtful persons for its originality and profoundness. The narrative of the little voyage, though faithful, is a very slender thread for such big beads and ingots as are strung on it. It is really a book of the results of the studies of years.

Would you like to print this book into your American Library? It is quite ready, and the whole can be sent you at once. It has never yet been offered to any publisher. If you wish to see the MS. I suppose Mr. Thoreau would readily send it to you. I am only desirous that you should propose to him good terms, and give his book the great advantages of being known which your circulation ensures.

Mr. Thoreau is the author of an Article on Carlyle, now printed and printing in Graham's last and coming Magazine, and some papers in the Dial; but he has done nothing half so good as his new book. He is well known to Mr. Hawthorne also.[214]

Although Wiley & Putnam declined to publish the book at any financial risk to themselves, Duyckinck did use his influence to help garner interest. He put a notice in *The Literary World*, which he edited: "Henry D. Thoreau, Esq., whose elaborate paper on Carlyle, now publishing in Graham's Magazine, is attracting considerable attention, has also completed a new work of which reports speak highly. It will probably be soon given to the public."[215]

When Emerson made his first voyage to Europe in 1831, he was a young widower who had resigned his ministerial profession. He went at the urging of friends who hoped it would restore his fragile physical and mental health. Having met Wordsworth and Coleridge, and, most important, Thomas Carlyle, Emerson's world changed, although he did not yet know in what way. His European journal shows a receptive mind, newly and continuously sparked and animated by all he experienced. People, places, and perspectives opened new ways of thinking and observing the world around him. His second voyage was at the invitation of his European friends, and although he did not like travelling and felt that long journeys did not "yield a fair share of reasonable hours,"[216] he eventually and reluctantly agreed. During his first visit, he wanted to meet certain people. On his second visit, people wanted to meet him.

Before going, however, there was this question: who would take care of his family and his house in his absence? When Emerson asked Thoreau at the end of August if he were willing to move back to the Emerson house during the lecture tour, it would have been surprising had

Thoreau given any answer other than yes. Based on how seminal we have historically made his time at Walden Pond, it was extraordinary how quickly Thoreau packed his bags and moved back into the town of Concord. Emerson was not sailing from Boston on the packet ship *Washington Irving* until October 5, yet Thoreau, rather than "suck out all the marrow"[217] of his time there, left Walden precipitously on September 6, one month before he was needed in the Emerson household.

Although Thoreau could, in all probability, have returned to Walden Pond after Emerson returned from Europe, there was no reason to do so. "What is once well done," he wrote, "is done forever."[218] There was no need to go back. He had, as he said, "several more lives to live, and could not spare any more time for that one."[219] It was now time for the writer's "long probation."[220] It was the time when, as Emerson said, "experience is converted into thought."[221] Thoreau described the process in a letter to H.G.O. Blake.

> Let me suggest a theme for you: to state to yourself precisely and completely what that walk over the mountains amounted to for you,—returning to this essay again and again, until you are satisfied that all that was important in your experience is in it. . . . Going up there and being blown on is nothing. We never do much climbing while we are there, but we eat our luncheon, etc., very much as at home. It is after we get home that we really go over the mountain, if ever. What did the mountain say? What did the mountain do?[222]

Ultimately it is not the climbing of the mountain but the understanding of what that experience on the mountain means that is crucial. Similarly, his two years at Walden

Pond, or his one night in jail, was in the end not as momentous and as transformative as the writing about those events. It was then that John Thoreau's son, Henry, who walked around Concord and made pencils and surveyed land, became Thoreau, and turned a few local and personal experiences into something universally representative and profoundly significant. "Perhaps he fell," as Emerson said all of us do, "into his way of living, without forecasting it much, but approved and confirmed it with later wisdom."[223]

Sometime in the fall of 1847, forty-five-year-old Sophia Ford,[224] who had joined the Alcott household two years earlier as tutor to the children, fell in love with Thoreau and proposed marriage. Thoreau was not flattered, confiding to Emerson,

> I have had a tragic correspondence, for the most part all on one side, with Miss Ford. She did really wish to—I hesitate to write—marry me. That is the way they spell it. Of course I did not write a deliberate answer. How could I deliberate upon it? I sent back as distinct a *no* as I have learned to pronounce after considerable practice, and I trust that this *no* has succeeded. Indeed, I wished that it might burst, like hollow shot, after it had struck and buried itself and make itself felt there. *There was no other way.* I really had anticipated no such foe as this in my career.[225]

Though she continued to correspond with Thoreau, he did not answer her letters and in one instance burned one immediately on reading it.[226] Ford, remaining true to her belief that their souls were twins and that they would unite in the spirit world,[227] continued unmarried until her death nearly forty years later.

Thoreau's letters to Emerson in Europe were often filled with mundane and necessary points of business in regard to Emerson's property, but he also regaled him with stories of his family, and how he, "such a hermit as I am" found "the experiment" as head of Emerson's household "good for society, so I do not regret my transient nor my permanent share in it." He found that "Lidian and I make very good housekeepers," and that Edward "very seriously asked me, the other day, 'Mr. Thoreau, will you be my father?' I am occasionally Mr. Rough-and-tumble with him that I may not miss *him*, and lest he should miss *you* too much. So you must come back soon, or you will be superseded."[228]

"I suppose you will like to hear of my book," Thoreau wrote Emerson toward the end of 1847, "though I have nothing worth writing about it. Indeed, for the last month or two I have forgotten it, but shall certainly remember it again." Publishers declined to release the book at any risk to themselves, though some were willing to print it if the author accepted the risk. "If I liked the book well enough, I should not delay; but for the present I am indifferent. I believe this is, after all, the course you advised,—to let it lie."[229]

Emerson replied, "But lest I should not say what is needful . . . I am not of opinion that your book should be delayed a month. I should print it at once, nor do I think that you would incur any risk in doing so that you cannot well afford. It is very certain to have readers and debtors here as well as there."[230] Emerson's encouragement may have pushed Thoreau to accept an offer from James Munroe & Co., publisher of *The Dial* in its final year, to print it at Thoreau's risk—which, when the book failed to sell, took him several years to pay.

On May 26, 1849, Thoreau went into Boston to pick up copies of his first book. In early June Theodore Parker invited Emerson to review *A Week on the Concord and Merrimack Rivers* for his *The Massachusetts Quarterly*. Emerson declined, saying, "I am not the man to write the Notice of Thoreau's book. I am of the same clan and parish. You must give it to a good foreigner." He then suggested possible reviewers who might do justice to the book: "E. P. Whipple has good literary insulation and is a superior critic. Will he not try his hand on this? If not, will not Starr King? If not the one or the other, why not send it to the New Yorkers, to Henry James, Parke Goodwin, or C. Dana? The book has rare claims, and we must have an American claim and ensign marked on it before it goes abroad for English opinions."[231] It was ultimately reviewed for Parker's journal by James Russell Lowell, who continued his condemnations of the author. Thoreau, "like most solitary men," Lowell wrote, "exaggerates the importance of his own thoughts."[232]

Thoreau was frustrated and disillusioned that Emerson had not, in his mind, done what he ought to support his first book. In the fall Thoreau wrote, among pages of strongly worded invective about friends, the more succinct, "I had a friend, I wrote a book, I asked my friend's criticism, I never got but praise for what was good in it—my friend became estranged from me and then I got blame for all that was bad,—and so I got at last the criticism which I wanted."[233] It is unlikely that Thoreau knew all that Emerson had done to promote the book, nor that Emerson knew of Thoreau's criticisms; Thoreau confided to his journal concerns he would not voice to his friend. In spite of it all, when Munroe sent Thoreau the unsold copies of his book, he met the occasion with humor. Four years after publication, Munroe wrote to him asking what should be done with the books, and Thoreau

> had them all sent to me here, and they have arrived to-
> day by express, filling the man's wagon,—706 copies
> out of an edition of 1000 which I bought of Munroe
> four years ago and have been ever since paying for, and
> have not quite paid for yet. The wares are sent to me at
> last, and I have an opportunity to examine my purchase.
> They are something more substantial than fame, as my
> back knows, which has borne them up two flights of
> stairs to a place similar to that to which they trace their
> origin. . . . I have now a library of nearly nine hundred
> volumes, over seven hundred of which I wrote myself.[234]

In November 1847 Lidian sent her husband a description of a domestic scene, complete with stage directions—"The three children and Mama at the worktable. Eddy on Mama's lap"—followed by some dialogue.

> Eddy. Write to Father I am a good Boy.
> Edie. I want Father to come home. . . . Mr. Thoreau puts
> Eddy in a chair, and then takes Eddy up in it, and carries
> it about the room. . . . Mr. Thoreau jumps us every night.
> Eddy. Mother, and tell him Mr. Thoreau jumped a chair
> over me tonight![235]

In December Waldo wrote Henry a letter that began with an appreciation for all he was doing.

> It is one of the best things connected with my coming
> hither that you could and would keep the homestead,
> that fireplace shines all the brighter, and has a certain
> permanent glimmer therefor. Thanks, evermore thanks

for the kindness which I well discern to the *youth* of the house, to my darling little horseman of pewter, leather, wooden, rocking and what other breeds, destined, I hope, to ride Pegasus yet, and I hope not destined to be thrown, to Edith who long ago drew from you verses which I carefully preserve, and to Ellen who by speech and now by letter I find old enough to be companionable, and to choose and reward her own friends in her own fashions.[236]

Henry was grateful for the letter.

My Dear Friend,

I thank you for your letter. I was very glad to get it—And I am glad again to write to you. However slow the steamer, no time intervenes between the writing and the reading of thoughts, but they come freshly to the most distant port.

I am here still, and very glad to be here—and shall not trouble you with my complaints because I do not fill my place better. I have had many good hours in the chamber at the head of the stairs—a solid time, it seems to me.[237]

Emerson's first letter to his friend in the new year opened with adulation before reporting on a talk he had heard. "Let who or what pass," he wrote, "there stands the dear Henry,—if indeed any body had a right to call him so,—erect, serene, and undeceivable. So let it ever be!"[238] Earlier that month Thoreau wrote that not only had he "read a part of the story of my excursion to Ktaadn to quite a large audience of men and boys, the other night, whom it interested," but "I have also written what will do for a lecture on Friendship."[239]

Between completion of the first draft and its eventual publication, Thoreau had opportunity to revise and expand his first book. His essay on friendship was placed in the Wednesday chapter of *A Week on the Concord and Merrimack Rivers* as a central theme. He wrote it in part out of loss, looking back at the friendship he had enjoyed with his brother, but also out of hope, looking at the potential of his friendship with Emerson. Drawing journal passages out of the more than a decade he and Emerson shared, he wrote of the expectations, disappointments, and possibilities of what he thought true friendship might still present.

"There are few even whom I should venture to call earnestly by their most proper names," Thoreau wrote in *A Week*. "A name pronounced is the recognition of the individual to whom it belongs. He who can pronounce my name aright, he can call me, and is entitled to my love and service."[240] With that idea in mind he addressed a letter to Emerson in February in a new way: "Dear Waldo,—For I think I have heard that that is your name . . . Whatever I may *call* you, I know you better than I know your name." He continued with thanks for what Emerson's essays meant to him. "I believe I never thanked you for your lectures, one and all, which I have heard formerly read here in Concord. I *know* I never have. There was some excellent reason each time why I did not; but it will never be too late. I have had that advantage, at least, over you in my education."[241]

Lidian had been unwell for a month, but Emerson had not known until Thoreau finally informed him of her slow recovery.

Lidian is too unwell to write to you and so I must tell you what I can about the children, and herself. I am afraid she has not told you how unwell she is, today perhaps we may say—has been. She has been confined to her chamber four or five weeks, and three or four weeks, at least to her bed—with the jaundice, accompanied with *constant* nausea, which makes life intolerable to her. This added to her general ill health has made her *very* sick. She is as yellow as saffron. The Doctor, who comes once a day does not let her read (nor can she now) nor *hear* much reading. She has written her letters to you till recently sitting up in bed—but he said that he would not come again if she did so. She has Abby and Almira to take care of her, and Mrs. Brown to read to her, and I also occasionally have something to read or to say. The Doctor says she must not expect to "take any comfort of her life" for a week or two yet.[242]

Toward the end of March things had come to a sudden impasse, with a slowly recovering Lidian writing her husband, "Henry is well, but won't write to you. I suppose because you don't write to him."[243] But letters crossed in the mails. As Lidian's letter was crossing the ocean, a letter from Waldo was on its way to Henry, beginning, "Your letter was very welcome."[244] Whatever may have caused this lapse is not clear from any extant correspondence. In May Thoreau wrote, "I am glad to find that you are expecting a line from me, since I have a better excuse for sending this hard scrawl."[245] When Emerson sailed home in July, landing in Boston at the end of the month, Thoreau lost no time in leaving Bush and moving back to his family's house.

Emerson was, perhaps they both were, cautious about renewing their friendship to its previous level after Emerson's return from Europe. "Henry Thoreau is like the woodgod," Emerson wrote shortly after his return, "who solicits the wandering poet and draws him into 'antres vast and deserts idle,' and bereaves him of his memory, and leaves him naked, plaiting vines and with twigs in his hand. Very seductive are the first steps from the town to the woods, but the end is want and madness."[246] It took some time before whatever issues they had experienced were resolved, or forgiven, or forgotten.

Thoreau was writing in his journal that he did "not feel permanently related to any one,"[247] and "When we separate finally and completely from one who has been our friend we separate with content—and without grief—as gently and naturally as night passes into day."[248] But Emerson did not show any similar concern that their friendship was permanently ruptured. He continued to do what he could for Thoreau's career. "I was at *South Danvers*," Emerson wrote Thoreau in early 1850,

> and promised Mr. C. Northend, Secretary of the Lyceum, to invite you for Monday 18th Feb. to read a lecture to his institution. I told him there were two lectures to describe Cape Cod, which interested him and his friends, and they hoped that the two might somehow be rolled into one to give them some sort of complete story of the journey. I hope it will not quite discredit my negotiation if I confess that they heard with joy that Concord people laughed till they cried, when it was read to them. . . . They will pay your expenses, and $10.00. . . . Do go if you can.[249]

Any internal conflict they were feeling toward each other may have been more on Thoreau's side. With Emerson, there remained a complete trust. "I leave town tomorrow," he wrote in 1850, "and must beg you, if any question arises between Mr. Bartlett and me, in regard to boundary lines, to act as my attorney, and I will be bound by any agreement you shall make."[250] When tragedy struck, any differences, real or imagined, were put aside.

On May 17, 1850, Margaret Fuller, her husband, Giovanni Ossoli, and their young son, Angelo, boarded the ship *Elizabeth* in Italy, heading home to America. The ship ran aground as it approached Fire Island off the coast of New York on July 19. Fuller, her husband, and their child all drowned. Emerson sent Thoreau to discover what remains he could, whether corporeal or literary. By the time news had reached Concord and Thoreau had reached Fire Island, there was little hope of recovering either. Thoreau wrote to Emerson from Fire Island, describing the wreck and what little he found.

I am writing this at the house of Smith Oakes, within one mile of the wreck. He is the one who rendered the most assistance. . . . Mr. Oakes and wife tell me (all the survivors came or were brought directly to their house) that the ship struck at 10 minutes after 4 AM. and all hands, being mostly in their night clothes made haste to the forecastle—the water coming in at once. There they remained, the passengers *in* the forecastle, the crew *above* it doing what they could. Every wave lifted the forecastle roof and washed over those within. The first man got ashore at 9, many from 9 to noon—. At floodtide about 3$\frac{1}{2}$ o'clock when the ship broke up entirely, they came out of the forecastle and Margaret sat with her back to the foremast with her hands over her knees—her husband and child already drowned—a great wave came and washed her off. . . .

I have visited the child's grave. . . .

In the meanwhile I shall do what I can to recover property and obtain particulars hereabouts.[251]

Thoreau wrote to H.G.O. Blake on his return about "a button which I ripped off the coat of the Marquis of Ossoli, on the seashore, the other day. Held up, it intercepts the light,—an actual button,—and yet all the life it is connected with is less substantial to me, and interests me less, than my faintest dream. Our thoughts are the epochs in our lives: all else is but as a journal of the winds that blew while we were here."[252] The importance of thought over all else, including human companionship, seemed to form from the loss he witnessed on Fire Island, as well as his perceived loss of his friendship with Emerson.

About a month after he returned from Fire Island, Thoreau told Emerson that people were less interesting than Nature.[253] "I do not know but a pine wood," Thoreau wrote in his journal, "is as substantial and as memorable a fact as a friend. I am more sure to come away from it cheered, than from those who come nearest to being my friends."[254] Nature became a substitute for what he failed to find on a personal level.

> I love nature partly *because* she is not man, but a retreat
> from him. None of his institutions control or pervade her.
> There a different kind of right prevails. In her midst I can
> be glad with an entire gladness. If this world was all man,
> I could not stretch myself, I should lose all hope. He is
> constraint, she is freedom to me. He makes me wish for
> another world. She makes me content with this. None
> of the joys she supplies is subject to his rules and defi-
> nitions. What he touches he taints. In thought he mor-
> alizes. One would think that no free, joyful labor was
> possible to him. How infinite and pure the least pleasure
> of which Nature is basis, compared with the congratula-
> tion of mankind! The joy which Nature yields is like that
> afforded by the frank words of one we love.[255]

This idea culminated in his 1857 statement that "All nature is my bride."[256] Early in the next year he wrote that it had been "long since a human friend has met me with such a glow" as he found in the Andromeda,"[257] and that "a man's relation to Nature must come very near to a personal one . . . when human friends fail or die, she must stand in the gap to him."[258]

From 1851 on, Thoreau's journal became a more fully realized part of not only his writing but also his life, and he began to see that a more introspective and thoughtful life might be more beneficial than what he found in society. "My acquaintances will sometimes wonder why," he wrote, "I will impoverish myself by living aloof from this or that company, but greater would be the impoverishment if I should associate with them."[259] "Associate reverently and as much as you can with your loftiest thoughts," he wrote early in 1852. "My thoughts are my company."[260]

Emerson continued to find it "an inexcusable fault" that Thoreau "is insignificant here in the town. He speaks at Lyceum or other meeting but somebody else speaks and his speech falls dead and is forgotten. He rails at the town doings and ought to correct and inspire them."[261] Thoreau did not take his talent far enough, being dismissed by Emerson as "a boy, and will be an old boy. Pounding beans is good to the end of pounding Empires, but not, if at the end of years, it is only beans."[262] He was wanting "a little ambition," Emerson wrote in 1851, and "instead of being the head of American engineers, he is captain of a huckleberry party."[263]

Thoreau continued to struggle with their relationship.

Ah, I yearn toward thee, my friend, but I have not confidence in thee. We do not believe in the same God. I am not thou; thou art not I. We trust each other to-day, but we distrust to-morrow. Even when I meet thee unexpectedly, I part from thee with disappointment. Though

I enjoy thee more than other men, yet I am more disappointed with thee than with others. I know a noble man; what is it hinders me from knowing him better? I know not how it is that our distrust, our hate, is stronger than our love. Here I have been on what the world would call friendly terms with one fourteen years, have pleased my imagination sometimes with loving him; and yet our hate is stronger than our love. Why are we related, yet thus unsatisfactorily? We almost are a sore to one another. Ah, I am afraid because thy relations are not my relations. Because I have experienced that in some respects we are strange to one another, strange as some wild creature. Ever and anon there will come the consciousness to mar our love that, change the theme but a hair's breadth, and we are tragically strange to one another. We do not know what hinders us from coming together. But when I consider what my friend's relations and acquaintances are, what his tastes and habits, then the difference between us gets named. I see that all these friends and acquaintances and tastes and habits are indeed my friend's self. In the first place, my friend is prouder than I am,—and I am very proud, perchance.[264]

Together they spoke about the isolation of the individual. "It would be hard to recall the rambles of last night's talk with Henry Thoreau," Emerson noted in October 1851,

But we stated over again, to sadness almost, the eternal loneliness. I found that though the stuff of Tragedy and of Romances is in a moral union of two superior persons, and the confidence of each in the other, for long years, out of sight and in sight, and against all appearances, is at last justified by victorious proof of probity to gods and men, causing a gush of joyful emotion, tears, glory, or what-not,—though there be for heroes this *moral union*, yet they, too, are still as far off as ever from an intellectual union, and this moral union is for comparatively low and external purposes, like the coöperation of a ship's crew or of a fire-club. But how insular and pathetically solitary are all the people we know![265]

"In regard to my friends," Thoreau wrote at the end of the year, "I feel that I know and have communion with a finer and subtler part of themselves which does not put me off when they put me off, which is not cold to me when they are cold, not till I am cold. I hold by a deeper and stronger tie than absence can sunder."[266] Throughout this period of perplexity, Thoreau stood by a certain "if you don't know what's wrong, I'm not going to tell you" stance, feeling like his "difficulties with my friends are such as no frankness will settle."

Others can confess and explain; I cannot. It is not that I am too proud, but that is not what is wanted. Friendship is the unspeakable joy and blessing that results to two or more individuals who from constitution sympathize; and natures are liable to no mistakes, but will know each other through thick and thin. Between two by nature alike and fitted to sympathize there is no veil and there can be no obstacle. Who are the estranged? Two friends explaining.

I feel sometimes as if I could say to my friends, "My friends, I am aware how I have outraged you, how I have seemingly preferred hate to love, seemingly treated others kindly and you unkindly, sedulously concealed my love, and sooner or later expressed all and more than all my hate." I can imagine how I might utter something like this in some moment never to be realized. But let me say frankly that at the same time I feel, it may be with too little regret, that I am under an awful necessity to be what I am. If the truth were known, which I do not know, I have no concern with those friends whom I misunderstand or who misunderstand me.

In the same entry Thoreau began to put blame on himself.

The fates only are unkind that keep us asunder, but my friend is ever kind. I am of the nature of stone. It takes the summer's sun to warm it.

My acquaintances sometimes imply that I am too cold; but each thing is warm enough of its kind. Is the stone too cold which absorbs the heat of the summer sun and does not part with it during the night? Crystals, though they be of ice, are not too cold to melt, but it was in melting that they were formed. Cold! I am most sensible of warmth in winter days. It is not the warmth of fire that you would have, but everything is warm and cold according to its nature. It is not that I am too cold, but that our warmth and coldness are not of the same nature; hence when I am absolutely warmest, I may be coldest to you. Crystal does not complain of crystal any more than the dove of its mate. You who complain that I am cold find Nature cold. To me she is warm. My heat is latent to you. Fire itself is cold to whatever is not of a nature to be warmed by it. A cool wind is warmer to a feverish man than the air of a furnace. That I am cold means that I am of another nature.[267]

"It is not words that I wish to hear or to utter," he wrote, "but relations that I seek to stand in."[268] By the end of 1851 he told himself to "treat your friends for what you know them to be. Regard no surfaces. Consider not what they did, but what they intended. Be sure, as you know them you are known of them again." After again blaming himself for their rift, Thoreau "sought an opportunity to make atonement, but the friend avoided me, and, with kinder feelings even than before, I was obliged to depart." At last he found his way through.

> I am resolved to know that one centrally, through thick and thin, and though we should be cold to one another, though we should never speak to one another, I will know that inward and essential love may exist even under a superficial cold, and that the law of attraction speaks louder than words. My true relation this instant shall be my apology for my false relation the last instant. I made haste to cast off my injustice as scurf. I own it least of anybody, for I have absolutely done with it. Let the idle and wavering and apologizing friend appropriate it. Methinks our estrangement is only like the divergence of the branches which unite in the stem.[269]

Although Thoreau still felt that he was "peacefully parting company with the best friend I ever had, by each pursuing his proper path," he also saw that "it is possible that we may have a better *understanding* now than when we were more at one. Not expecting such essential agreement as before. Simply our paths diverge."[270] It was a moment of resignation and acceptance, and he was ready to accept a new period in his friendship with Emerson.

At the beginning of 1852 Thoreau was showing an uncharacteristic reserve and restraint. When Emerson shared a letter from the sculptor Horatio Greenough on making architectural ornaments have a "core of truth, a necessity and hence a beauty," Thoreau responded that it was fine from Greenough's point of view but "little better than the common dilettantism." He was "afraid," he admitted to his journal, "I should say hard things if I said more."[271] In his journal he put the harsher criticisms he would not utter to Emerson, still fluctuating between placing responsibility outward, stating that Emerson is "too grand for me,"[272] and inward: "If I have not succeeded in my friendships, it was because I demanded more of them and did not put up with what I could get; and I got no more partly because I gave so little."[273]

When Thoreau asked in his journal in August 1852, "Are my friends aware how disappointed I am?"[274] the answer was painfully clear. During this period Thoreau was constantly writing of his personal turmoil about their friendship, while Emerson was, in comparison, relatively silent about it. He continued to recognize that Thoreau "gives me, in flesh and blood and pertinacious Saxon belief, my own ethics. He is far more real, and daily practically obeying them, than I; and fortifies my memory at all times with an affirmative experience which refuses to be set aside."[275] There is little, however, to show Emerson experiencing any sort of crisis similar to Thoreau's. He did suffer annoyances with Thoreau, such as his disposition "to maximize the minimum," which Emerson scorned by saying, "that will take him some days."[276] Thoreau, Emerson noted, "sturdily pushes his economy into houses and thinks it the false mark of the gentleman that he is to pay much for his food. He ought to pay little for his food. Ice,—he must have ice!"[277] "Henry Thoreau says he values," Emerson wrote, "only the man who goes directly to his needs; who, wanting wood, goes to the woods and brings it home; or to the river, and collects the drift, and brings it in his boat to his door, and burns it: not him who keeps shop, that he may buy wood.

One is pleasing to reason and imagination; the other not."[278] "Henry is military," Emerson concluded.

> He seemed stubborn and implacable; always manly and wise, but rarely sweet. One would say that, as Webster could never speak without an antagonist, so Henry does not feel himself except in opposition. He wants a fallacy to expose, a blunder to pillory, requires a little sense of victory, a roll of the drums, to call his powers into full exercise.[279]

One afternoon, finding Thoreau complaining of "Clough or somebody that he or they recited to every one at table the paragraph just read by him and by them in the last newspaper and studiously avoided everything private," Emerson sardonically quipped, "I should think he was complaining of one H.D.T."[280]

Perhaps Emerson avoided the despair that Thoreau felt because each of Emerson's acquaintances contributed only one part of the whole that made up his family of friends. "I find in my platoon," he wrote, "contrasted figures; as, my brothers, and Everett, and Caroline, and Margaret, and Elizabeth, and Jones Very, and Sam Ward, and Henry Thoreau, and Alcott, and Channing. Needs all these and many more to represent my relations."[281]

At the end of 1853 after Emerson had delivered his lecture "The Anglo-American," Thoreau told him that he regretted "that whatever was written for a lecture, or whatever succeeded with the audience was bad." Emerson defended his position: "I am ambitious to write something which all can read, like *Robinson Crusoe*. . . . Henry objected, of course, and vaunted the better lectures which only reached a few persons."[282] In "Life without Principle," Thoreau re-iterated his stance, "If you would get money as a writer or lecturer, you must be popular, which is to go down per-pendicularly."[283] At supper with the Emersons one evening, Edith asked Thoreau whether "his lecture would be a nice interesting story, such as she wanted to hear, or whether it was one of those old philosophical things that she did not care about?" Thoreau turned to her, and then "bethought himself," Emerson said, seeing him "trying to believe that he had matter that might fit Edith and Edward, who were to sit up and go to the lecture, if it was a good one for them."[284]

When *Walden* was published in August 1854, Emerson praised his friend's book, writing to one person that "it is cheerful, sparkling, readable, with all kinds of merits, and rising sometimes to very great heights," and joking that the "little pond sinks in these very days as tremulous at its hu-man fame."[285] In June 1855 Emerson began soliciting money for the Alcott Fund—a life annuity to help support the ever-struggling Alcott Family—something that prompted the self-sufficient Thoreau to ask "fairly enough, when is it that the man is to begin to provide for himself?"[286]

"It is curious," Emerson wrote with a heightened sense of annoyance in 1856, "that Thoreau goes to a house to say with little preface what he has just read or observed, delivers it in lump, is quite inattentive to any comment or thought which any of the company offer on the matter, nay, is merely interrupted by it, and, when he has finished his report de-parts with precipitation."[287] "If I knew only Thoreau," he said around the same time,

I should think coöperation of good men impossible. Must we always talk for victory, and never once for truth, for comfort, and joy? Centrality he has, and penetration, strong understanding, and the higher gifts,—the insight of the real, or from the real, and the moral rectitude that belongs to it; but all this and all his resources of wit and invention are lost to me, in every experiment, year after year, that I make, to hold intercourse with his mind. Always some weary captious paradox to fight you with, and the time and temper wasted.[288]

On a walk with Emerson in the spring of 1857 Thoreau demonstrated how to cut a strip of bark from a white birch "to show how a naturalist would make the best box to carry a plant or other specimen requiring care, and thought the woodman would make a better hat of birch-bark than of felt,—hat, with cockade of lichens thrown in. I told him the Birkebeiners of the Heimskringla had been before him." The next day Emerson noted in his journal, "We will make a book on walking, 't is certain, and have easy lessons for beginners. 'Walking in ten Lessons.'"[289]

In early 1858 Emerson wrote that he was "specially sensible" of Thoreau's merits as a surveyor, "as he has just now by better surveying quite innocently made 60 rods of woodland for me, and left the adjacent lot, which he was measuring, larger than the deed gave it. There's a surveyor for you!"[290] Emerson's faith in Thoreau's surveying skills let his friend play a practical joke on him later that year when Sam Staples bought Kettell Farm next to the Emerson home. Thoreau ran the lines for him and found that a ditch Staples had dug, following the line of Emerson's orchard and meadow, was incorrectly located. What was thought by all to be part of Emerson's land was actually his new neighbor's property. Although the error was to no one's blame or discredit, Thoreau found it an opportunity to tease his friend.

"We'll call Emerson down and show it to him," he said. Staples had no interest in the issue and told Thoreau to "let it be as is," but Thoreau insisted, "I'll get Emerson down." Thoreau went up to the house and got Emerson to follow him down to the property line.

Standing on the border of the two properties, Thoreau taunted his friend, "I didn't think this of you, Mr. Emerson, stealing so much land of Staples here." Emerson was troubled by the dispute, offering right away to buy the land from Staples, who would hear none of it.

"I dug the ditch there supposing the hedge was the line," Staples said. "'Twan't your fault. 'Twas the man you bought of showed you where to put the hedge. Let it be as the ditch is now." Thoreau delighted in the joke.[291] In his next book Emerson wrote, "Every man takes care that his neighbor shall not cheat him. But a day comes when he begins to care that he do not cheat his neighbor."[292]

John Brown visited Concord for the first time in March 1857. While the *New-York Tribune* carried many pro-Brown reports of his exploits, stories of the Pottawatomie Massacre had also been in circulation for the past year. How much the Concordians knew, or believed, of his past is irrelevant. Brown was clear in his intentions for the future. "He believes in two articles,—two instruments, shall I say?—the Golden Rule and the Declaration of Independence," Emerson wrote, "and he used this expression in a conversation here concerning them, 'Better a whole generation of men, women and children should pass away by a violent death than that one word of either should be violated in this country.'"[293] And Thoreau wrote it was Brown's "peculiar doctrine that a man has a perfect right to interfere by force with the slaveholder, in order to rescue the slave. I agree with him. They who are continually shocked by slavery have some right to be shocked by the violent death of the slaveholder, but no others."[294] Both Emerson and Thoreau accepted that violence was not always to be avoided, and they had been readied for Brown's visit by such circumstances as the passage of the Fugitive Slave Act and return of the fugitive Anthony Burns to slavery.

When Brown returned to Concord two years later, he had "added a flowing beard, which gives the soldierly air, and port of an apostle," Alcott said, and he had "the martyr's temper and purpose."[295] It was five months before his raid on Harper's Ferry. Thoreau and Emerson were both firmly in support of his plans, although they did not know the exact nature of what those would be. Alcott noted that some "contribute something in aid of his plans without asking particulars."[296] It may not have mattered. When the news of what Brown had done came to Concord in October, Thoreau wrote in his journal, "I do not complain of any tactics that are effective of good, whether one wields the quill or the sword, but I shall not think him mistaken who quickest succeeds to liberate the slave. I will judge of the tactics by the fruits."[297]

Both friends were in complete accord over what they deemed a selfless act of personal sacrifice for the sake of humanity. Thoreau wrote that the crucifixion of Christ and the hanging of John Brown "are the two ends of a chain which is not without its links. He is not Old Brown any longer; he is an angel of light."[298] And Emerson agreed, calling Brown "that new saint than whom none purer or more brave was ever led by love of men into conflict and death,—the new saint awaiting his martyrdom, and who, if he shall suffer, will make the gallows glorious like the cross."[299]

Thoreau lectured on "The Character and Actions of Capt. John Brown" at the end of October in Concord. Emerson said it was read "with great force and effect, and though the audience was of widely different parties, it was heard without a murmur of dissent."[300] When Emerson heard that Frederick Douglass might not be able to speak in Boston due to his connection with Brown, he lost no time in promoting Thoreau as a replacement, writing to the organizer of the lecture series, Charles W. Slack, "I understand that there is some doubt about Mr. Douglass's keeping his engagement for Tuesday next. If there is a vacancy, I think you cannot do a greater public good than to send for Mr. Thoreau, who has read last night here a discourse on the history and character of Captain John Brown, which ought to be heard or read by every man in the Republic."[301]

John Brown was executed on December 2, 1859. A service for him was held in the Concord Town Hall, where Emerson and Thoreau among others read "appropriate passages from Brown's words, from the poets, and from the Scriptures."[302] That same day Frank Sanborn, one of Brown's Secret Six financial supporters, received a message that one of Brown's sons was in Boston. After hastily getting to Boston, Sanborn found instead Francis Jackson Merriam, who had joined Brown's army, avoided arrest, and escaped to Canada, but soon returned to Boston "to raise another expedition against the slave-holders. He was quite unfit to lead or even join in such an affair, being weak in body and almost distracted in mind; and I insisted that he should return at once to Canada."[303] Agreeing, Merriam mistakenly took a train that brought him no farther than Concord, arriving at Sanborn's door, wanted, with a reward out for his arrest. Sanborn went to Emerson and asked for the loan of his horse and a covered wagon, to be made ready at sunrise. He then went to Thoreau to ask him to drive the wagon from Emerson's house to Sanborn's, to take a "Mr. Lockwood" to the station in South Acton and put him on board a train bound for Canada. Neither Emerson nor Thoreau had any prior knowledge of the reasons for this clandestine adventure, but trusting Sanborn, and the need for secrecy, agreed to what they could only have suspected was an illegal situation.

Merriam, according to Sanborn, "was in a flighty state of mind, and though he had agreed to go back to Canada, and knew his own life depended on it, could not keep to that purpose. He insisted to Mr. Thoreau that he must see Mr. Emerson before he left Concord, must lay before him the plan of invading the South, and must consult him also about certain moral and religious questions that troubled his mind."[304] Thoreau listened, all the while continuing on toward South Acton, with Merriam growing suspicious.

"I don't know but *you* are Emerson," he said. "Are you? You look somewhat like him."

"No," Thoreau assured him, "I am not."

"Well, then," Merriam cried, jumping out of the wagon, "I am going back to Concord."

Merriam questioned Thoreau several more times before he told himself, "But then Emerson wouldn't lie." Thoreau was able to get Merriam back on the wagons then safely boarded on the train, and was soon reporting to Sanborn that "Mr. Lockwood had taken passage for Montreal."[305]

The next day memorial services for John Brown were held at the Music Hall in Boston, where Emerson read his essay "Morals," which was not written for this occasion but must have seemed as if it had been, with Emerson telling his audience:

Great men serve us, as insurrections do, in tyrannical governments. The world would run into endless routine, and forms incrust forms, till the life was gone. But the perpetual supply of new genius shocks us with thrills of life. It happens now and then in the ages, that a soul is born which has no weakness of self; which offers no impediment to the divine spirit; which comes down into nature as if only for the benefit of souls; and all its thoughts are perceptions of things as they are, without any infirmity of earth.[306]

At the end of 1859 Caroline Dall came to Concord to lecture on "Lives of Noted Women." Taking tea with the Emersons and a few others beforehand, she asked who might come out to hear her. A woman lecturing was not common.

Sanborn asked, "I suppose that Thoreau will come?"

"No. I saw him this morning," Emerson replied, before sharing one of Thoreau's sweepingly dismissive exaggerations, "He says women never have anything to say." Emerson had become used to such remarks. He had noted more than a decade earlier that "Thoreau sometimes appears only as a *gendarme*, good to knock down a cockney with, but," he continued, "without that power to cheer and establish which makes the value of a friend."[307] Thoreau, too, was "aware of his stubborn contradictory attitude into which almost any conversation threw him," Emerson wrote in his journal after Thoreau died.[308]

Margaret Fuller had published her "The Great Lawsuit. Man versus Men. Woman versus Women" in the July 1843 *Dial*. It was the precursor to her 1845 book *Women in the Nineteenth Century*, which Dall would call "doubtless the most brilliant, complete, and scholarly statement ever made upon this subject."[309] Fuller's tract placed the position of women as clearly and undeniably parallel with that of the enslaved. Thoreau, who Emerson said "will never like anything," wrote that it was "a noble piece, rich extempore writing, talking with pen in hand."[310] Emerson saw that it "will teach us all to revise our habits of thinking on this head."[311]

Partway through her lecture that evening Dall noticed a man enter wearing a green baize jacket, "who looked like a working man . . . and seated himself on the end of the very last bench by the door." Her habit was to speak to the furthest person in the room, who was now, although she didn't then know it, Thoreau. As she mingled after the lecture, she overheard Emerson say to the man, "Why, Thoreau, I thought you was not coming," to which he replied, "But *this* woman had something to say!" He told her afterwards, Dall recalled, "that he had been on the river all day and dropped in on his way home to see what I looked like and 'had to say.' I thought it a pleasant victory then, for he waited to persuade me to remain over the next day and spend it at his home with himself, his mother and sister. It was a day I shall never forget, filled to the brim with charming talk."[312]

Thoreau's opinion about women has often been considered misogynistic. He derived "no pleasure from talking with a young woman half an hour simply because she has regular features."[313] The reason he talked with any person, male or female, was for the intellect he found there. This he had found in Dall, Fuller, and Emerson's aunt, Mary Moody Emerson, of whom he wrote,

> She is singular, among women at least, in being really and perseveringly interested to know what thinkers think. She relates herself surely to the intellectual where she goes. . . . In short, she is a genius, as woman seldom is, reminding you less often of her sex than any woman whom I know.[314]

Emerson, too, had respect for the acuity of women. Women often made up his circle when meeting for conversation. It was a superior mind which attracted them, no matter in whom it was embodied, and such minds were not easily found. "Superior women are rare anywhere, as superior men are," Emerson said.[315] On the issue of whether women should have the vote, Emerson's answer was simple: "'T is idle to refuse them a vote on the ground of incompetency. I wish our masculine voting were so good that we had any right to doubt their equal discretion. They could not easily give worse votes, I think, than we do."[316] Emerson easily dismissed the male-centered perspective when he wrote, "If women feel wronged, then they are wronged."[317]

Both men took the common conception that men were intellectual and women emotional—"We commonly say," Emerson wrote, "Man represents Intellect; and Woman, Love."[318]—but they could also see that the world was not perfectly binary. As Thoreau put it, "Man is continually saying to woman, Why will you not be more wise? Woman is continually saying to man, Why will you not be more loving? It is not in their wills to be wise or to be loving; but, unless each is both wise and loving, there can be neither wisdom nor love."[319] Emerson agreed with this androgynous approach to human nature. He wrote that there are, in each person, "mind and heart, Intellect and morals . . . One is the man, the other the woman. . . . These elements always coexist in every normal individual, but one predominates."[320] Or as he also wrote, "A highly endowed man with good intellect and good conscience is a Man-woman."[321]

In 1858 tragedy struck the Alcott family when Elizabeth Alcott—"Beth" of Louisa May Alcott's *Little Women*—died from scarlet fever. Thoreau and Emerson were pallbearers. Two years later they shared another, more celebratory event with the Alcotts. On May 23, 1860, eldest daughter Anna Alcott married John Pratt in the parlor at Orchard House. It was the thirtieth anniversary of her parents' marriage. All the guests were reported to have kissed the bride, shared the wedding cake, and drunk the wedding wine. The Emersons gave them a silver cake basket as a wedding present. Thoreau's name does not appear on Anna's list of gifts.[322]

In August at the Emersons', while Thoreau was entertaining the family with stories about Mount Monadnock, Emerson and their cat, Milcah, slipped away in pursuit of something. It was a bat hidden behind a picture in the dining room. When it flew off, Thoreau caught it, and while it struggled to escape, Lidian offered it her finger. "There, Batty," she said, "you shall have something to bite if it will make you feel better, I'm sure." The bat was held briefly under a glass dish while Thoreau identified it as a hoary bat and then set it free outside.[323]

The winter of 1860 was cold, wet, and snowy. Many people were ill, including Alcott, from whom Thoreau caught a cold when they were planning John Brown's memorial service. "I took a severe cold about the 3 of Dec.," Thoreau wrote in February 1861, "which at length resulted in a kind of bronchitis, so that I have been confined to the house ever since, excepting a very few experimental trips as far as the P.O. in some particularly mild noons."[324] Thoreau's journal, often a barometer of his physical health, is blank from the 4th until the 22nd. Bronchitis, or chronic bronchitis, was a euphemism used for tuberculosis, and Ellery Channing was clear about the consumptive nature of Thoreau's illness: "he is reduced much in stature."[325] Channing, who had begun reading medical texts and making a study of Thoreau's condition, reported in April that

Henry's bronchitis is very obstinate. It does not perceptibly mend; it is understood that the physician advises a warmer climate. I have still confidence that Henry may recover from this very obstinate attack, knowing how perfectly obstinate he also is. . . . Henry has lost much flesh . . . All air at all harsh affects him very much. He is also I judge far from strong as he had on Sunday morning last a fainting time. I say, I think he will recover, because he is a singular constitution and acts by himself, but if you were sick as he, I should not set your life at a pin's fee.[326]

In May, Emerson dined with Thoreau and Horace Mann Jr., who were planning a trip to Minnesota for Thoreau's health. The next day Emerson provided Thoreau with a "little list of names of good men whom you may chance to see" in case the travelers needed assistance of any sort.[327] "I am still as much an invalid as when you and Theophilus Brown were here," Thoreau wrote H.G.O. Blake before he left in mid-May,

if not more of one, and at this rate there is danger that the cold weather may come again, before I get over my bronchitis. The doctor accordingly tells me that I must "clear out" to the West Indies, or elsewhere,—he does not seem to care much where. But I decide against the West Indies, on account of their muggy heat in the summer, and the South of Europe, on account of the expense of time and money, and have at last concluded that it will be most expedient for me to try the air of Minnesota, say somewhere about St Paul. I am only waiting to be well enough to start. Hope to get off within a week or ten days.[328]

The excursion did little for Thoreau's health. Robert Collyer, who Thoreau visited in Chicago, wrote that he would "pause with a pathetic patience to master the trouble in his chest."[329]

In July Thoreau returned home to Concord from Minnesota. It was clear to him, as it was to everyone else, that whatever time was left in him was limited. On seeing him shortly after his return, Daniel Moncure Conway said Thoreau was "sadly out of health,"[330] and Simon Brown had "no doubt but he is in the first stage of consumption."[331] In a quietly prophetic passage Thoreau wrote Daniel Ricketson, "If I do not mend very quickly I shall be obliged to go to another climate again very soon."[332]

He left the house infrequently. Special events would draw him out: a final visit in August to Daniel Ricketson in New Bedford, a send-off dinner, also in August, for Edward Emerson heading off to Harvard, and occasional visits with friends. Recalling Thoreau's joy over his music box nearly twenty years earlier, the Hawthornes loaned him their own music box to soothe him during his final days.[333]

In September Channing was writing, with a significant underscoring, "*He is no better.*"[334] He had "not the least faith in" Josiah Bartlett—the man who misdiagnosed the severity of John's cut—as Thoreau's physician, even though Thoreau "has and concludes to follow him. The doctor says there is nothing the matter with Henry's lungs . . . but that it is all in his throat . . . I think he has made up his mind to sink or swim under the village Asclepius."[335]

For a while into autumn, too weak to walk, Thoreau would take a ride in a wagon every other day or so, courtesy of his neighbor Ebenezer Rockwood Hoar. His journal, once the almost daily repository for his thoughts, contains fewer than a dozen entries after his July return, the final entry written in early November.

At the first of the new year, Alcott noted that it was "sad to find him failing and feeble. . . . But the most he may hope for is to prepare his manuscripts for others' editing, and take his leave of them and us."[336] Channing found Thoreau "greatly decreased if it was possible in flesh. I do not think he weighs to-day but a very little and a few days since, his pulse was at 56."[337] Emerson felt "ever threatened by the decay of Henry Thoreau," writing, "As we live longer, it looks as if our company were picked out to die first, and we live on in a lessening minority."[338] Preparing for the inevitable task of writing a eulogy, Emerson began to gather thoughts and memories about his friend.

As Thoreau declined, Emerson noted that he "remains erect, calm, self-subsistent, before me, and I read him not only truly in his Journal, but he is not long out of mind when I walk, and, as to-day, row upon the pond."[339] Despite his weakening, Thoreau always tried to participate in conversations. When Emerson told him about things happening beyond his window view, such as walking across Walden Pond on the ice on the first of April, Thoreau told him he had known the ice to hold as late as April 18. When Emerson reported of a purple finch he'd heard, Thoreau recalled hearing a blue snowbird on Monadnock. "Thoreau tells me," Emerson wrote in his journal, that chickadees "are very sociable with wood-choppers, and will take crumbs from their hands."[340]

Sam Staples told Emerson he had never "spent an hour with more satisfaction. Never saw a man dying with so much pleasure and peace. Thinks that very few men in Concord know Mr. Thoreau; finds him serene and happy."[341] Emerson then recalled something Thoreau had said to him, something that could have been a summing up of their friendship.

Henry praised to me lately the manners of an old, established, calm, well-behaved river, as perfectly distinguished from those of a new river. A new river is a torrent; an old one slow and steadily supplied. What happens in any part of the old river relates to what befals in every other part of it. 'T is full of compensations, resources, and reserved funds.[342]

Thoreau died on the morning on May 8, 1862. His sister, Sophia, wrote that she could "never be grateful enough for the gentle, easy exit which was granted him. At seven o'clock Tuesday morning he became restless and desired to be moved . . . A little after eight he asked to be raised quite up, his breathing grew fainter and fainter, and without the slightest struggle, he left us at nine o'clock."[343]

Emerson's obituary for Thoreau was published the same day in the *Boston Daily Advertiser.*

He was a man of stoic temperament, highly intellectual, of a perfect probity, full of practical skill, an expert woodsman and boatman, acquainted with the use of tools, a good planter and cultivator, when he saw fit to plant, but without any taste for luxury, without the least ambition to be rich, or to be popular, and almost without sympathy in any of the common motives of men around him. He led the life of a philosopher, subordinating all other pursuits and so-called duties to his pursuit of knowledge and to his own estimate of duty. He was a man of firm mind and direct dealing, never disconcerted, and not to be bent by any inducement from his own course. He had a penetrating insight into men with whom he conversed, and was not to be deceived or used by any party, and did not conceal his disgust at any duplicity. As he was incapable of any the least dishonesty or untruth, he had nothing to hide, and kept his haughty independence to the end. And when we now look back at the solitude of this erect and spotless person, we lament that he did not live long enough for all men to know him.[344]

May 9, the day of Thoreau's funeral, was clear and calm. The service was held at the First Parish Church, "a thing Henry would not have liked," Louisa May Alcott wrote, "but Emerson said his sorrow was so great he wanted all the world to mourn with him." There were those who said that Thoreau was an infidel who should not be buried from the church as he did not attend it in life, but she knew that "if ever a man was a real Christian it was Henry, and I think his own wise and pious thoughts read by one who loved him"—Bronson Alcott—"and whose own life was a beautiful example of religious faith, convinced many and touched the hearts of all."[345] Sophia felt that her brother was "honored" by such a public funeral from the church.[346]

"The death of friends," Thoreau wrote, "should inspire us as much as their lives."[347] Emerson may have hoped that his eulogy, written out of a profound grief, would achieve what he said Thoreau's did for John Brown when "his earnest eulogy of the hero was heard by all respectfully, by many with a sympathy that surprised themselves."[348] For the most part he succeeded, wanting to show his neighbors the Thoreau he knew and loved.

Emerson's eulogy was delivered with a "broken, tender voice."[349] Sophia described it as an "address as no other man could have done. It is a source of great satisfaction that one so gifted knew and loved my brother and is prepared to speak such brave words about him at this time."[350] Annie Fields, wife of publisher James T. Fields, thought his address "made the simple ceremony one never to be forgotten,"[351] while Louisa May Alcott thought it was "good in itself but not appropriate to the time or place."[352]

Gathering journal passages about Thoreau written over the vast expanse of their friendship, covering the best moments and the worst, reiterating his own hopes and disappointments, Emerson offered a full portrait. His loss did not allow him to gloss over the less agreeable aspects of Thoreau's personality and disposition that he had experienced. Had the eulogy stayed in Concord, it may not have mattered, but publishing it in *The Atlantic Monthly* brought it to the world, cementing a portrait of Thoreau that even in our day is difficult to shake.

Out of the entirety of Emerson's thoughtful and expansive eulogy, full of love, praise, and unbounded admiration, posterity has repeatedly quoted this as Emerson's summation: "I cannot help counting it a fault in him that he had no ambition. Wanting this, instead of engineering for all America, he was the captain of a huckleberry-party."[353] But in the very next paragraph Emerson was unsure if these "foibles" he saw were "real or apparent"[354] and continued on to recognize the best in his friend till he reached his true summation.

> The country knows not yet, or in the least part, how great a son it has lost. It seems an injury that he should leave in the midst his broken task which none else can finish, a kind of indignity to so noble a soul that he should depart out of Nature before yet he has been really shown to his peers for what he is. . . . His soul was made for the noblest society; he had in a short life exhausted the capabilities of this world; wherever there is knowledge, wherever there is virtue, wherever there is beauty, he will find a home.[355]

Truth was always the cornerstone of whatever Emerson wrote, and this was no exception. Emerson learned later that people "were dissatisfied with my notice of him in the *Atlantic* after his death: they did not want me to place any bounds to his genius,"[356] but he was paying the highest honor to his friend by acknowledging in an honest portrait something Thoreau said in his first book, "The rarest quality in an epitaph is truth."[357]

In early June, Emerson and Alcott dined together, discussing "Thoreau a good deal."[358] Emerson had been reading Thoreau's journal. He referred to one entry, from October 1852, in which Thoreau heard the laugh of the loon, calling, but never to be reached. It may have reminded him of his lost friend. Emerson wrote to his son Edward, "I saw yesterday a loon in Walden, but silent."[359] When the "Parker Fraternity" met in Boston at the end of the month, he read his piece that would soon appear in *The Atlantic Monthly*, expanded from the eulogy. Thoreau was never long out of Emerson's thoughts.

At the beginning of July, Ellen was writing her brother Edward that "Father is constantly engaged now in writing and reading about Mr. Thoreau."[360] Emerson had been reading, among other things, selections from Thoreau's journals prepared by Ellery Channing. "If we should ever print Henry's journals," Emerson wrote in his journal, "you may look for a plentiful crop of naturalists. Young men of sensibility must fall an easy prey to the charming of Pan's pipe."[361]

One quotation in Channing's selection stumped him— "Some circumstantial evidence is very strong, as when you find a trout in the milk."—and he thought it would be a good "question for a gameparty," hoping the players might provide the solution to this conundrum. His daughter

Ellen, however, understood it instantly "and considered it so self evident as to be not worth mentioning, and long afterward Mother said 'Or a mouse.' Then I explained to her that wasn't the same thing, that it meant the milk was watered. Whereupon Father said he hadn't thought of that before, of course that was right. I was amazed that he shouldn't have seen it, but on trying the experiment I find that very few people do."[362]

That summer Rebecca Harding Davis, whose *Life in the Iron Mills* had been published the previous year in *The Atlantic Monthly*, came to Concord to meet Hawthorne and others. Hawthorne warned Davis that when she met Emerson he would talk to her about his pears. "You may begin at Plato or the day's news, and he will come around to pears."[363] But it wasn't pears he wanted to talk about. It was Thoreau. "I wish Thoreau had not died before you came. He was an interesting study," Emerson told her.

"Why?" she asked.

"Why? Thoreau?" Davis described Emerson hesitating, "thinking, going apparently to the bottom of the matter," before he responded, "Henry often reminded me of an animal in human form. He had the eye of a bird, the scent of a dog, the most acute, delicate intelligence—but no soul. No." Emerson shook his head. "Henry could not have had a human soul."[364]

Emerson had such moments in which he grappled with the personality of Thoreau. While editing Thoreau's correspondence for *Letters to Various Persons*, Emerson had removed the salutations and closings, but Sophia insisted "that all kind beginnings and endings of Mr. Thoreau's letters, and little messages to friends being left out give a too cold idea of him, agreeing with the popular notion that he wanted affection."[365] In July 1864 Emerson began a new notebook, labelled "HT." In collecting these pieces about his friend, he found that "Thoreau was with difficulty sweet."[366]

His overall admiration of his friend's work, however, continued to grow as he came to sincerely understand that in some ways Thoreau's achievements were greater than his own. It was not humility but perception. When Sophia died in 1876, Thoreau's manuscripts were passed on to H.G.O. Blake, to whom Emerson wrote, "I can well understand that he should vex tender persons by his conversation, but his books, I confide, must and will find a multitude of readers."[367] In reading Thoreau's journals, Emerson rediscovered the true difference between himself and his friend.

> I am very sensible of the vigor of his constitution. That oaken strength which I noted whenever he walked, or worked, or surveyed wood-lots, the same unhesitating hand with which a field-laborer accosts a piece of work, which I should shun as a waste of strength, Henry shows in his literary task. He has muscle, and ventures on and performs feats which I am forced to decline. In reading him, I find the same thought, the same spirit that is in me, but he takes a step beyond, and illustrates by excellent images that which I should have conveyed in a sleepy generality. 'T is as if I went into a gymnasium, and saw youths leap, climb, and swing with a force unapproachable,—though their feats are only continuations of my initial grapplings and jumps.[368]

Emerson had thought something similar a decade earlier. "Thoreau gives me," he wrote in 1852, "in flesh and blood and pertinacious Saxon belief, my own ethics. He is far more real, and daily practically obeying them, than I; and fortifies my memory at all times with an affirmative experience which refuses to be set aside."[369]

When it was proposed at a town meeting in 1874 to name a street for him, Emerson countered the idea by suggesting instead Thoreau Street, which was then adopted.[370] Receiving a copy of *Bedford's Monthly Magazine* containing a "very friendly notice of myself," he found that the author

> seems to me to have been misinformed. The only pain he gives me is in his estimate of Thoreau, whom he underrates. Thoreau was a superior genius. I read his books and manuscripts always with new surprise at the range of his topics and the novelty and depth of his thought. A man of large reading, of quick perception, of great practical courage and ability,—who grew greater every day, and, had his short life been prolonged, would have found few equals to the power and wealth of his mind.[371]

Emerson lost no opportunity to read Thoreau's works to others. At one gathering Emerson was asked "to read something, Shakespeare was suggested, but he collected a whole set of accounts of Mr. Thoreau from his old books and read them."[372]

In October of 1878 Anne Burrows Gilchrist, the English writer and friend of Walt Whitman, visited Concord for a brief period, spending two evenings in the company of the seventy-five-year-old Emerson and his family. She wrote that his "memory fails somewhat as to recent names and topics, but as is usual in such cases, all the mental impressions that were made when he was in full vigour remain clear and strong."[373]

As they chatted, Emerson called to Lidian in the next room, "What was the name of my best friend?"

"Henry Thoreau," she answered.

"Oh, yes," Emerson repeated. "Henry Thoreau."[374]

PART II

Thoreau

Friendship[1]

(from *A Week on the Concord and Merrimack Rivers*)

While we float here, far from that tributary stream on whose banks our Friends and kindred dwell, our thoughts, like the stars, come out of their horizon still; for there circulates a finer blood than Lavoisier has discovered the laws of,—the blood, not of kindred merely, but of kindness, whose pulse still beats at any distance and forever.

> True kindness is a pure divine affinity,
> Not founded upon human consanguinity.
> It is a spirit, not a blood relation,
> Superior to family and station.

After years of vain familiarity, some distant gesture or unconscious behavior, which we remember, speaks to us with more emphasis than the wisest or kindest words. We are sometimes made aware of a kindness long passed, and realize that there have been times when our Friends' thoughts of us were of so pure and lofty a character that they passed over us like the winds of heaven unnoticed; when they treated us not as what we were, but as what we aspired to be. There has just reached us, it may be, the nobleness of some such silent behavior, not to be forgotten, not to be remembered, and we shudder to think how it fell on us cold, though in some true but tardy hour we endeavor to wipe off these scores.

In my experience, persons, when they are made the subject of conversation, though with a Friend, are commonly the most prosaic and trivial of facts. The universe seems bankrupt as soon as we begin to discuss the character of individuals. Our discourse all runs to slander, and our limits grow narrower as we advance. How is it that we are impelled to treat our old Friends so ill when we obtain new ones? The housekeeper says, I never had any new crockery in my life but I began to break the old. I say, let us speak of mushrooms and forest trees rather. Yet we can sometimes afford to remember them in private.

Lately, alas, I knew a gentle boy,
　　Whose features all were cast in Virtue's mould,
As one she had designed for Beauty's toy,
　　But after manned him for her own stronghold.

On every side he open was as day,
　　That you might see no lack of strength within,
For walls and ports do only serve alway
　　For a pretence to feebleness and sin.

Say not that Caesar was victorious,
　　With toil and strife who stormed the House of Fame,
In other sense this youth was glorious,
　　Himself a kingdom wheresoe'er he came.

No strength went out to get him victory,
　　When all was income of its own accord;
For where he went none other was to see,
　　But all were parcel of their noble lord.

He forayed like the subtile haze of summer,
　　That stilly shows fresh landscapes to our eyes,

And revolutions works without a murmur,
    Or rustling of a leaf beneath the skies.

So was I taken unawares by this,
    I quite forgot my homage to confess;
Yet now am forced to know, though hard it is,
    I might have loved him had I loved him less.

Each moment as we nearer drew to each,
    A stern respect withheld us farther yet,
So that we seemed beyond each other's reach,
    And less acquainted than when first we met.

We two were one while we did sympathize,
    So could we not the simplest bargain drive;
And what avails it now that we are wise,
    If absence doth this doubleness contrive?

Eternity may not the chance repeat,
    But I must tread my single way alone,
In sad remembrance that we once did meet,
    And know that bliss irrevocably gone.

The spheres henceforth my elegy shall sing,
    For elegy has other subject none;
Each strain of music in my ears shall ring
    Knell of departure from that other one.

Make haste and celebrate my tragedy;
    With fitting strain resound ye woods and fields;
Sorrow is dearer in such case to me
    Than all the joys other occasion yields.

———

Is 't then too late the damage to repair?
>   Distance, forsooth, from my weak grasp hath reft
The empty husk, and clutched the useless tare,
>   But in my hands the wheat and kernel left.

If I but love that virtue which he is,
>   Though it be scented in the morning air,
Still shall we be truest acquaintances,
>   Nor mortals know a sympathy more rare.

Friendship is evanescent in every man's experience, and remembered like heat lightning in past summers. Fair and flitting like a summer cloud,—there is always some vapor in the air, no matter how long the drought; there are even April showers. Surely from time to time, for its vestiges never depart, it floats through our atmosphere. It takes place, like vegetation in so many materials, because there is such a law, but always without permanent form, though ancient and familiar as the sun and moon, and as sure to come again. The heart is forever inexperienced. They silently gather as by magic, these never failing, never quite deceiving visions, like the bright and fleecy clouds in the calmest and clearest days. The Friend is some fair floating isle of palms eluding the mariner in Pacific seas. Many are the dangers to be encountered, equinoctial gales and coral reefs, ere he may sail before the constant trades. But who would not sail through mutiny and storm, even over Atlantic waves, to reach the fabulous retreating shores of some continent man? The imagination still clings to the faintest tradition of

THE ATLANTIDES.

The smothered streams of love, which flow
More bright than Phlegethon, more low,

Island us ever, like the sea,
In an Atlantic mystery.
Our fabled shores none ever reach,
No mariner has found our beach,
Scarcely our mirage now is seen,
And neighboring waves with floating green,
Yet still the oldest charts contain
Some dotted outline of our main;
In ancient times midsummer days
Unto the western islands' gaze,
To Teneriffe and the Azores,
Have shown our faint and cloud-like shores.

But sink not yet, ye desolate isles,
Anon your coast with commerce smiles,
And richer freights ye'll furnish far
Than Africa or Malabar.
Be fair, be fertile evermore,
Ye rumored but untrodden shore,
Princes and monarchs will contend
Who first unto your land shall send,
And pawn the jewels of the crown
To call your distant soil their own.

Columbus has sailed westward of these isles by the mariner's compass, but neither he nor his successors have found them. We are no nearer than Plato was. The earnest seeker and hopeful discoverer of this New World always haunts the outskirts of his time, and walks through the densest crowd uninterrupted, and, as it were, in a straight line.

Sea and land are but his neighbors,
And companions in his labors,
Who on the ocean's verge and firm land's end

Doth long and truly seek his Friend.
Many men dwell far inland,
But he alone sits on the strand.
Whether he ponders men or books,
Always still he seaward looks,
Marine news he ever reads,
And the slightest glances heeds,
Feels the sea breeze on his cheek,
At each word the landsmen speak,
In every companion's eye
A sailing vessel doth descry;
In the ocean's sullen roar
From some distant port he hears,
Of wrecks upon a distant shore,
And the ventures of past years.

Who does not walk on the plain as amid the columns of Tadmore of the desert? There is on the earth no institution which Friendship has established; it is not taught by any religion; no scripture contains its maxims. It has no temple, nor even a solitary column. There goes a rumor that the earth is inhabited, but the shipwrecked mariner has not seen a footprint on the shore. The hunter has found only fragments of pottery and the monuments of inhabitants.

However, our fates at least are social. Our courses do not diverge; but as the web of destiny is woven it is fulled, and we are cast more and more into the centre. Men naturally, though feebly, seek this alliance, and their actions faintly foretell it. We are inclined to lay the chief stress on likeness and not on difference, and in foreign bodies we admit that there are many degrees of warmth below blood heat, but none of cold above it.

Mencius says: "If one loses a fowl or a dog, he knows well how to seek them again; if one loses the sentiments of his heart, he does not know how to seek them again. . . . The duties of practical philosophy consist only in seeking after those sentiments of the heart which we have lost; that is all."

One or two persons come to my house from time to time, there being proposed to them the faint possibility of intercourse. They are as full as they are silent, and wait for my plectrum to stir the strings of their lyre. If they could ever come to the length of a sentence, or hear one, on that ground they are dreaming of! They speak faintly, and do not obtrude themselves. They have heard some news, which none, not even they themselves, can impart. It is a wealth they can bear about them which can be expended in various ways. What came they out to seek?

No word is oftener on the lips of men than Friendship, and indeed no thought is more familiar to their aspirations. All men are dreaming of it, and its drama, which is always a tragedy, is enacted daily. It is the secret of the universe. You may thread the town, you may wander the country, and none shall ever speak of it, yet thought is everywhere busy about it, and the idea of what is possible in this respect affects our behavior toward all new men and women, and a great many old ones. Nevertheless, I can remember only two or three essays on this subject in all literature. No wonder that the Mythology, and Arabian Nights, and Shakespeare, and Scott's novels entertain us,—we are poets and fablers and dramatists and novelists ourselves. We are continually acting a part in a more interesting drama than any written. We are dreaming that our Friends are our *Friends*, and that we are our Friends' *Friends*. Our actual Friends are but distant relations of those to whom we are pledged. We never exchange more than three words with a Friend in our lives on that level to which our thoughts and feelings almost habitually rise. One goes forth prepared to say,

"Sweet Friends!" and the salutation is, "Damn your eyes!" But never mind; faint heart never won true Friend. O my Friend, may it come to pass once, that when you are my Friend I may be yours.

Of what use the friendliest dispositions even, if there are no hours given to Friendship, if it is forever postponed to unimportant duties and relations? Friendship is first, Friendship last. But it is equally impossible to forget our Friends, and to make them answer to our ideal. When they say farewell, then indeed we begin to keep them company. How often we find ourselves turning our backs on our actual Friends, that we may go and meet their ideal cousins. I would that I were worthy to be any man's Friend.

What is commonly honored with the name of Friendship is no very profound or powerful instinct. Men do not, after all, *love* their Friends greatly. I do not often see the farmers made seers and wise to the verge of insanity by their Friendship for one another. They are not often transfigured and translated by love in each other's presence. I do not observe them purified, refined, and elevated by the love of a man. If one abates a little the price of his wood, or gives a neighbor his vote at town-meeting, or a barrel of apples, or lends him his wagon frequently, it is esteemed a rare instance of Friendship. Nor do the farmers' wives lead lives consecrated to Friendship. I do not see the pair of farmer Friends of either sex prepared to stand against the world. There are only two or three couples in history. To say that a man is your Friend, means commonly no more than this, that he is not your enemy. Most contemplate only what would be the accidental and trifling advantages of Friendship, as that the Friend can assist in time of need, by his substance, or his influence, or his counsel; but he who foresees such advantages in this relation proves himself blind to its real advantage, or indeed wholly inexperienced in the relation itself. Such services are particular and me-nial, compared with the perpetual and all-embracing ser-vice which it is. Even the utmost good-will and harmony and practical kindness are not sufficient for Friendship, for Friends do not live in harmony merely, as some say, but in melody. We do not wish for Friends to feed and clothe our bodies,—neighbors are kind enough for that,—but to do the like office to our spirits. For this few are rich enough, however well disposed they may be. For the most part we stupidly confound one man with another. The dull distin-guish only races or nations, or at most classes, but the wise man, individuals. To his Friend a man's peculiar character appears in every feature and in every action, and it is thus drawn out and improved by him.

Think of the importance of Friendship in the education of men.

"He that hath love and judgment too,
Sees more than any other doe."

It will make a man honest; it will make him a hero; it will make him a saint. It is the state of the just dealing with the just, the magnanimous with the magnanimous, the sin-cere with the sincere, man with man.

And it is well said by another poet,—

"Why love among the virtues is not known,
Is that love is them all contract in one."

All the abuses which are the object of reform with the philanthropist, the statesman, and the housekeeper are un-consciously amended in the intercourse of Friends. A Friend is one who incessantly pays us the compliment of expecting from us all the virtues, and who can appreciate them in us.

It takes two to speak the truth,—one to speak, and another to hear. How can one treat with magnanimity mere wood and stone? If we dealt only with the false and dishonest, we should at last forget how to speak truth. Only lovers know the value and magnanimity of truth, while traders prize a cheap honesty, and neighbors and acquaintance a cheap civility. In our daily intercourse with men, our nobler faculties are dormant and suffered to rust. None will pay us the compliment to expect nobleness from us. Though we have gold to give, they demand only copper. We ask our neighbor to suffer himself to be dealt with truly, sincerely, nobly; but he answers no by his deafness. He does not even hear this prayer. He says practically, I will be content if you treat me as "no better than I should be," as deceitful, mean, dishonest, and selfish. For the most part, we are contented so to deal and to be dealt with, and we do not think that for the mass of men there is any truer and nobler relation possible. A man may have *good* neighbors, so called, and acquaintances, and even companions, wife, parents, brothers, sisters, children, who meet himself and one another on this ground only. The state does not demand justice of its members, but thinks that it succeeds very well with the least degree of it, hardly more than rogues practice; and so do the neighborhood and the family. What is commonly called Friendship even is only a little more honor among rogues.

But sometimes we are said to *love* another, that is, to stand in a true relation to him, so that we give the best to, and receive the best from, him. Between whom there is hearty truth, there is love; and in proportion to our truthfulness and confidence in one another, our lives are divine and miraculous, and answer to our ideal. There are passages of affection in our intercourse with mortal men and women, such as no prophecy had taught us to expect, which transcend our earthly life, and anticipate Heaven for us. What is this Love that may come right into the middle of a prosaic Goffstown day, equal to any of the gods? that discovers a new world, fair and fresh and eternal, occupying the place of the old one, when to the common eye a dust has settled on the universe? which world cannot else be reached, and does not exist. What other words, we may almost ask, are memorable and worthy to be repeated than those which love has inspired? It is wonderful that they were ever uttered. They are few and rare, indeed, but, like a strain of music, they are incessantly repeated and modulated by the memory. All other words crumble off with the stucco which overlies the heart. We should not dare to repeat these now aloud. We are not competent to hear them at all times.

The books for young people say a great deal about the *selection* of Friends; it is because they really have nothing to say about *Friends*. They mean associates and confidants merely. "Know that the contrariety of foe and Friend proceeds from God." Friendship takes place between those who have an affinity for one another, and is a perfectly natural and inevitable result. No professions nor advances will avail. Even speech, at first, necessarily has nothing to do with it; but it follows after silence, as the buds in the graft do not put forth into leaves till long after the graft has taken. It is a drama in which the parties have no part to act. We are all Mussulmen and fatalists in this respect. Impatient and uncertain lovers think that they must say or do something kind whenever they meet; they must never be cold. But they who are Friends do not do what they *think* they must, but what they *must*. Even their Friendship is to some extent but a sublime phenomenon to them.

The true and not despairing Friend will address his Friend in some such terms as these.

"I never asked thy leave to let me love thee,—I have a right. I love thee not as something private and personal, which is *your own*, but as something universal and worthy of love, *which I have found*. O, how I think of you! You are purely good,—you are infinitely good. I can trust you forever. I did not think that humanity was so rich. Give me an opportunity to live."

"You are the fact in a fiction,—you are the truth more strange and admirable than fiction. Consent only to be what you are. I alone will never stand in your way."

"This is what I would like,—to be as intimate with you as our spirits are intimate,—respecting you as I respect my ideal. Never to profane one another by word or action, even by a thought. Between us, if necessary, let there be no acquaintance."

"I have discovered you; how can you be concealed from me?"

The Friend asks no return but that his Friend will religiously accept and wear and not disgrace his apotheosis of him. They cherish each other's hopes. They are kind to each other's dreams.

Though the poet says, "'T is the preëminence of Friendship to impute excellence," yet we can never praise our Friend, nor esteem him praiseworthy, nor let him think that he can please us by any *behavior*, or ever *treat* us well enough. That kindness which has so good a reputation elsewhere can least of all consist with this relation, and no such affront can be offered to a Friend, as a conscious good-will, a friendliness which is not a necessity of the Friend's nature.

The sexes are naturally most strongly attracted to one another, by constant constitutional differences, and are most commonly and surely the complements of each other. How natural and easy it is for man to secure the attention of woman to what interests himself. Men and women of equal culture, thrown together, are sure to be of a certain value to one another, more than men to men. There exists already a natural disinterestedness and liberality in such society, and I think that any man will more confidently carry his favorite books to read to some circle of intelligent women, than to one of his own sex. The visit of man to man is wont to be an interruption, but the sexes naturally expect one another. Yet Friendship is no respecter of sex; and perhaps it is more rare between the sexes than between two of the same sex.

Friendship is, at any rate, a relation of perfect equality. It cannot well spare any outward sign of equal obligation and advantage. The nobleman can never have a Friend among his retainers, nor the king among his subjects. Not that the parties to it are in all respects equal, but they are equal in all that respects or affects their Friendship. The one's love is exactly balanced and represented by the other's. Persons are only the vessels which contain the nectar, and the hydrostatic paradox is the symbol of love's law. It finds its level and rises to its fountain-head in all breasts, and its slenderest column balances the ocean.

> "And love as well the shepherd can
> As can the mighty nobleman."

The one sex is not, in this respect, more tender than the other. A hero's love is as delicate as a maiden's.

Confucius said, "Never contract Friendship with a man who is not better than thyself." It is the merit and preservation of Friendship, that it takes place on a level higher than the actual characters of the parties would seem to warrant. The rays of light come to us in such a curve that every man whom we meet appears to be taller than he actually is. Such foundation has civility. My Friend is that one whom I can associate with my choicest thought. I always assign to him a nobler employment in my absence than I ever find him engaged in; and I imagine that the hours which he devotes to me were snatched from a higher society. The sorest insult which I ever received from a Friend was, when he behaved with the license which only long and cheap acquaintance allows to one's faults, in my presence, without shame, and still addressed me in friendly accents. Beware, lest thy Friend learn at last to tolerate one frailty of thine, and so an obstacle be raised to the progress of thy love. There are times when we have had enough even of our Friends, when we begin inevitably to profane one another, and must withdraw religiously into solitude and silence, the better to prepare ourselves for a loftier intimacy. Silence is the ambrosial night in the intercourse of Friends, in which their sincerity is recruited and takes deeper root.

Friendship is never established as an understood relation. Do you demand that I be less your Friend that you may know it? Yet what right have I to think that another cherishes so rare a sentiment for me? It is a miracle which requires constant proofs. It is an exercise of the purest imagination and the rarest faith. It says by a silent but eloquent behavior, "I will be so related to thee as thou canst imagine; even so thou mayest believe. I will spend truth,—all my wealth on thee,"—and the Friend responds silently through his nature and life, and treats his Friend with the same divine courtesy. He knows us literally through thick and thin. He never asks for a sign of love, but can distinguish it by the features which it naturally wears. We never need to stand upon ceremony with him with regard to his visits. Wait not till I invite thee, but observe that I am glad to see thee when thou comest. It would be paying too dear for thy visit to ask for it. Where my Friend lives there are all riches and every attraction, and no slight obstacle can keep me from him. Let me never have to tell thee what I have not to tell. Let our intercourse be wholly above ourselves, and draw us up to it.

The language of Friendship is not words, but meanings. It is an intelligence above language. One imagines endless conversations with his Friend, in which the tongue shall be loosed, and thoughts be spoken without hesitancy or end; but the experience is commonly far otherwise. Acquaintances may come and go, and have a word ready for every occasion; but what puny word shall he utter whose very breath is thought and meaning? Suppose you go to bid farewell to your Friend who is setting out on a journey; what other outward sign do you know than to shake his hand? Have you any palaver ready for him then? any box of salve to commit to his pocket? any particular message to send by him? any statement which you had forgotten to make?—as if you could forget anything.—No, it is much that you take his hand and say Farewell; that you could easily omit; so far custom has prevailed. It is even painful, if he is to go, that he should linger so long. If he must go, let him go quickly. Have you any *last* words? Alas, it is only the word of words, which you have so long sought and found not; *you* have not a *first* word yet. There are few even whom I should venture to call earnestly by their most proper names. A name pronounced is the recognition of the individual to whom it belongs. He who can pronounce my name aright, he can call me, and is entitled to my love and service. Yet reserve is the freedom and abandonment of lovers. It is the reserve of what is hostile or indifferent in their natures, to give place to what is kindred and harmonious.

The violence of love is as much to be dreaded as that of hate. When it is durable it is serene and equable. Even its famous pains begin only with the ebb of love, for few are indeed lovers, though all would fain be. It is one proof of a man's fitness for Friendship that he is able to do without that which is cheap and passionate. A true Friendship is as wise as it is tender. The parties to it yield implicitly to the guidance of their love, and know no other law nor kindness. It is not extravagant and insane, but what it says is something established henceforth, and will bear to be stereotyped. It is a truer truth, it is better and fairer news, and no time will ever shame it, or prove it false. This is a plant which thrives best in a temperate zone, where summer and winter alternate with one another. The Friend is a *necessarius*, and meets his Friend on homely ground; not on carpets and cushions, but on the ground and on rocks they will sit, obeying the natural and primitive laws. They will meet without any outcry, and part without loud sorrow. Their relation implies such qualities as the warrior prizes; for it takes a valor to open the hearts of men as well as the gates of castles. It is not an idle sympathy and mutual consolation merely, but a heroic sympathy of aspiration and endeavor.

> "When manhood shall be matched so
>   That fear can take no place,
> Then weary *works* make warriors
>   Each other to embrace."

The Friendship which Wawatam testified for Henry the fur-trader, as described in the latter's "Adventures," so almost bare and leafless, yet not blossomless nor fruitless, is remembered with satisfaction and security. The stern, imperturbable warrior, after fasting, solitude, and mortification of body, comes to the white man's lodge, and affirms that he is the white brother whom he saw in his dream, and adopts him henceforth. He buries the hatchet as it regards his friend, and they hunt and feast and make maple-sugar together. "Metals unite from fluxility; birds and beasts from motives of convenience; fools from fear and stupidity; and just men at sight." If Wawatam would taste the "white man's milk" with his tribe, or take his bowl of human broth made of the trader's fellow-countrymen, he first finds a place of safety for his Friend, whom he has rescued from a similar fate. At length, after a long winter of undisturbed and happy intercourse in the family of the chieftain in the wilderness, hunting and fishing, they return in the spring to Michilimackinac to dispose of their furs; and it becomes necessary for Wawatam to take leave of his Friend at the Isle aux Outardes, when the latter, to avoid his enemies, proceeded to the Sault de Sainte Marie, supposing that they were to be separated for a short time only. "We now exchanged farewells," says Henry, "with an emotion entirely reciprocal. I did not quit the lodge without the most grateful sense of the many acts of goodness which I had experienced in it, nor without the sincerest respect for the virtues which I had witnessed among its members. All the family accompanied me to the beach; and the canoe had no sooner put off than Wawatam commenced an address to the Kichi Manito, beseeching him to take care of me, his brother, till we should next meet. We had proceeded to too great a distance to allow of our hearing his voice, before Wawatam had ceased to offer up his prayers." We never hear of him again.

Friendship is not so kind as is imagined; it has not much human blood in it, but consists with a certain disregard for men and their erections, the Christian duties and humanities, while it purifies the air like electricity. There may be the sternest tragedy in the relation of two more than usually innocent and true to their highest instincts. We may call it an essentially heathenish intercourse, free and irresponsible in its nature, and practising all the virtues gratuitously. It is not the highest sympathy merely, but a pure and lofty society, a fragmentary and godlike intercourse of ancient date, still kept up at intervals, which, remembering itself, does not hesitate to disregard the humbler rights and duties of humanity. It requires immaculate and godlike qualities full-grown, and exists at all only by condescension and anticipation of the remotest future. We love nothing which is merely good and not fair, if such a thing is possible. Nature puts some kind of blossom before every fruit, not simply a calyx behind it. When the Friend comes out of his heathenism and superstition, and breaks his idols, being converted by the precepts of a newer testament; when he forgets his mythology, and treats his Friend like a Christian, or as he can afford, then Friendship ceases to be Friendship, and becomes charity; that principle which established the almshouse is now beginning with its charity at home, and establishing an almshouse and pauper relations there.

As for the number which this society admits, it is at any rate to be begun with one, the noblest and greatest that we know, and whether the world will ever carry it further,—whether, as Chaucer affirms,—

> "There be mo sterres in the skie than a pair,"

remains to be proved;

> "And certaine he is well begone
> Among a thousand that findeth one."

We shall not surrender ourselves heartily to any while we are conscious that another is more deserving of our love. Yet Friendship does not stand for numbers; the Friend does not count his Friends on his fingers; they are not numerable. The more there are included by this bond, if they are indeed included, the rarer and diviner the quality of the love that binds them. I am ready to believe that as private and intimate a relation may exist by which three are embraced, as between two. Indeed, we cannot have too many friends; the virtue which we appreciate we to some extent appropriate, so that thus we are made at last more fit for every relation of life. A base Friendship is of a narrowing and exclusive tendency, but a noble one is not exclusive; its very superfluity and dispersed love is the humanity which sweetens society, and sympathizes with foreign nations; for though its foundations are private, it is, in effect, a public affair and a public advantage, and the Friend, more than the father of a family, deserves well of the state.

The only danger in Friendship is that it will end. It is a delicate plant, though a native. The least unworthiness, even if it be unknown to one's self, vitiates it. Let the Friend know that those faults which he observes in his Friend his own faults attract. There is no rule more invariable than that we are paid for our suspicions by finding what we suspected. By our narrowness and prejudices we say, I will have so much and such of you, my Friend, no more. Perhaps there are none charitable, none disinterested, none wise, noble, and heroic enough, for a true and lasting Friendship.

I sometimes hear my Friends complain finely that I do not appreciate their fineness. I shall not tell them whether I do or not. As if they expected a vote of thanks for every fine thing which they uttered or did. Who knows but it was finely appreciated. It may be that your silence was the finest thing of the two. There are some things which a man never speaks of, which are much finer kept silent about. To the highest communications we only lend a silent ear. Our finest relations are not simply kept silent about, but buried under a positive depth of silence never to be revealed. It may be that we are not even yet acquainted. In human intercourse the tragedy begins, not when there is misunderstanding about words, but when silence is not understood. Then there can never be an explanation. What avails it that another loves you, if he does not understand you? Such love is a curse. What sort of companions are they who are presuming always that their silence is more expressive than yours? How foolish, and inconsiderate, and unjust, to conduct as if you were the only party aggrieved! Has not your Friend always equal ground of complaint? No doubt my Friends sometimes speak to me in vain, but they do not know what things I hear which they are not aware that they have spoken. I know that I have frequently disappointed them by not giving them words when they expected them, or such as they expected. Whenever I see my Friend I speak to him; but the expecter, the man with the ears, is not he. They will complain too that you are hard. O ye that would have the cocoa-nut wrong side outwards, when next I weep I will let you know. They ask for words and deeds, when a true relation is word and deed. If they know not of these things, how can they be informed? We often forbear to confess our feelings, not from pride, but for fear that we could not continue to love the one who required us to give such proof of our affection.

I know a woman who possesses a restless and intelligent mind, interested in her own culture, and earnest to enjoy the highest possible advantages, and I meet her with pleasure as a natural person who not a little provokes me, and I suppose is stimulated in turn by myself. Yet our acquaintance plainly does not attain to that degree of confidence and sentiment which women, which all, in fact, covet. I am glad to help her, as I am helped by her; I like very well to know her with a sort of stranger's privilege, and hesitate to visit her often, like her other Friends. My nature pauses here, I do not well know why. Perhaps she does not make the highest demand on me, a religious demand. Some, with whose prejudices or peculiar bias I have no sympathy, yet inspire me with confidence, and I trust that they confide in me also as a religious heathen at least,—a good Greek. I, too, have principles as well founded as their own. If this person could conceive that, without wilfulness, I associate with her as far as our destinies are coincident, as far as our Good Geniuses permit, and still value such intercourse, it would be a grateful assurance to me. I feel as if I appeared careless, indifferent, and without principle to her, not expecting more, and yet not content with less. If she could know that I make an infinite demand on myself, as well as on all others, she would see that this true though incomplete intercourse, is infinitely better than a more unreserved but falsely grounded one, without the principle of growth in it. For a companion, I require one who will make an equal demand on me with my own genius. Such a one will always be rightly tolerant. It is suicide, and corrupts good manners to welcome any less than this. I value and trust those who love and praise my aspiration rather than my performance. If you would not stop to look at me, but look whither I am looking, and farther, then my education could not dispense with your company.

> My love must be as free
> > As is the eagle's wing,
> Hovering o'er land and sea
> > And everything.

> I must not dim my eye
> > In thy saloon,
> I must not leave my sky
> > And nightly moon.

> Be not the fowler's net
> > Which stays my flight,

And craftily is set
> T' allure the sight.

But be the favoring gale
> That bears me on,
And still doth fill my sail
> When thou art gone.

I cannot leave my sky
> For thy caprice,
True love would soar as high 1
> As heaven is.

The eagle would not brook
> Her mate thus won,
Who trained his eye to look
> Beneath the sun.

Few things are more difficult than to help a Friend in matters which do not require the aid of Friendship, but only a cheap and trivial service, if your Friendship wants the basis of a thorough practical acquaintance. I stand in the friendliest relation, on social and spiritual grounds, to one who does not perceive what practical skill I have, but when he seeks my assistance in such matters, is wholly ignorant of that one with whom he deals; does not use my skill, which in such matters is much greater than his, but only my hands. I know another, who, on the contrary, is remarkable for his discrimination in this respect; who knows how to make use of the talents of others when he does not possess the same; knows when not to look after or oversee, and stops short at his man. It is a rare pleasure to serve him, which all laborers know. I am not a little pained by the other kind of treatment. It is as if, after the friendliest and most ennobling intercourse, your Friend should use you as a hammer, and drive a nail with your head, all in good faith; notwithstanding that you are a tolerable carpenter, as well as his good Friend, and would use a hammer cheerfully in his service. This want of perception is a defect which all the virtues of the heart cannot supply:—

> The Good how can we trust?
> Only the Wise are just.
> The Good we use,
> The Wise we cannot choose.
> These there are none above;
> The Good they know and love,
> But are not known again
> By those of lesser ken.
> They do not charm us with their eyes,
> But they transfix with their advice;
> No partial sympathy they feel,
> With private woe or private weal,
> But with the universe joy and sigh
> Whose knowledge is their sympathy.

Confucius said: "To contract ties of Friendship with any one, is to contract Friendship with his virtue. There ought not to be any other motive in Friendship." But men wish us to contract Friendship with their vice also. I have a Friend who wishes me to see that to be right which I know to be wrong. But if Friendship is to rob me of my eyes, if it is to darken the day, I will have none of it. It should be expansive and inconceivably liberalizing in its effects. True Friendship can afford true knowledge. It does not depend on darkness and ignorance. A want of discernment cannot be an ingredient in it. If I can see my Friend's virtues more distinctly than another's, his faults too are made more conspicuous by contrast. We have not so good a right to hate any as our Friend. Faults are not the less faults because they are invariably balanced by corresponding virtues, and for a fault there is no excuse, though it may appear greater than it is in many ways. I have never known one who could bear criticism, who could not be flattered, who would not bribe his judge, or was content that the truth should be loved always better than himself.

If two travelers would go their way harmoniously together, the one must take as true and just a view of things as the other, else their path will not be strewn with roses. Yet you can travel profitably and pleasantly even with a blind man, if he practises common courtesy, and when you converse about the scenery will remember that he is blind but that you can see; and you will not forget that his sense of hearing is probably quickened by his want of sight. Otherwise you will not long keep company. A blind man, and a man in whose eyes there was no defect, were walking together, when they came to the edge of a precipice. "Take care, my friend," said the latter, "here is a steep precipice; go no farther this way." "I know better," said the other, and stepped off.

It is impossible to say all that we think, even to our truest Friend. We may bid him farewell forever sooner than complain, for our complaint is too well grounded to be uttered. There is not so good an understanding between any two, but the exposure by the one of a serious fault in the other will produce a misunderstanding in proportion to its heinousness. The constitutional differences which always exist, and are obstacles to a perfect Friendship, are forever a forbidden theme to the lips of Friends. They advise by their whole behavior. Nothing can reconcile them but love. They are fatally late when they undertake to explain and treat with one another like foes. Who will take an apology for a Friend? They must apologize like dew and frost, which are off again with the sun, and which all men know in their hearts to be beneficent. The necessity itself for explanation,—what explanation will atone for that?

True love does not quarrel for slight reasons, such mistakes as mutual acquaintances can explain away, but, alas, however slight the apparent cause, only for adequate and fatal and everlasting reasons, which can never be set aside. Its quarrel, if there is any, is ever recurring, notwithstanding the beams of affection which invariably come to gild its tears; as the rainbow, however beautiful and unerring a sign, does not promise fair weather forever, but only for a season. I have known two or three persons pretty well, and yet I have never known advice to be of use but in trivial and transient matters. One may know what another does not, but the utmost kindness cannot impart what is requisite to make the advice useful. We must accept or refuse one another as we are. I could tame a hyena more easily than my Friend. He is a material which no tool of mine will work. A naked savage will fell an oak with a firebrand, and wear a hatchet out of a rock by friction, but I cannot hew the smallest chip out of the character of my Friend, either to beautify or deform it.

The lover learns at last that there is no person quite transparent and trustworthy, but every one has a devil in him that is capable of any crime in the long run. Yet, as an Oriental philosopher has said, "Although Friendship between good men is interrupted, their principles remain unaltered. The stalk of the lotus may be broken, and the fibres remain connected."

Ignorance and bungling with love are better than wisdom and skill without. There may be courtesy, there may be even temper, and wit, and talent, and sparkling conversation, there may be good-will even,—and yet the humanest and divinest faculties pine for exercise. Our life without love is like coke and ashes. Men may be pure as alabaster and Parian marble, elegant as a Tuscan villa, sublime as Niagara, and yet if there is no milk mingled with the wine at their entertainments, better is the hospitality of Goths and Vandals.

My Friend is not of some other race or family of men, but flesh of my flesh, bone of my bone. He is my real brother. I see his nature groping yonder so like mine. We do not live far apart. Have not the fates associated us in many ways? It says, in the Vishnu Purana: "Seven paces together is sufficient for the friendship of the virtuous, but thou and I have dwelt together." Is it of no significance that we have so long partaken of the same loaf, drank at the same fountain, breathed the same air summer and winter, felt the same heat and cold; that the same fruits have been pleased to refresh us both, and we have never had a thought of different fibre the one from the other!

> Nature doth have her dawn each day,
>   But mine are far between;
> Content, I cry, for sooth to say,
>   Mine brightest are, I ween.
>
> For when my sun doth deign to rise,
>   Though it be her noontide,
> Her fairest field in shadow lies,
>   Nor can my light abide.
>
> Sometimes I bask me in her day,
>   Conversing with my mate,

But if we interchange one ray,
    Forthwith her heats abate.

Through his discourse I climb and see,
    As from some eastern hill,
A brighter morrow rise to me
    Than lieth in her skill.

As 't were two summer days in one,
    Two Sundays come together,
Our rays united make one sun,
    With fairest summer weather.

As surely as the sunset in my latest November shall translate me to the ethereal world, and remind me of the ruddy morning of youth; as surely as the last strain of music which falls on my decaying ear shall make age to be forgotten, or, in short, the manifold influences of nature survive during the term of our natural life, so surely my Friend shall forever be my Friend, and reflect a ray of God to me, and time shall foster and adorn and consecrate our Friendship, no less than the ruins of temples. As I love nature, as I love singing birds, and gleaming stubble, and flowing rivers, and morning and evening, and summer and winter, I love thee, my Friend.

But all that can be said of Friendship is like botany to flowers. How can the understanding take account of its friendliness?

Even the death of Friends will inspire us as much as their lives. They will leave consolation to the mourners, as the rich leave money to defray the expenses of their funerals, and their memories will be incrusted over with sublime and pleasing thoughts, as monuments of other men are overgrown with moss; for our Friends have no place in the graveyard.

This to our cis-Alpine and cis-Atlantic Friends.

Also this other word of entreaty and advice to the large and respectable nation of Acquaintances, beyond the mountains;—Greeting.

My most serene and irresponsible neighbors, let us see that we have the whole advantage of each other; we will be useful, at least, if not admirable, to one another. I know that the mountains which separate us are high, and covered with perpetual snow, but despair not. Improve the serene winter weather to scale them. If need be, soften the rocks with vinegar. For here lie the verdant plains of Italy ready to receive you. Nor shall I be slow on my side to penetrate to your Provence. Strike then boldly at head or heart or any vital part. Depend upon it, the timber is well seasoned and tough, and will bear rough usage; and if it should crack, there is plenty more where it came from. I am no piece of crockery that cannot be jostled against my neighbor without danger of being broken by the collision, and must needs ring false and jarringly to the end of my days, when once I am cracked; but rather one of the old-fashioned wooden trenchers, which one while stands at the head of the table, and at another is a milking-stool, and at another a seat for children, and finally goes down to its grave not unadorned with honorable scars, and does not die till it is worn out. Nothing can shock a brave man but dullness. Think how many rebuffs every man has experienced in his day; perhaps has fallen into a horse-pond, eaten fresh-water clams, or worn one shirt for a week without washing. Indeed, you cannot receive a shock unless you have an electric affinity for that which shocks you. Use me, then, for I am useful in my way, and stand as one of many petitioners, from toad-stool and henbane up to dahlia and violet, supplicating to be put to my use, if by any means ye may find me serviceable; whether for a medicated drink or bath, as balm and laven-der; or for fragrance, as verbena and geranium; or for sight, as cactus; or for thoughts, as pansy. These humbler, at least, if not those higher uses.

Ah, my dear Strangers and Enemies, I would not forget you. I can well afford to welcome you. Let me subscribe myself Yours ever and truly,—your much obliged servant. We have nothing to fear from our foes; God keeps a stand-ing army for that service; but we have no ally against our Friends, those ruthless Vandals.

Once more to one and all,—
    "Friends, Romans, Countrymen, and Lovers."

> Let such pure hate still underprop
> Our love, that we may be
> Each other's conscience.
> And have our sympathy
> Mainly from thence.

> We'll one another treat like gods,
> And all the faith we have
> In virtue and in truth, bestow
> On either, and suspicion leave
> To gods below.

> Two solitary stars,—
> Unmeasured systems far

Between us roll,
But by our conscious light we are
Determined to one pole.

What need confound the sphere,—
Love can afford to wait,
For it no hour's too late
That witnesseth one duty's end,
Or to another doth beginning lend.

It will subserve no use,
More than the tints of flowers,
Only the independent guest
Frequents its bowers,
Inherits its bequest.

No speech though kind has it,
But kinder silence doles
Unto its mates,
By night consoles,
By day congratulates.

What saith the tongue to tongue?
What heareth ear of ear?
By the decrees of fate
From year to year,
Does it communicate.

Pathless the gulf of feeling yawns,—
No trivial bridge of words,
Or arch of boldest span,
Can leap the moat that girds
The sincere man.

No show of bolts and bars
Can keep the foeman out,
Or 'scape his secret mine
Who entered with the doubt
That drew the line.

No warder at the gate
Can let the friendly in,
But, like the sun, o'er all
He will the castle win,
And shine along the wall.

There's nothing in the world I know
That can escape from love,
For every depth it goes below,
And every height above.

It waits as waits the sky,
Until the clouds go by,
Yet shines serenely on
With an eternal day,
Alike when they are gone,
And when they stay.

Implacable is Love,—
Foes may be bought or teased
From their hostile intent,
But he goes unappeased
Who is on kindness bent.

Selected Writings on Friendship

For a man to act himself, he must be perfectly free; otherwise he is in danger of losing all sense of responsibility or of self-respect. Now when such a state of things exists, that the sacred opinions one advances in argument are apologized for by his friends, before his face, lest his hearers receive a wrong impression of the man,—when such gross injustice is of frequent occurrence, where shall we look, and not look in vain, for men, deeds, thoughts? As well apologize for the grape that it is sour, or the thunder that it is noisy, or the lightning that it tarries not.

—Thoreau to Helen Thoreau, October 27, 1837[2]

The utmost nearness to which men approach each other amounts barely to a mechanical contact. As when you rub two stones together, though they emit an audible sound, yet do they not actually touch each other. . . .

Let ours be like the meeting of two planets, not hastening to confound their jarring spheres, but drawn together by the influence of a subtle attraction, soon to roll diverse in their respective orbits, from this their perigee, or point of nearest approach.

—Scraps from a Lecture on "Society"
written March 14, 1838[3]

Two sturdy oaks I mean, which side by side
    Withstand the winter's storm,
        And, spite of wind and tide,

Grow up the meadow's pride,
    For both are strong.

Above they barely touch, but, undermined
    Down to their deepest source,
    Admiring you shall find
    Their roots are intertwined
      Insep'rably.

—Journal, 8 April 1838[4]

What though friends misinterpret your conduct, if it is right in sight of God and Nature.

—Journal, July 15, 1838[5]

Then first I conceive of a true friendship, when some rare specimen of manhood presents itself.

—Journal, Fall 1839[6]

I need not ask any man to be my friend, more than the sun the earth to be attracted by him. It is not his to give, nor mine to receive. I cannot pardon my enemy; let him pardon himself.

—Journal, Fall 1839[7]

Commonly we degrade Love and Friendship by presenting them under the aspect of a trivial dualism.

—Journal, Fall 1839[8]

What matter a few words more or less with my friend,— with all mankind;—they will still be my friends in spite of themselves. Let them stand aloof if they can! As though the most formidable distance could rob me of any real sympathy or advantage! No, when such interests are at stake, time, and distance, and difference fall into their own places.

—Journal, Fall 1839[9]

But alas! to be actually separated from that parcel of heaven we call our friend, with the suspicion that we shall no more meet in nature, is source enough for all the elegies that ever were written. But the true remedy will be to recover our friend again piecemeal, wherever we can find a feature, as Æetes gathered up the members of his son, which Medea had strewn in her path.   —Journal, Fall 1839[10]

The more complete our sympathy, the more our senses are struck dumb, and we are repressed by a delicate respect, so that to indifferent eyes we are least his friend, because no vulgar symbols pass between us. On after thought, perhaps, we come to fear that we have been the losers by such seeming indifference, but in truth that which withholds us is the bond between us.   —Journal, Fall 1839[11]

My friend will be as much better than myself as my aspiration is above my performance.   —Journal, Fall 1839[12]

Friends.
They are like air bubbles on water, hastening to flow together.   —Journal, January 26, 1840[13]

Constantly, as it were through a remote skylight, I have glimpses of a serene friendship-land, and know the better why brooks murmur and violets grow.

This conjunction of souls, like waves which meet and break, subsides also backward over things, and gives all a fresh aspect.   —Journal, January 26, 1840[14]

A friend in history looks like some premature soul. The nearest approach to a community of love in these days is like the distant breaking of waves on the seashore. An ocean there must be, for it washes our beach.

This alone do all men sail for, trade for, plow for, preach for, fight for.   —Journal, January 29, 1840[15]

All romance is grounded on friendship. What is this rural, this pastoral, this poetical life but its invention? Does not the moon shine for Endymion? Smooth pastures and mild airs are for some Corydon and Phyllis. Paradise belongs to Adam and Eve. Plato's republic is governed by Platonic love.   —Journal, February 18, 1840[16]

On the death of a friend, we should consider that the fates through confidence have devolved on us the task of a double living, that we have henceforth to fulfill the promise of our friend's life also, in our own, to the world.
                              —Journal, February 28, 1840[17]

We will warm us at each other's fire. Friendship is not such a cold refining process as a double sieve, but a glowing furnace in which all impurities are consumed.
                              —Journal, June 25, 1840[18]

Unless we meet religiously, we prophane one another. What was once consecrated ground round the temple, we have used as no better than a domestic court.

Our friend's is as holy a shrine as any God's, to be approached with sacred love and awe. Veneration is the measure of Love. Our friend answers ambiguously, and sometimes before the question is propounded, like the oracle of Delphi. He forbears to ask explanation, but doubts and surmises darkly with full faith, as we silently ponder our fates.

In no presence are we so susceptible to shame. Our hour is a sabbath, our abode a temple, our gifts peace offerings, our conversation a communion, our silence a prayer. In prophanity we are absent, in holiness near, in sin estranged, in innocence reconciled.   —Journal, June 27, 1840[19]

Of all phenomena, my own race are the most mysterious and undiscoverable. For how many years have I striven to meet one, even on common manly ground, and have not succeeded!   —Journal, June 29, 1840[20]

Friends will have to be introduced each time they meet. They will be eternally strange to one another, and when they have mutually appropriated their value for the last hour, they will go and gather a new measure of strangeness for the next. They are like two boughs crossed in the wood, which play backwards and forwards upon one another in the wind, and only wear into each other, but never the sap of the one flows into the pores of the other, for then the wind would no more draw from them those strains which enchanted the wood. They are not two united, but rather one divided.   —Journal, January 29, 1841[21]

How much does it concern you, the good opinion of your friend? Therein is the measure of fame. For the herd of men multiplied many times will never come up to the value of one friend.   —Journal, February 2, 1841[22]

One may discover a new side to his most intimate friend when for the first time he hears him speak in public. He will be stranger to him as he is more familiar to the audience. The longest intimacy could not foretell how he would behave then. When I observe my friend's conduct toward others, then chiefly I learn the traits in his character, and in each case I am unprepared for the issue.
          —Journal, February 6, 1841[23]

The most I can do for my friend is simply to be his friend. I have no wealth to bestow on him. If he knows that I am happy in loving him, he will want no other reward. Is not Friendship divine in this?

—Journal, February 7, 1841[24]

My friend will show such a noble confidence that I shall aspire to the society of his good opinion. Never presume men less that you may make them more. So far as we respond to our ideal estimate of each other do we have profitable intercourse.

—Journal, February 7, 1841[25]

You demand that I be less your friend that you may know it.

—Journal, February 19, 1841[26]

Nothing will reconcile friends but love.

—Journal, February 19, 1841[27]

If my world is not sufficient without thee, my friend, I will wait till it is and then call thee. You shall come to a palace, not to an almshouse.

—Journal, February 26, 1841[28]

Friendship

Now we are partners in such legal trade,
We'll look to the beginnings, not the ends,
Nor to pay-day, knowing truth wealth is made
For current stock and not for dividends.

—Journal, March 30, 1841[29]

Friends are the ancient and honorable of the earth.

—Journal, April 8, 1841[30]

Friendship's Steadfastness

True friendship is so firm a league
That's maintenance falls into the even tenor
Of our lives, and is no tie,
But the continuance of our life's thread.

If I would safely keep this new-got pelf,
I have no care henceforth but watch myself,
For lo! it goes untended from my sight,
Waxes and wanes secure with the safe star of night.

See with what liberal step it makes its way,
As we could well afford to let it stray
Throughout the universe, with the sun and moon,
Which would dissolve allegiance as soon.

Shall I concern myself for fickleness,
And undertake to make my friends more sure,
When the great gods out of sheer kindliness,
Gave me this office for a sinecure?

—Journal, April 11, 1841[31]

My friend, my friend, I'd speak so frank to thee that thou wouldst pray me to keep back some part, for fear I robbed myself. To address thee delights me, there is such cleanness in the delivery. I am delivered of my tale, which, told to strangers, still would linger on my lips as if untold, or doubtful how it ran. —Journal, March 11, 1842[32]

The sad memory of departed friends is soon incrusted over with sublime and pleasing thoughts, as their monuments are overgrown with moss. Nature doth thus kindly heal every wound. —Journal, March 13, 1842[33]

My friend is cold and reserved because his love for me is waxing and not waning. These are the early processes; the particles are just beginning to shoot in crystals. If the mountains came to me, I should no longer go to the mountains. So soon as that consummation takes place which I wish, it will be past. Shall I not have a friend in reserve? Heaven is to come. I hope this is not it.

Words should pass between friends as the lightning passes from cloud to cloud. I don't know how much I assist in the economy of nature when I declare a fact. Is it not an important part in the history of the flower that I tell my friend where I found it? We do not wish friends to feed and clothe our bodies,—neighbors are kind enough for that,—but to do the like offices to ourselves. We wish to spread and publish ourselves, as the sun spreads its rays; and we toss the new thought to the friend, and thus it is dispersed. Friends are those twain who feel their interests to be one. Each knows that the other might as well have said what he said. All beauty, all music, all delight springs from apparent dualism but real unity. My friend is my real brother. I see his nature groping yonder like my own. Does there go one whom I know? then I go there.

The field where friends have met is consecrated forever. Man seeks friendship out of the desire to realize a home here. As the Indian thinks he receives into himself the courage and strength of his conquered enemy, so we add to ourselves all the character and heart of our friends. He is my creation. I can do what I will with him. There is no possibility of being thwarted; the friend is like wax in the rays that fall from our own hearts.

The friend does not take my word for anything, but he takes me. He trusts me as I trust myself. We only need be as true to others as we are to ourselves, that there may be ground enough for friendship. In the beginnings of friendship,—for it does not grow,—we realize such love and justice as are attributed to God.

Very few are they from whom we derive any *in*forma- tion. The most only announce and tell tales, but the friend *in*-forms.   —Journal, March 20, 1842[34]

I care not for the man or his designs who would make the highest use of me short of an all-adventuring friendship. I wish by the behavior of my friend toward me to be led to have such regard for myself as for a box of precious oint- ment. I shall not be so cheap to myself if I see that another values me.   —Journal, March 25, 1842[35]

What a man does, compared with what he is, is but a small part. To require that our friend possess a certain skill is not to be satisfied till he is something less than our friend.

Friendship should be a great promise, a perennial springtime.   —Journal, March 28, 1842[36]

If ever our idea of a friend is realized it will be in some broad and generous natural person, as frank as the daylight, in whose presence our behavior will be as simple and un- constrained as the wanderer amid the recesses of these hills.
                     —Journal, 1837–47[37]

I am sometimes made aware of a kindness which may have long since been shown, which surely memory can- not retain, which reflects its light long after its heat. I realize, my friend, that there have been times when thy thoughts of me have been of such lofty kindness that they passed over me like the winds of heaven unnoticed, so pure that they presented no object to my eyes, so generous and universal that I did not detect them. Thou hast loved me for what I was not, but for what I aspired to be. We shudder to think of the kindness of our friend which has fallen on us cold, though in some true but tardy hour we have awakened. There has just reached me the kindness of some acts, not to be forgotten, not to be remembered. I wipe off these scores at midnight, at rare intervals, in moments of insight and gratitude.

—Journal, 1837–47[38]

As with two eyes we see and with two ears we hear, with the like advantage is man added to man. Making no complaint, offering no encouragement, one human being is made aware of the neighboring and contemporaneous existence of another. Such is the tenderness of friendship. We never recognize each other as finite and imperfect beings, but with a smile and as strangers. My intercourse with men is governed by the same laws with my intercourse with nature. —Journal, 1837–47[39]

Nothing makes the earth seem so spacious as to have friends at a distance; they make the latitudes and longitudes.

—Thoreau to Lidian Emerson, May 22, 1843[40]

Who has not imagined to himself a country inn, where the traveler shall really feel *in*, and at home, and at his public house, who was before at his private house?—whose host is indeed a *host*, and a *lord* of the *land*, a self-appointed brother of his race . . . a man of such universal sympathies, and so broad and genial a human nature, that he would fain sacrifice the tender but narrow ties of private friendship to a broad, sunshiny, fair-weather-and-foul friendship for his race. —"The Landlord"[41]

I have been to see Henry James. . . . I know of no one so patient and determined to have the good of you. It is almost friendship, such plain and human dealing.

—Thoreau to Emerson, June 8, 1843[42]

My very dear friend,—I have only read a page of your letter, and have come out to the top of the hill at sunset, where I can see the ocean, to prepare to read the rest. It is fitter that it should hear it than the walls of my chamber. The very crickets here seem to chirp around me as they did not before. I feel as if it were a great daring to go on and read the rest, and then to live accordingly. There are more than thirty vessels in sight going to sea. I am almost afraid to look at your letter. I see that it will make my life very steep, but it may lead to fairer prospects than this.

You seem to me to speak out of a very clear and high heaven, where any one may be who stands so high. Your voice seems not a voice, but comes as much from the blue heavens as from the paper.

My dear friend, it was very noble in you to write me so trustful an answer. It will do as well for another world as for this; such a voice is for no particular time nor person, but it makes him who may hear it stand for all that is lofty and true in humanity. The thought of you will constantly elevate my life; it will be something always above the horizon to behold, as when I look up at the evening star. I think I know your thoughts without seeing you, and as well here as in Concord. You are not at all strange to me.

I could hardly believe, after the lapse of one night, that I had such a noble letter still at hand to read,—that it was not some fine dream. I looked at midnight to be sure that it was real. I feel that I am unworthy to know you, and yet they will not permit it wrongfully.

I, perhaps, am more willing to deceive by appearances

than you say you are; it would not be worth the while to tell how willing; but I have the power perhaps too much to forget my meanness as soon as seen, and not be incited by permanent sorrow. My actual life is unspeakably mean compared with what I know and see that it might be. Yet the ground from which I see and say this is some part of it. It ranges from heaven to earth, and is all things in an hour. The experience of every past moment but belies the faith of each present. We never conceive the greatness of our fates. Are not these faint flashes of light which sometimes obscure the sun their certain dawn?

My friend, I have read your letter as if I was not reading it. After each pause I could defer the rest forever. The thought of you will be a new motive for every right action. You are another human being whom I know, and might not our topic be as broad as the universe? What have we to do with petty rumbling news? We have our own great affairs. Sometimes in Concord I found my actions dictated, as it were, by your influence, and though it led almost to trivial Hindoo observances, yet it was good and elevating. To hear that you have sad hours is not sad to me. I rather rejoice at the richness of your experience. Only think of some sadness away in Pekin,—unseen and unknown there. What a mine it is! Would it not weigh down the Celestial Empire, with all its gay Chinese? Our sadness is not sad, but our cheap joys. Let us be sad about all we see and are, for so we demand and pray for better. It is the constant prayer and whole Christian religion. I could hope that you would get well soon, and have a healthy body for this world, but I know this cannot be; and the Fates, after all, are the accomplishers of our hopes. Yet I do hope that you may find it a worthy struggle, and life seem grand still through the clouds.

What wealth is it to have such friends that we cannot

think of them without elevation! And we can think of them any time and anywhere, and it costs nothing but the lofty disposition. I cannot tell you the joy your letter gives me, which will not quite cease till the latest time. Let me accompany your finest thought.

I send my love to my other friend and brother, whose nobleness I slowly recognize.

—Thoreau to Lidian Emerson, June 20, 1843[43]

I love men with the same distinction that I love woman—as if my friend were of some third sex—some other or stranger and still my friend. —Journal, May 5, 1846[44]

In what concerns you much, do not think that you have companions: know that you are alone in the world.

—Thoreau to Harrison Gray Otis Blake,
March 27, 1848[45]

The movements of the eyes express the perpetual and unconscious courtesy of the parties. It is said that a rogue does not look you in the face, neither does an honest man look at you as if he had his reputation to establish. I have seen some who did not know when to turn aside their eyes in meeting yours. A truly confident and magnanimous spirit is wiser than to contend for the mastery in such encounters. Serpents alone conquer by the steadiness of their gaze. My friend looks me in the face and sees me, that is all.

—*A Week on the Concord and Merrimack Rivers*[46]

I dreamed this night of an event which had occurred long before. It was a difference with a Friend, which had not ceased to give me pain, though I had no cause to blame myself. But in my dream ideal justice was at length done me for his suspicions, and I received that compensation which I had never obtained in my waking hours. I was unspeakably soothed and rejoiced, even after I awoke, because in dreams we never deceive ourselves, nor are deceived, and this seemed to have the authority of a final judgment.

—*A Week on the Concord and Merrimack Rivers*[47]

My friends mistake when they communicate facts to me with so much pains. Their presence, even their exaggerations and loose statements, are equally good facts for me. I have no respect for facts even except when I would use them, and for the most part I am independent of those which I hear, and can afford to be inaccurate, or, in other words, to substitute more present and pressing facts in their place. —*A Week on the Concord and Merrimack Rivers*[48]

When I came out of prison. . . . I saw to what extent the people among whom I lived could be trusted as good neighbors and friends; that their friendship was for summer weather only; that they did not greatly propose to do right; that they were a distinct race from me by their prejudices and superstitions, as the Chinamen and Malays are; that in their sacrifices to humanity they ran no risks, not even to their property; that after all they were not so noble but they treated the thief as he had treated them, and hoped, by a certain outward observance and a few prayers, and by walking in a particular straight though useless path from time to time, to save their souls. —*"Civil Disobedience"*[49]

He whom we associate with our daily affairs is our acquaintance. He whom we associate with our social joys is what the world commonly calls our friend. He whom we associate with our Elysium is beloved by us.

—*Journal, after May 26, 1849*[50]

I have a friend whom I heartily love, whom I would always treat tenderly; who, indeed, is so transfigured to me that I dare not identify the ideal with the actual. The fit time has never come for that. If I could believe that my friend would tenderly and wisely enough sustain the declaration of my love I should make him privy to my dreams, but I fear that some more terrestrial cousin may be introduced, that if ideals can thus commingle, actuals will begin to obtrude themselves.

I am afraid to contrast my dreams so rudely with the actual day, to tell them by daylight. I was never so near my friend when he was bodily present, as when he was absent. And yet I am indirectly accused by this friend of coldness and disingenuousness, when I cannot speak for warmth and sincerity.

If what I might tell my friend is what he does not already know, it will no longer be true when I have told it.

I do desire nothing so much as to tell my love, yet as my love is rare so is the opportunity to declare it. Can it be that my friend is but a suggestion and hint of a friend whom I have never seen?

Is it a use I make of my friends which necessarily transcends their privity (consciousness)? They sometimes even demand to be admitted to my solitary joy, ask why I smile, but I see too plainly that if I degraded my ideal to an identity with any actual mortal whose hand is to be grasped there would be an end of our fine relations. I would be related to my friend by the most etherial part of our natures alone, and what else is quite obedient to this.

—Journal, after May 26, 1849[51]

It is not enough that my friend is good—he must be wise. Our intercourse is likely to be a tragedy with that one who cannot measure us. Where there is not discernment the behavior even of a pure soul may in effect amount to coarseness. In a difference with a friend I have felt that our intercourse was prophaned when that friend made haste come to speech about it. I am more grieved that my friend can so easily give utterance to his wounded feelings than by what he says. Such a wound cannot be permanently healed.

—Journal, after May 26, 1849[52]

I had tenderly cherished the flower of our friendship till one day my friend treated it as a weed. It did not survive the shock but drooped and withered from that hour. A friend avoids the subject of friendship in conversation. It is a very sacred relation which is not liable to a vulgar difference.

—Journal, after May 26, 1849[53]

To have a brother or a sister—to have a gold mine on your farm—to find diamonds in the gravel heaps before your door—how rare these things are.

To share the day with you—to inhabit the earth. Whether to have a god or goddess for companion in your walks or to walk alone, with hinds and villains and carles. Would not a friend enhance the beauty of the landscape as much as a deer or hare? Every thing would acknowledge and serve such a relation, the corn in the field and the cranberries in the meadows. The flowers and the birds would bloom and sing with a new impulse. There would be more fair days in the year.

What a difference whether you have a brother on earth or not, whether in all your walks you meet only strangers or in one house is one who knows you and whom you know.

—Journal, after September 11, 1849[54]

We never have the benefit of our friend's criticism, and none is so severe and searching until he is estranged from us.

No one appreciates our virtues like our friend, yet methinks that I do not receive from my friend that criticism which is most valuable and indispensable to me until he is estranged from me. He who knows best what we are, knows what we are not. He will never tell me the fatal truth which it concerns me most to know until he is estranged from me and then the harmless truth will be shot with a poisoned arrow, will have a poisoned barb.

When we are such friends and have such for our friends that our love is not partiality, that truth is not crowded out or postponed or delayed, there will be *Friendship*.

Now first we are dealt with absolutely. This truth without that poison and we were friends still and indeed.

The fruit of partiality is enmity.

I had a friend, I wrote a book, I asked my friend's criticism, I never got but praise for what was good in it—my friend became estranged from me and then I got blame for all that was bad,—and so I got at last the criticism which I wanted.

While my friend was my friend he flattered me, and I never heard the truth from him, but when he became my enemy he shot it to me on a poisoned arrow.

There is as much hatred as love in the world. Hate is a good critic.

When two can treat each other with absolute truth, then there will be but those two in the world. Then men will no longer be divided but be one as God is.

—Journal, after September 11, 1849[55]

Why should we be related as mortals merely, as limited to one state of existence? Our lives are immortal, our transmigrations are infinite; the virtue that we are lives ever, the vice dieth ever. Shall I exhibit to my friend a human

narrowness? To what purpose mythology? The petty tragedy or comedy of our human life, we can sit spectators of
it; let it pass. I would meet my friend not in the light or
shadow of our human life alone but as daimons. We should
not be less tender and human, sympathizing for this because we should meet intimately as essences.

I should consider this friend of mine is a *Great* fellow;
my knowledge of him, our intercourse, is not to be limited to a few of Nature's revolutions, a few paltry summers
and winters. No! no! We are Great fellows; we shall be a
long time together. I do not despair of knowing him better.
Ours is a tragedy of more than 5 acts. This is not the fifth
act in our tragedy. No, no! blow high, blow low, I will come
upon my feet, and holding my friend by the hand. The un-
dertaker will have a dusty time that undertakes to bury me.
I go with the party of the gods. What falsehoods men do
tell. They say that life's a fallacy. They are benighted, they
are ineffectual men who walk in the valley of the shadow
of Death. I am not a-going to be a man merely. I will be
Hari—

Not a little snivelling, hugging, hoping *pro tempore*,
loving, exaggerating. A friendship which will survive despair and the grave thereafter and laugh at such sweet pains
as a man hangs himself for.

—Journal, after October 15, 1849[56]

My friend may do whate'er he may
And I shall love him any day
If he doth it from love.
But let him do whate'er he will
I think that I must hate him still
If lower motives move.

—Journal, after October 28, 1849[57]

How happens it that one we love can ever do us wrong?—
for thinking wrong and doing wrong are one.

—Journal, after October 28, 1849

Over fineness in this relation is one with coarseness, for it is
only by the heart that it is refined.

The tenderest love is the most vulnerable, but it is the
most immortal.

A lover never hears anything that he is told, for that is
commonly either false or stale, but he hears things taking
place as moles mining in the ground.

I think that if I lived on a desolate island all my life I
should not the less know the sentiment of friendship.

And methinks I have never met with one who was prepared to be quite ideally related to me by sympathy and
kindness, a mystic relation. Methinks that instant that I
met my mate, I should have no reserve. I should give the
whole of myself to that society. I should have no duty aside
from that.

One who could bear to be so wonderfully and beautifully exaggerated from day to day. I would take my friend
out of his low self and set him higher, infinitely higher, and
there know him.

It would seem as if men were as much afraid of love as
of hate.

Such love is aweful to them they have lower engagements, they have near ends to serve, they have not imagination enough to be thus employed about a man but must be
coopering a barrel for employment.

There is always danger of losing sight of what our
friend is absolutely, while considering what he is to us
alone.

—Journal, after October 28, 1849[58]

It is not always that I hate my friends.

—Journal, January 5, 1850[59]

My friend cannot invite nor repel me, when he *will*. It is easy to "pass the compliment" but only he who is rightly related to me can invite me. He makes his invitations cheap by asking me to call and see him when he is not at home.

To invite my friend is to draw him gently but strongly toward me by my sympathy and love—such an invitation is irresistible—not to ask him to come to me when my apathy or antipathy repels him. I feel a yearning toward him. Then the billet is written. Then the invitation sent.

If you are inviting in this sense the rocks and trees will come to you. If therefore my neighbor does not come to me I know that there is no such attraction between us, we have no such affinity for one another. I do not draw him strongly enough and hence I have no right to go to him.

My love for another is my affinity for him, it is the love of quick lime for water. It is an enlargement of myself. I am pleased at the extension of my domains.

An invitation to which I did not attend! what an outrage! Do not the stones yield to gravity?

If we would put our invitation into words, who shall tell us what we would say?

There is no interpreter between us and our consciousness.

I have no satisfaction in the visits of some of my acquaintances because they do not make themselves at home. Sit down and sit heavy though you break my chairs. If you have leisure to be met, I will meet you. I will not take you on the wing. If you have any engagement, fulfill it and leave me. Unless you abound in leisure as the creator when he made this globe—Farewell.

You are a rare bird, but, as was said of the bird of

Paradise, never alight on the earth. Give me a barn door fowl rather which goes honestly to roost.

But what though you are a bird of Paradise, if you never alight on the earth. You are a fabulous bird to me.

Make your will before you come to see me, that there may be no interruption. Take leave of your wife and children, receive extreme unction. One *friend* will go *professedly* to see another and if in five minutes he has not success, he will take his hat and come away saying to himself that after such a disappointment he will *never* try again. The sportsman will lie curled up and motionless an hour or more under a bush in the snow in a winter afternoon, waiting for a partridge to come out of the woods to bud on an apple tree.

The first goes home without any game in his bag; the last is rarely disappointed, muffled up and rubbing his hands and feet to keep them warm.

He who remembers engagements is not here.

Watching under a bush till the stars come out, with no companion but his fowling piece.

Though the seasons quicken their pace I will not be hurried. —Journal, after January 5, 1850[60]

You had been dealing with an imaginary mate.

The quarrels of lovers are beneficent. Each one yields to a true instinct.

Methinks that I carry into friendship the tenderness and nicety of a lover.

We lose our friends when we cease to be friends, not when they die. Then they depart, then we are sad and go into mourning for them. Death is no separation compared with that which takes place when we cease to have confidence in one with whom we have walked in confidence. When we cease to love one whom we had loved; when we know him no more; when we look for him and cannot find him, how completely is he departed! No things can be farther asunder than friends estranged. Our courses inevitably diverge, and we feel the fibres being rent. What can restore him to life for me? This miracle was never performed. Shall I *never* see him more? What fate has driven a wedge between us? Friends estranged are buried alive to one another. . . .

Let us endeavor, then, to save the lives of our friends as long as we can.

Two were not made to travel in company always. Where are they who were once our friends but are so no longer? Where are we whose friend is dead? Are we in this life?

If you would know what it is to be separated from those we love, think not of death but of estrangement. Whom we have once seen we shall never see again; whom we have never seen we shall see 'ere long.

Friends meet and part as when two pilgrims who have walked together many days in sweet society, sharing the adventures of the road with mutual aid and entertainment, reach a point where their courses diverge and linger there awhile, and then bidding each other farewell, one goes this road and the other that, and as they withdraw they mutually turn to wave a last farewell and watch each other's retreating figure, until at last they are concealed from one another by a bend in the road and the sun goes down behind the mountains leaving each alone.

And they are sorry to part but their duty calls them different ways. And one climbs upon a rock that he may see his late fellow-traveller a little longer, and freely communicating their thoughts and feelings.

I can excuse any offence against the heart but not against the imagination. The imagination knows and remembers and controls the heart. My heart may still yearn toward the valley but my imagination will not permit me to jump off the precipice that debars me from it, for it has had its wings clipt and cannot fly.

My imagination is wounded and cannot fly, for the imagination never forgets. It is a *re-membering*, for the imagination is not foundationless but most reasonable. It uses all the knowledge of the intellect. It has a real though not actual basis. It is grounded on reality.

We hesitate to name our friends, our brothers and our sisters, for the name attaches but to a part of them and when they who bear the name are gone, we find that friend is not gone with them, for they are more than half ideal. It would be taking names in vain. We are not aware of the uses to which we put each other.

If I valued my friends less I should visit them oftener.

Ask and ye shall receive, but asking is not merely the form of asking; we must ask as purely and undesignedly as we would that another should give.

My so-called friend comes near to being my greatest enemy, for when he deceives me, he deceives me more than any. He betrays as an enemy has no opportunity to.

There is no kind of cheating, no dishonesty so fatal to all society as the disposition to get more than you give; to get the whole of your friend while you give him but a part of yourself; to meet him with designs upon him who comes without design; to make a conscious use of that relation whose fruit surpasses utility, and inspires to unconscious nobleness.

That man is not my friend who for any reason withholds from me what I bestow on him.

One man wishes me to be the friend of his whim. I'll be the inveterate and relentless foe of it whenever it comes in my way.

One wishes me to prove to him that I am his friend,

and then he says he will be mine. How can I prove it him in such a case? How can I prove what is not true?

I am more reinforced when I renounce entirely a hesitating and unreliable friendship than when I surround myself with such allies.

My friend died long ago; why follow a body to the graveyard? Why toll the bell today? Its knell has died away.

There still remain his clothes. Shall we have a third service *when they* are decayed?

—Journal, after January 5, 1850[61]

There are few to whom Friendship is a sufficiently sacred relation. Most are prepared for a vulgar quarrel and truce. I cherish so many fancies about it, and so religiously, that I never get to speech on the subject.

—Journal, 1848–1850[62]

I do not wish for intimacy for its own sake. Two may more strongly attract at the same moment that they repel each other, than if they attracted merely—they make an appointment. —Journal, after April 1, 1850[63]

Is your friend such a one that an increase of worth on your part will surely make him more your friend?

—Journal, after April 19, 1850[64]

I do not feel permanently related to any one.

—Journal, after April 19, 1850[65]

When we separate finally and completely from one who has been our friend we separate with content—and without grief—as gently and naturally as night passes into day.

—Journal, after April 19, 1850[66]

When our companions fail us we transfer our love instantaneously to a worthy object, as the sunlight which falls on the walls and fences, when those are removed, falls instantaneously on the mountains and spires in the horizon.

—Journal, 1848–1850[67]

Actually I have no friend. I am very distant from all actual persons. —Journal, 1848–1850[68]

A friend in need is not a friend indeed. What we need is a friend. All the world are our friends then. He is not our friend who visits us only when we are sick, but he whose preventive visits keep us well,—who never lets us need.

—Journal, 1848–1850[69]

Woe to him who wants a companion, for he is unfit to be the companion even of himself.

We inspire friendship in men when we have contracted friendship with the gods.

When we cease to sympathize with and to be personally related to men, and begin to be universally related, then we are capable of inspiring others with the sentiment of love for us. —Journal, June 1850[70]

As for missing friends,—fortunate perhaps is he who has any to miss, whose place a thought will not supply. I have an ideal friend in whose place actual persons sometimes stand for a season. The last I may often miss, but the first I recover when I am myself again. What if we do miss one another? have we not agreed upon a rendezvous? While each travels his own way through the wood with serene and inexpressible joy, though it be on his hands and knees over the rocks and fallen trees, he cannot but be on the right way; there is no wrong way to him. I have found myself as well off when I have fallen into a quagmire, as in an armchair in the most hospitable house. The prospect was pretty much the same. Without anxiety let us wander on, admiring whatever beauty the woods exhibit.

Do you know on what bushes a little peace, faith, and contentment grow? Go a-berrying early and late after them. Miss our friends! It is not easy to get rid of them.

—Journal, 1850[71]

Ah, my friend, what if I do not answer thee? I hear thee. Thou canst speak; I cannot. I hear and forget to answer. I am occupied with hearing. I awoke and thought of thee; thou wast present to my mind. How camest thou there? Was I not present to thee likewise?   —Journal, 1850[72]

I love my friends very much, but I find that it is of no use to go to see them. I hate them commonly when I am near them. They belie themselves and deny me continually.

—Journal, November 16, 1850[73]

I have certain friends whom I visit occasionally, but I commonly part from them early with a certain bitter-sweet sentiment. That which we love is so mixed and entangled with that we hate in one another that we are more grieved and disappointed, aye, and estranged from one another, by meeting than by absence. Some men may be my acquaintances merely, but one whom I have been accustomed to regard, to idealize, to have dreams about as a friend, and mix up intimately with myself, can never degenerate into an acquaintance. I must know him on that higher ground or not know him at all. We do not confess and explain, because we would fain be so intimately related as to understand each other without speech. Our friend must be broad. His must be an atmosphere coextensive with the universe, in which we can expand and breathe. For the most part we are smothered and stifled by one another. I go and see my friend and try his atmosphere. If our atmospheres do not mingle, if we repel each other strongly, it is of no use to stay.

—Journal, November 24, 1850[74]

Our thoughts are with those among the dead into whose sphere we are rising, or who are now rising into our own. Others we inevitably forget, though they be brothers and sisters. Thus the departed may be nearer to us than when they were present. At death our friends and relations either draw nearer to us and are found out, or depart further from us and are forgotten. Friends are as often brought nearer together as separated by death.

—Journal, December 24, 1850[75]

I lose my friends, of course, as much by my own ill treatment and ill valuing of them, prophaning of them, cheapening of them, as by their cheapening of themselves, till at last, when I am prepared to do them justice, I am permitted to deal only with the memories of themselves, their ideals still surviving in me, no longer with their actual selves. We exclude ourselves, as the child said of the stream in which he bathed head or foot. —Journal, January 1851[76]

Fatal is the discovery that our friend is fallible, that he has prejudices. He is, then, only prejudiced in our favor. What is the value of his esteem who does not justly esteem another?

Alas! Alas! when my friend begins to deal in confessions, breaks silence, makes a theme of friendship (which then is always something past), and descends to merely human relations! As long as there is a spark of love remaining, cherish that alone. Only *that* can be kindled into a flame. I thought that friendship, that love was still possible between us. I thought that we had not withdrawn very far asunder. But now that my friend rashly, thoughtlessly, profanely speaks, *recognizing* the distance between us, that distance seems infinitely increased.

Of our friends we do not incline to speak, to complain, to others; we would not disturb the foundations of confidence that may still be.

—Journal, February 15, 1851[77]

To obtain to a true relation to one human creature is enough to make a year memorable. —Journal, March 30, 1851[78]

Having treated my friend ill, I wished to apologize; but, not meeting him, I made an apology to myself.

—Journal, April 22, 1851[79]

Every man, perhaps, is inclined to think his own situation singular in relation to friendship. Our thoughts would imply that other men *have* friends, though we have not. But I do not know of two whom I can speak of as standing in this relation to one another. Each one makes a standing offer to mankind, "On such and such terms I will give myself to you;" but it is only by a miracle that his terms are ever accepted.

We have to defend ourselves even against those who are nearest to friendship with us.

What a difference it is!—to perform the pilgrimage of life in the society of a mate, and not to have an acquaintance among all the tribes of men!

What signifies the census—this periodical numbering of men—to one who has no friend?

I distinguish between my *actual* and my *real*

communication with individuals. I *really* communicate with my friends and congratulate myself and them on our relation and rejoice in their presence and society oftenest when they are personally absent. I remember that not long ago, as I laid my head on my pillow for the night, I was visited by an inexpressible joy that I was permitted to know and be related to such mortals as I was then actually related to; and yet no special event that I could think of had occurred to remind me of any with whom I was connected, and by the next noon, perchance, those essences that had caused me joy would have receded somewhat. I experienced a remarkable gladness in the thought that they existed. Their existence was then blessed to me. Yet such has never been my actual waking relation to any.

Every one experiences that, while his relation to another actually may be one of distrust and disappointment, he may still have relations to him ideally and so really, in spite of both. He is faintly conscious of a confidence and satisfaction somewhere, and all further intercourse is based on this experience of success.

The very dogs and cats incline to affection in their relation to man. It often happens that a man is more humanely related to a cat or dog than to any human being. What bond is it relates us to any animal we keep in the house but the bond of affection? In a degree we grow to love one another.

—Journal, April 29, 1851[80]

I find that I postpone all actual intercourse with my friends to a certain real intercourse which takes place commonly when we are actually at a distance from one another.

—Journal, June 15, 1851[81]

Now at least the moon is full, and I walk alone, which is best by night, if not by day always. Your companion must sympathize with the present mood. The conversation must be located where the walkers are, and vary exactly with the scene and events and the contour of the ground. Farewell to those who will talk of nature unnaturally, whose presence is an interruption. I know but one with whom I can walk. I might as well be sitting in a bar-room with them as walk and talk with most. We are never side by side in our thoughts, and we cannot bear each other's silence. Indeed, we cannot be silent. We are forever breaking silence, that is all, and mending nothing. How can they keep together who are going different ways!

—Journal, July 12, 1851[82]

O my dear friends, I have not forgotten you. I will know you to-morrow.   —Journal, July 16, 1851[83]

I thank you, God. I do not deserve anything, I am unworthy of the least regard; and yet I am made to rejoice. I am impure and worthless, and yet the world is gilded for my delight and holidays are prepared for me, and my path is strewn with flowers. But I cannot thank the Giver; I cannot even whisper my thanks to those human friends I have. It seems to me that I am more rewarded for my expectations than for anything I do or can do. . . . And why should I speak to my friends? for how rarely is it that I am I; and are they, then, they?

—Journal, August 17, 1851[84]

My home, then, to a certain extent is the place where I keep my thick coat and my tent and some books which I cannot carry; where, next, I can depend upon meeting some friends; and where, finally, I, even I, have established myself in business. But this last in my case is the least important qualification of a home.   —Journal, August 19, 1851[85]

In regard to my friends, I feel that I know and have communion with a finer and subtler part of themselves which does not put me off when they put me off, which is not cold to me when they are cold, not till I am cold. I hold by a deeper and stronger tie than absence can sunder.

—Journal, December 12, 1851[86]

I come from contact with certain acquaintances, whom even I am disposed to look toward as possible friends. It oftenest happens that I come from them wounded. Only they can wound me seriously, and that perhaps without their knowing it. —Journal, December 14, 1851[87]

I do not know but a pine wood is as substantial and as memorable a fact as a friend. I am more sure to come away from it cheered, than from those who come nearest to being my friends....

When they who have aspired to be friends cease to sympathize, it is the part of religion to keep asunder.

One of the best men I know often offends me by uttering made words—the very best words, of course, or dinner speeches, most smooth and gracious and fluent repartees, a sort of talking to Buncombe, a dash of polite conversation, a graceful bending, as if I were Master Slingsby of promising parts, from the University. O would you but be simple and downright! Would you but cease your palaver! It is the misfortune of being a gentleman and famous. The conversation of gentlemen after dinner! One of the best of men and wisest, to whom this diabolical formality will adhere. Repeating himself, shampooing himself! Passing the time of day, as if he were just introduced! No words are so tedious. Never a natural or simple word or yawn. It produces an appearance of phlegm and stupidity in me the auditor.

I am suddenly the closest and most phlegmatic of mortals, and the conversation comes to naught. Such speeches as an ex-Member of Congress might make to an ex-Member of Parliament.

To explain to a friend is to suppose that you are not intelligent of one another. If you are not, to what purpose will you explain?

My acquaintances will sometimes wonder why I will impoverish myself by living aloof from this or that company, but greater would be the impoverishment if I should associate with them.　　—Journal, December 17, 1851[88]

My difficulties with my friends are such as no frankness will settle. There is no precept in the New Testament that will assist me. My nature, it may be, is secret. Others can confess and explain; I cannot. It is not that I am too proud, but that is not what is wanted. Friendship is the unspeakable joy and blessing that results to two or more individuals who from constitution sympathize; and natures are liable to no mistakes, but will know each other through thick and thin. Between two by nature alike and fitted to sympathize there is no veil and there can be no obstacle. Who are the estranged? Two friends explaining.

I feel sometimes as if I could say to my friends, "My friends, I am aware how I have outraged you, how I have seemingly preferred hate to love, seemingly treated others kindly and you unkindly, sedulously concealed my love, and sooner or later expressed all and more than all my hate." I can imagine how I might utter something like this in some moment never to be realized. But let me say frankly that at the same time I feel, it may be with too little regret, that I am under an awful necessity to be what I am. If the truth were known, which I do not know, I have no concern with those friends whom I misunderstand or who misunderstand me.

The fates only are unkind that keep us asunder, but my friend is ever kind. I am of the nature of stone. It takes the summer's sun to warm it.

My acquaintances sometimes imply that I am too cold; but each thing is warm enough of its kind. Is the stone too cold which absorbs the heat of the summer sun and does not part with it during the night? Crystals, though they be of ice, are not too cold to melt, but it was in melting that they were formed. Cold! I am most sensible of warmth in winter days. It is not the warmth of fire that you would have, but everything is warm and cold according to its nature. It is not that I am too cold, but that our warmth and coldness are not of the same nature; hence when I am absolutely warmest, I may be coldest to you. Crystal does not complain of crystal any more than the dove of its mate. You who complain that I am cold find Nature cold. To me she is warm. My heat is latent to you. Fire itself is cold to whatever is not of a nature to be warmed by it. A cool wind is warmer to a feverish man than the air of a furnace. That I am cold means that I am of another nature.

—Journal, December 21, 1851[89]

If I am thus seemingly cold compared with my companion's warm, who knows but mine is a less transient glow, a steadier and more equable heat, like that of the earth in spring, in which the flowers spring and expand? It is not words that I wish to hear or to utter, but relations that I seek to stand in; and it oftener happens, methinks, that I go away unmet, unrecognized, ungreeted in my offered relation, than that you are disappointed of words. If I can believe that we are related to one another as truly and gloriously as I have imagined, I ask nothing more, and words are not required to convince me of this. I am disappointed of relations, you of words.

—Journal, December 22, 1851[90]

It would give me such joy to know that a friend had come to see me, and yet that pleasure I seldom if ever experience.

—Journal, December 23, 1851[91]

I do not lay myself open to my friends!? The owner of the casket locks it, and unlocks it. Treat your friends for what you know them to be. Regard no surfaces. Consider not what they did, but what they intended. Be sure, as you know them you are known of them again. Last night I treated my dearest friend ill. Though I could find some excuse for myself, it is not such excuse as under the circumstances could be pleaded in so many words. Instantly I blamed myself, and sought an opportunity to make atonement, but the friend avoided me, and, with kinder feelings even than before, I was obliged to depart. And now this morning I feel that it is too late to speak of the trifle, and, besides, I doubt now in the cool morning, if I have a right to suppose such intimate and serious relations as afford a basis for the apology I had conceived, for even magnanimity must ask this poor earth for a field. The virtues even wait for invitation. Yet I am resolved to know that one centrally, through thick and thin, and though we should be cold to one another, though we should never speak to one another, I will know that inward and essential love may exist even under a superficial cold, and that the law of attraction speaks louder than words. My true relation this instant shall be my apology for my false relation the last instant. I made haste to cast off my injustice as scurf. I own it least of anybody, for I have absolutely done with it. Let the idle and wavering and apologizing friend appropriate it.

Methinks our estrangement is only like the divergence of the branches which unite in the stem.

—Journal, December 31, 1851[92]

I have so much faith in the power of truth to communicate itself, that I should not believe a friend if he should tell me that he had given credit to an unjust rumor concerning me. Suspect! Ah! yes, you may suspect a thousand things, but I well know that that which you suspect most confidently of all, is just the truth. Your other doubts but flavor this your main suspicion; they are the condiments which, taken alone, do simply bite the tongue.

—Journal, January 1, 1852[93]

Live a purer, a more thoughtful and laborious life, more true to your friends and neighbors, more noble and magnanimous, and that will be better than a wild walk. To live in relations of truth and sincerity with men is to dwell in a frontier country. What a wild and unfrequented wilderness that would be!   —Journal, January 12, 1852[94]

We forget to strive and aspire, to do better ever than is expected of us. I cannot stay to be congratulated. I would leave the world behind me. We must withdraw from our flatterers, even from our friends. They drag us down. It is rare that we use our thinking faculty as resolutely as an Irishman his spade. To please our friends and relatives we turn out our silver ore in cartloads, while we neglect to work our mines of gold known only to ourselves far up in the Sierras, where we pulled up a bush in our mountain walk, and saw the glittering treasure. Let us return thither. Let it be the price of our freedom to make that known.

—Journal, January 13, 1852[95]

If I am too cold for human friendship, I trust I shall not soon be too cold for natural influences. It appears to be a law that you cannot have a deep sympathy with both man and nature. Those qualities which bring you near to the one estrange you from the other.   —Journal, April 11, 1852[96]

It is hard for a man to take money from his friends for any service. This suggests how all men should be related.
                                        —Journal, April 11, 1852[97]

Nature must be viewed humanly to be viewed at all; that is, her scenes must be associated with humane affections, such as are associated with one's native place, for instance. She is most significant to a lover. A lover of Nature is preëminently a lover of man. If I have no friend, what is Nature to me? She ceases to be morally significant.
                                        —Journal, June 30, 1852[98]

There are enough who will flatter me with sweet words, and anon use bitter ones to balance them, but they are not my friends. Simple sincerity and truth are rare indeed. One acquaintance criticises me to my face, expecting every moment that I will become his friend to pay for it. I hear my acquaintance thinking his criticism aloud. We love to talk with those who can make a good guess at us, not with those who talk to us as if we were somebody else all the while. Our neighbors invite us to be amiable toward their vices. How simple is the law of love! One who loves us accordingly, and anon we come together and succeed together without let or hindrance.   —Journal, September 9, 1852[99]

Considering how few poetical friendships there are, it is remarkable that so many are married. It would seem as if men yielded too easy an obedience to nature without consulting their genius. One may be drunk with love without being any nearer to finding his mate. There is more of good nature than of good sense at the bottom of most marriages. But the good nature must have the counsel of the good spirit or Intelligence. If common sense had been consulted, how many marriages would never have taken place; if uncommon or divine sense, how few marriages such as we witness would ever have taken place!

Our love may be ascending or descending. . . .

Is your friend such a one that an increase of worth on your part will surely make her more your friend? Is she retained—is she attracted by more nobleness in you,—by more of that virtue which is peculiarly yours; or is she indifferent and blind to that? Is she to be flattered and won by your meeting her on any other than the ascending path? Then duty requires that you separate from her.

Love must be as much a light as a flame. . . .

In love and friendship the imagination is as much exercised as the heart; and if either is outraged the other will be estranged. It is commonly the imagination which is wounded first, rather than the heart,—it is so much the more sensitive. . . .

In our intercourse with one we love, we wish to have answered those questions at the end of which we do not raise our voice; against which we put no interrogation-mark,— answered with the same unfailing, universal aim toward every point of the compass.

I require that thou knowest everything without being told anything. I parted from my beloved because there was one thing which I had to tell her. She *questioned* me. She should have known all by sympathy. That I had to tell it her was the difference between us,—the misunderstanding. . . .

There is danger that we lose sight of what our friend is absolutely, while considering what she is to us alone. . . .

I need thy hate as much as thy love. Thou wilt not repel me entirely when thou repellest what is evil in me. . . .

It is not enough that we are truthful; we must cherish and carry out high purposes to be truthful about. . . .

What a difference, whether, in all your walks, you meet only strangers, or in one house is one who knows you, and whom you know. To have a brother or a sister! To have a gold mine on your farm! To find diamonds in the gravel heaps before your door! How rare these things are! To share the day with you,—to people the earth. Whether to have a god or a goddess for companion in your walks, or to walk alone with hinds and villains and carles. Would not a friend enhance the beauty of the landscape as much as a deer or hare? Everything would acknowledge and serve such a relation; the corn in the field, and the cranberries in the meadow. The flowers would bloom, and the birds sing, with a new impulse. There would be more fair days in the year.

—"Love" (September 1852)[100]

My friend is he who can make a good guess at me, hit me on the wing.   —Journal, September 21, 1852[101]

We must love our friend so much that she shall be associated with our purest and holiest thoughts alone.

—"Chastity and Sensuality" (September 1852)[102]

My friend is one whom I meet, who takes me for what I am. A stranger takes me for something else than I am. We do not speak, we cannot communicate, till we find that we are recognized. The stranger supposes in our stead a third person whom we do not know, and we leave him to converse with that one. It is suicide for us to become abetters in mis-apprehending ourselves. Suspicion creates the stranger and substitutes him for the friend. I cannot abet any man in misapprehending myself.

What men call social virtues, good fellowship, is commonly but the virtue of pigs in a litter, which lie close together to keep each other warm. It brings men together in crowds and mobs in barrooms and elsewhere, but it does not deserve the name of virtue.

—Journal, October 23, 1852[103]

Trench says that "'rivals', in the primary sense of the word, are those who dwell on the banks of the same stream" or "on opposite banks," but as he says, in many words, since the use of water-rights is a fruitful source of contention between such neighbors, the word has acquired this secondary sense. My friends are my *rivals* on the Concord, in the primitive sense of the word. There is no strife between us respecting the use of the stream. The Concord offers many privileges, but none to quarrel about. It is a peaceful, not a brawling, stream. It has not made *rivals* out of neighbors *that lived on its banks*, but friends. My friends are my *rivals*; we dwell on opposite banks of the stream, but that stream is the Concord, which flows without a ripple or a murmur, without a rapid or a brawl, and offers no petty privileges to quarrel about.   —Journal, January 16, 1853[104]

To be supported by the charity of friends or a government pension is to go into the almshouse.

—Journal, March 13, 1853[105]

Nothing is more saddening than an ineffectual and proud intercourse with those of whom we expect sympathy and encouragement. I repeatedly find myself drawn toward certain persons but to be disappointed. No concessions which are not radical are the least satisfaction. By myself I can live and thrive, but in the society of incompatible friends I starve. To cultivate their society is to cherish a sore which can only be healed by abandoning them. . . .

No fields are so barren to me as the men of whom I expect everything but get nothing. In their neighborhood I experience a painful yearning for society, which cannot be satisfied, for the hate is greater than the love.

—Journal, April 3, 1853[106]

In dreams the links of life are united: we forget that our friends are dead; we know them as of old.

—Journal, May 23, 1853[107]

I have some good friends from whom I am wont to part with disappointment, for they neither care what I think nor mind what I say. The greatest compliment that was ever paid me was when one asked me what I *thought*, and attended to my answer.   —Journal, January 27, 1854[108]

If he is your friend, you may have to consider that he loves you, but perchance he also loves gingerbread.

—Journal, February 16, 1854[109]

I only know myself as a human entity; the scene, so to speak, of thoughts and affections; and am sensible of a certain doubleness by which I can stand as remote from myself as from another. However intense my experience, I am conscious of the presence and criticism of a part of me, which, as it were, is not a part of me, but spectator, sharing no experience, but taking note of it; and that is no more I than it is you. When the play, it may be the tragedy, of life is over, the spectator goes his way. It was a kind of fiction, a work of the imagination only, so far as he was concerned. This doubleness may easily make us poor neighbors and friends sometimes. —*Walden*[110]

I had three chairs in my house; one for solitude, two for friendship, three for society. —*Walden*[111]

We should never stand upon ceremony with sincerity. We should never cheat and insult and banish one another by our meanness, if there were present the kernel of worth and friendliness. —*Walden*[112]

Do not trouble yourself much to get new things, whether clothes or friends. Turn the old; return to them. Things do not change; we change. Sell your clothes and keep your thoughts. God will see that you do not want society. —*Walden*[113]

What if we feel a yearning to which no breast answers? I walk alone. My heart is full. Feelings impede the current of my thoughts. I knock on the earth for my friend. I expect to meet him at every turn; but no friend appears, and perhaps none is dreaming of me. I am tired of frivolous society, in which silence is forever the most natural and the best manners. I would fain walk on the deep waters, but my companions will only walk on shallows and puddles. I am naturally silent in the midst of twenty from day to day, from year to year. I am rarely reminded of their presence. Two yards of politeness do not make society for me. One complains that I do not take his jokes. I took them before he had done uttering them, and went my way. One talks to me of his apples and pears, and I depart with my secret untold. His are not the apples that tempt me. —Journal, June 11, 1855[114]

I had two friends. The one offered me friendship on such terms that I could not accept it, without a sense of degradation. He would not meet me on equal terms, but only be to some extent my patron. He would not come to see me, but was hurt if I did not visit him. He would not readily accept a favor, but would gladly confer one. He treated me with ceremony occasionally, though he could be simple and downright sometimes; and from time to time acted a part, treating me as if I were a distinguished stranger; was on stilts, using made words. Our relation was one long tragedy, yet I did not directly speak of it. I do not believe in complaint, nor in explanation. The whole is but too plain, alas, already. We grieve that we do not love each other, that we cannot confide in each other. I could not bring myself to speak, and so recognize an obstacle to our affection.

I had another friend, who, through a slight obtuseness, perchance, did not recognize a fact which the dignity of friendship would by no means allow me to descend so far as to speak of, and yet the inevitable effect of that ignorance was to hold us apart forever.   —Journal, March 4, 1856[115]

I think to say to my friend, There is but one interval between us. You are on one side of it, I on the other. You know as much about it as I,—how wide, how impassable it is. I will endeavor not to blame you. Do not blame me. There is nothing to be said about it. Recognize the truth, and pass over the intervals that are bridged.

Farewell, my friends, my path inclines to this side the mountain, yours to that. For a long time you have appeared further and further off to me. I see that you will at length disappear altogether. For a season my path seems lonely without you. The meadows are like barren ground. The memory of me is steadily passing away from you. My path grows narrower and steeper, and the night is approaching. Yet I have faith that, in the definite future, new suns will rise, and new plains expand before me, and I trust that I shall therein encounter pilgrims who bear that same virtue that I recognized in you, who will be that very virtue that was you. I accept the everlasting and salutary law, which was promulgated as much that spring that I first knew you, as this that I seem to lose you.

My former friends, I visit you as one walks amid the columns of a ruined temple. You belong to an era, a civilization and glory, long past. I recognize still your fair proportions, notwithstanding the convulsions which we have felt, and the weeds and jackals that have sprung up around. I come here to be reminded of the past, to read your inscriptions, the hieroglyphics, the sacred writings. We are no longer the representatives of our former selves.

Love is a thirst that is never slaked. Under the coarsest rind, the sweetest meat. If you would read a friend aright, you must be able to read through something thicker and opaquer than horn. If you can read a friend, all languages will be easy to you. Enemies publish themselves. They declare war. The friend never declares his love.

—Journal, March 28, 1856[116]

If my friend would take a quarter part the pains to show me himself that he does to show me a piece of roast beef, I should feel myself irresistibly invited. He says,—

"Come and see
Roast beef and me."

I find the beef fat and well done, but him rare.

—Journal, May 19, 1856[117]

How I love the simple, reserved countrymen, my neighbors, who mind their own business and let me alone, who never waylaid nor shot at me, to my knowledge, when I crossed their fields, though each one has a gun in his house! For nearly twoscore years I have known, at a distance, these long-suffering men, whom I never spoke to, who never spoke to me, and now feel a certain tenderness for them, as if this long probation were but the prelude to an eternal friendship. —Journal, December 3, 1856[118]

And now another friendship is ended. I do not know what has made my friend doubt me, but I know that in love there is no mistake, and that every estrangement is well founded. But my destiny is not narrowed, but if possible the broader for it. The heavens withdraw and arch themselves higher. I am sensible not only of a moral, but even a grand physical pain, such as gods may feel, about my head and breast, a certain ache and fullness. This rending of a tie, it is not my work nor thine. It is no accident that we mind; it is only the awards of fate that are affecting. I know of no æons, or periods, no life and death, but these meetings and separations. My life is like a stream that is suddenly dammed and has no outlet; but it rises the higher up the hills that shut it in, and will become a deep and silent lake. Certainly there is no event comparable for grandeur with the eternal separation—if we may conceive it so—from a being that we have known. I become in a degree sensible of the meaning of finite and infinite. What a grand significance the word "never" acquires! With one with whom we have walked on high ground we cannot deal on any lower ground ever after. We have tried for so many years to put each other to this immortal use, and have failed. Undoubtedly our good genii have mutually found the material unsuitable. We have hitherto paid each other the highest possible compliment; we have recognized each other constantly as divine, have afforded each other that opportunity to live that no other wealth or kindness can afford. And now, for some reason inappreciable by us, it has become necessary for us to withhold this mutual aid. Perchance there is none beside who knows us for a god, and none whom we know for such. Each man and woman is a veritable god or goddess, but to the mass of their fellows disguised. There is only one in each case who sees through the disguise. That one who does not stand so near to any man as to see the divinity in him is truly alone. I am perfectly sad at parting from you. I could better have the earth taken away from under my feet, than the thought of you from my mind. One while I think that some great injury has been done, with which you are implicated, again that you are no party to it. I fear that there may be incessant tragedies, that one may treat his fellow as a god but receive somewhat less regard from him. I now almost for the first time *fear* this. Yet I believe that in the long run there is no such inequality.

—Journal, February 8, 1857[119]

A man cannot be said to succeed in this life who does not satisfy one friend.   —Journal, February 19, 1857[120]

I say in my thought to my neighbor, who was once my friend, "It is of no use to speak the truth to you, you will not hear it. What, then, shall I say to you?" At the instant that I seem to be saying farewell forever to one who has been my friend, I find myself unexpectedly near to him, and it is our very nearness and dearness to each other that gives depth and significance to that forever. Thus I am a helpless prisoner, and these chains I have no skill to break. While I think I have broken one link, I have been forging another.

I have not yet known a friendship to cease, I think. I fear I experienced its decaying. Morning, noon, and night, I suffer a physical pain, an aching of the breast which unfits me for my tasks. It is perhaps intense at evening. With respect to Friendship I feel like a wreck that is driving before the gale, with a crew suffering from hunger and thirst, not knowing what shore, if any, they may reach, so long have I *breasted* the conflicting waves of this sentiment, my seams open, my timbers laid bare. I float on Friendship's sea simply because my specific gravity is less than its, but no longer that stanch and graceful vessel that careered so buoyantly over it. My planks and timbers are scattered. At most I hope to make a sort of raft of Friendship, on which, with a few of our treasures, we may float to some firm land.

That aching of the breast, the grandest pain that man endures, which no ether can assuage.

You cheat me, you keep me at a distance with your manners. I know of no other dishonesty, no other devil. Why this doubleness, these compliments? They are the worst of lies. A lie is not worse between traders than a compliment between friends. I would not, I cannot speak. I will let you *feel* my thought, my feeling.

Friends! they are united for good and for evil. They can delight each other as none other can. They can distress each other as none other can. Lying on lower levels is but a trivial offense compared with civility and compliments on the level of Friendship.

I visit my friend for joy, not for disturbance. If my coming hinders him in the least conceivable degree, I will exert myself to the utmost to stay away, I will get the Titans to help me stand aloof, I will labor night and day to construct a rampart between us. If my coming casts but the shadow of a shadow before it, I will retreat swifter than the wind and more untrackable. I will be gone irrevocably, if possible, before he fears that I am coming.

If the teeth ache they can be pulled. If the heart aches, what then? Shall we pluck it out?

Must friends then expect the fate of those Oriental twins,—that one shall at last bear about the corpse of the other, by that same ligature that bound him to a living companion?

Look before you leap. Let the isthmus be cut through, unless sea meets sea at exactly the same level, unless a perfect understanding and equilibrium has been established from the beginning around Cape Horn and the unnamed northern cape. What a tumult! It is Atlantic and Atlantic, or it is Atlantic and Pacific.

—Journal, February 23, 1857[121]

If I should make the least concession, my friend would spurn me. I am obeying his law as well as my own.

Where is the actual friend you love? Ask from what hill the rainbow's arch springs! It adorns and crowns the earth.

Our friends are our kindred, of our species. There are very few of our species on the globe.

Between me and my friend what unfathomable distance! All mankind, like motes and insects, are between us.

If my friend says in his mind, I will *never* see you again, I translate it of necessity into *ever.* That is its definition in Love's lexicon.

Those whom we can love, we can hate; to others we are indifferent.   —Journal, February 24, 1857[122]

I have several friends and acquaintances who are very good companions in the house or for an afternoon walk, but whom I cannot make up my mind to make a longer excursion with.   —Journal, June 3, 1857[123]

The price of friendship is the total surrender of yourself; no lesser kindness, no ordinary attentions and offerings will buy it. There is forever that purchase to be made with that wealth which you possess, yet only once in a long while are you *advertised* of such a commodity. I sometimes awake in the night and think of friendship and its possibilities, a new life and revelation to me, which perhaps I had not experienced for many months. Such transient thoughts have been my nearest approach to realization of it, thoughts which I know of no one to communicate to. I suddenly erect myself in my thoughts, or find myself erected, infinite degrees above the possibility of ordinary endeavors, and see for what grand stakes the game of life may be played. Men, with their indiscriminate attentions and ceremonious goodwill, offer you trivial baits, which do not tempt; they are not serious enough either for success or failure. I wake up in the night to these higher levels of life, as to a day that begins to dawn, as if my intervening life had been a long night. I catch an echo of the great strain of Friendship played somewhere, and feel compensated for months and years of commonplace. I rise into a diviner atmosphere, in which simply to exist and breathe is a triumph, and my thoughts inevitably tend toward the grand and infinite, as aeronauts report that there is ever an upper current hereabouts which sets toward the ocean. If they rise high enough they go out to sea, and behold the vessels seemingly in mid-air like themselves. It is as if I were serenaded, and the highest and truest compliments were paid me. The universe gives three cheers.

Friendship is the fruit which the year should bear; it lends its fragrance to the flowers, and it is in vain if we get only a large crop of apples without it. This experience makes us unavailable for the ordinary courtesy and intercourse of men. We can only recognize them when they rise to that level and realize our dream.   —Journal, July 13, 1857[124]

I see two great fish hawks (*possibly* blue herons) slowly beating northeast against the storm, by what a curious tie circling ever near each other and in the same direction. . . . Where is my mate, beating against the storm with me?

—Journal, October 26, 1857[125]

Ah, my friends, I know you better than you think, and love you better, too. The day after never, we will have an explanation.

—Journal, November 8, 1857[126]

A man is worth most to himself and to others, whether as an observer, or poet, or neighbor, or friend, where he is most himself, most contented and at home.

—Journal, November 20, 1857[127]

Going to the Andromeda Ponds, I was greeted by the warm brown-red glow of the *Andromeda calyculata* toward the sun. I see where I have been through, the more reddish under sides apparently being turned up. It is long since a human friend has met me with such a glow.

—Journal, January 3, 1858[128]

To insure health, a man's relation to Nature must come very near to a personal one; he must be conscious of a friendliness in her; when human friends fail or die, she must stand in the gap to him.

—Journal, January 23, 1858[129]

I will take another walk to the Cliff, another row on the river, another skate on the meadow, be out in the first snow, and associate with the winter birds. Here I am at home. In the bare and bleached crust of the earth I recognize my friend. . . .

I want nothing new, if I can have but a tithe of the old secured to me. I will spurn all wealth beside. Think of the consummate folly of attempting to go away from *here!* When the constant endeavor should be to get nearer and nearer *here.* Here are all the friends I ever had or shall have, and as friendly as ever. Why, I never had any quarrel with a friend but it was just as sweet as unanimity could be. I do not think we budge an inch forward or backward in relation to our friends. How many things can you go away from?

—Journal, November 1, 1858[130]

How long we will follow an illusion! On meeting that one whom I call my friend, I find that I had imagined something that was not there. I am sure to depart sadder than I came. Nothing makes me so dejected as to have met my friends, for they make me doubt if it is possible to have any friends. I feel what a fool I am. I cannot conceive of persons more strange to me than they actually are; not thinking, not believing, not doing as I do; interrupted by me. My only distinction must be that I am the greatest bore they ever had. Not in a single thought agreed; regularly balking one another. But when I get far away, my thoughts return to them. That is the way I *can* visit them. Perhaps it is unaccountable to me why I care for them. Thus I am taught that my friend is not an actual person. When I have withdrawn and am alone, I forget the actual person and remember only my ideal. Then I have a friend again. I am not so ready to perceive the illusion that is in Nature. I certainly come nearer, to say the least, to an actual and joyful intercourse with her. Every day I have more or less communion with her, *as I think.* At least, I do not feel as if I must withdraw out of nature. I feel like a welcome guest. Yet, strictly speaking, the same must be true of nature and of man; our ideal is the only real. It is not the finite and temporal that satisfies or concerns us in either case.

I associate the idea of friendship, methinks, with the

person the most foreign to me. This illusion is perpetuated, like superstition in a country long after civilization has been attained to. We are attracted toward a particular person, but no one has discovered the laws of this attraction. When I come nearest to that other *actually*, I am wont to be surprised at my selection. It may be enough that we have met *some time*, and now can never forget it. Some time or other we paid each other this wonderful compliment, looked largely, humanly, divinely on one another, and now are fated to be acquaintances forever. In the case of nature I am not so conscious of this unsatisfied yearning.

—Journal, November 3, 1858[131]

I have lately got back to that glorious society called Solitude, where we meet our friends continually, and can imagine the outside world also to be peopled. Yet some of my acquaintance would fain hustle me into the almshouse for *the sake of society*, as if I were pining for that diet, when I seem to myself a most befriended man, and find constant employment. However, they do not believe a word I say. They have got a club, the handle of which is in the Parker House at Boston, and with this they beat me from time to time, expecting to make me tender or minced meat, so fit for a club to dine off....

The doctors are all agreed that I am suffering for want of society. Was never a case like it. First, I did not know that I was suffering at all. Secondly, as an Irishman might say, I had thought it was indigestion of the society I got.

—Thoreau to Harrison Gray Otis Blake,
January 1, 1859[132]

I perceive that we partially die ourselves through sympathy at the death of each of our friends or near relatives. Each such experience is an assault on our vital force. It becomes a source of wonder that they who have lost many friends still live. —Journal, February 3, 1859[133]

When we have experienced many disappointments, such as the loss of friends, the notes of birds cease to affect us as they did. —Journal, February 5, 1859[134]

Sometimes in our prosaic moods, life appears to us but a certain number more of days like those which we have lived, to be cheered not by more friends and friendship but probably fewer and less. —Journal, February 13, 1859[135]

Have just read "Counterparts, or the Cross of Love," by the author of "Charles Auchester." It is very interesting— its illustration of Love and Friendship—as showing how much we can know of each other through sympathy merely, without any of the ordinary information. You know about a person who deeply interests you more than you can be told. A look, a gesture, an act, which to everybody else is insignificant tells you more about that one than words can. (How language is always found to serve best the highest moods, and expression of the highest truths!) If he wished to conceal something from you it would be apparent. It is as if a bird told you. Something of moment occurs. Your friend designs that it shall be a secret to you. Vain wish! You will know it, and his design. He says consciously nothing about it, yet as he is necessarily affected by it, its effect is visible to you. From this effect you infer the cause. Have you not already anticipated a thousand possible accidents? Can you be surprised? You unconsciously through sympathy make the right supposition. No other will account for precisely this behavior. You are disingenuous, and yet your knowledge exceeds the woodcraft of the cunningest hunter. It is as if you had a sort of trap, knowing the haunts of your game, what lures attract it, and its track, etc. You have foreseen how it will behave when it is caught, and now you only behold what you anticipated.

Sometimes from the altered manner of our friend, which no cloak can possibly conceal, we know that something has happened, and what it was, all the essential particulars, though it would be a long story to tell,—though it may involve the agency of four or five persons who never breathed it to you. Yet you are sure, as if you had detected all their tracks in the wood. You are the more sure because, in the case of love, effects follow their causes more inevitably than usual, this being a controlling power. Why, a friend tells all with a look, a tone, a gesture, a presence, a friendliness. He is present when absent.

—Journal, February 20, 1859[136]

Obey your calling rather, and it will not be whither your neighbors and kind friends and patrons expect or desire, but be true nevertheless, and choose not, nor go whither they call you.　　　　—"Reform and the Reformers"[137]

Give me for my friends and neighbors wild men, not tame ones.　　　　　—"Walking"[138]

Thoreau on Emerson

At R.W.Es.

The charm of the Indian to me is that he stands free and unconstrained in Nature, is her inhabitant and not her guest, and wears her easily and gracefully. But the civilized man has the habits of the house. His house is a prison, in which he finds himself oppressed and confined, not sheltered and protected. He walks as if he sustained the roof; he carries his arms as if the walls would fall in and crush him, and his feet remember the cellar beneath. His muscles are never relaxed. It is rare that he overcomes the house, and learns to sit at home in it, and roof and floor and walls support themselves, as the sky and trees and earth.

It is a great art to saunter.

—Journal, April 26, 1841[139]

The richest gifts we can bestow are the least marketable. We hate the kindness which we understand. A noble person confers no such gift as his whole confidence: none so exalts the giver and the receiver; it produces the truest gratitude. Perhaps it is only essential to friendship that some vital trust should have been reposed by the one in the other. I feel addressed and probed even to the remote parts of my being when one nobly shows, even in trivial things, an implicit faith in me. When such divine commodities are so near and cheap, how strange that it should have to be each day's discovery! A threat or a curse maybe forgotten, but this mild trust translates me. I am no more of this earth;

it acts dynamically; it changes my very substance. I cannot do what before I did. I cannot be what before I was. Other chains may be broken, but in the darkest night, in the remotest place, I trail this thread. Then things cannot *happen.* What if God were to confide in us for a moment! Should we not then be gods?

How subtle a thing is this confidence! Nothing sensible passes between; never any consequences are to be apprehended should it be misplaced. Yet something has transpired. A new behavior springs; the ship carries new ballast in her hold. A sufficiently great and generous trust could never be abused. It should be cause to lay down one's life,—which would not be to lose it. Can there be any mistake up there? Don't the gods know where to invest their wealth? Such confidence, too, would be reciprocal. When one confides greatly in you, he will feel the roots of an equal trust fastening themselves in him. When such trust has been received or reposed, we dare not speak, hardly to see each other; our voices sound harsh and untrustworthy. We are as instruments which the Powers have dealt with. Through what straits would we not carry this little burden of a magnanimous trust! Yet no harm could possibly come, but simply faithlessness. Not a feather, not a straw, is intrusted; that packet is empty. It is only *committed* to us, and, as it were, all things are committed to us.

The kindness I have longest remembered has been of this sort,—the sort unsaid; so far behind the speaker's lips that almost it already lay in my heart. It did not have far to go to be communicated. The gods cannot misunderstand, man cannot explain. We communicate like the burrows of foxes, in silence and darkness, under ground. We are undermined by faith and love. How much more full is Nature where we think the empty space is than where we place the solids!—full of fluid influences. Should we ever communicate but by these? The spirit abhors a vacuum more than Nature. There is a tide which pierces the pores of the air. These aerial rivers, let us not pollute their currents. What meadows do they course through? How many fine mails there are which traverse their routes! He is privileged who gets his letter franked by them.

I believe these things.

—Thoreau to Emerson, February 12, 1843[140]

He who is not touched by the poetry of Channing—Very— Emerson and the best pieces of Bryant may be sure he has not drunk deep of the Pierian spring.

—Journal, August 25, 1843[141]

Of Emerson's Essays I should say that they were not poetry—that they were not written exactly at the right crisis though inconceivably near to it.

—Journal, December 2, 1846[142]

Emerson again is a critic, poet, philosopher, with talent not so conspicuous, not so adequate to his task; but his field is still higher, his task more arduous. Lives a far more intense life; seeks to realize a divine life; his affections and intellect equally developed. Has advanced farther, and a new heaven opens to him. Love and Friendship, Religion, Poetry, the Holy are familiar to him. The life of an Artist; more variegated, more observing, finer perception; not so robust, elastic; practical enough in his own field; faithful, a judge of men. There is no such general critic of men and things, no such trustworthy and faithful man. More of the divine realized in him than in any. A poetic critic, reserving the unqualified nouns for the gods.

—Journal, Winter 1846–1847[143]

Emerson has special talents unequalled. The divine in man has had no more easy, methodically distinct expression. His personal influence upon young persons greater than any man's. In his world every man would be a poet, Love would reign, Beauty would take place, Man and Nature would harmonize.   —Journal, Winter 1846–47[144]

Emerson does not consider things in respect to their essential utility, but an important partial and relative one, as works of art perhaps. His probes pass one side of their centre of gravity. His exaggeration is of a part, not of the whole.   —Journal, Winter 1846–47[145]

Dear Waldo,—For I think I have heard that that is your name,—my letter which was put last into the leathern bag arrived first. Whatever I may *call* you, I know you better than I know your name, and what becomes of the fittest name if in any sense you are here with him who *calls*, and not there simply to be called?

I believe I never thanked you for your lectures, one and all, which I have heard formerly read here in Concord. I *know* I never have. There was some excellent reason each time why I did not; but it will never be too late. I have had that advantage, at least, over you in my education.
                    —Thoreau to Emerson, February 23, 1848[146]

As for missing friends,—fortunate perhaps is he who has any to miss, whose place a thought will not supply. I have an ideal friend in whose place actual persons sometimes stand for a season. The last I may often miss, but the first I recover when I am myself again.   —Journal, July–August 1850[147]

As for missing friends,—what if we do miss one another? have we not agreed on a rendezvous? While each wanders his own way through the wood, without anxiety, ay, with serene joy, though it be on his hands and knees, over rocks and fallen trees, he cannot but be in the right way. There is no wrong way to him. How can he be said to miss his friend, whom the fruits still nourish and the elements sustain? A man who missed his friend at a turn, went on buoyantly, dividing the friendly air, and humming a tune to himself, ever and anon kneeling with delight to study each little lichen in his path, and scarcely made three miles a day for friendship.

—Thoreau to Harrison Gray Otis Blake,
August 9, 1850[148]

Ah, I yearn toward thee, my friend, but I have not confidence in thee. We do not believe in the same God. I am not thou; thou art not I. We trust each other to-day, but we distrust to-morrow. Even when I meet thee unexpectedly, I part from thee with disappointment. Though I enjoy thee more than other men, yet I am more disappointed with thee than with others. I know a noble man; what is it hinders me from knowing him better? I know not how it is that our distrust, our hate, is stronger than our love. Here I have been on what the world would call friendly terms with one fourteen years, have pleased my imagination sometimes with loving him; and yet our hate is stronger than our love. Why are we related, yet thus unsatisfactorily? We almost are a sore to one another. Ah, I am afraid because thy relations are not my relations. Because I have experienced that in some respects we are strange to one another, strange as some wild creature. Ever and anon there will come the consciousness to mar our love that, change the theme but a hair's breadth, and we are tragically strange to one another. We do not know what hinders us from coming together. But when I consider what my friend's relations and acquaintances are, what his tastes and habits, then the difference between us gets named. I see that all these friends and acquaintances and tastes and habits are indeed my friend's self. In the first place, my friend is prouder than I am,—and I am very proud, perchance.   —Journal, October 10, 1851[149]

My friend will be bold to conjecture; he will guess bravely at the significance of my words.
                    —Journal, October 27, 1851[150]

I bethought myself, while my fire was kindling, to open one of Emerson's books, which it happens that I rarely look at, to try what a chance sentence out of that could do for me; thinking, at the same time, of a conversation I had with him the other night, I finding fault with him for the stress he had laid on some of Margaret Fuller's whims and super-stitions, but he declaring gravely that she was one of those persons whose experience warranted her attaching im-portance to such things,—as the *Sortes Virgilianae*, for in-stance, of which her numerous friends could tell remarkable instances. At any rate, I saw that he was disposed to regard such things more seriously than I. The first sentence which I opened upon in his book was this: "If, with a high trust, he can thus submit himself, he will find that ample returns are poured into his bosom out of what seemed hours of ob-struction and loss. Let him not grieve too much on account of unfit associates. . . . In a society of perfect sympathy, no word, no act, no record, would be. He will learn that it is not much matter what he reads, what he does. Be a scholar, and he shall have the scholar's part of everything," etc., etc.

Most of this responded well enough to my mood, and this would be as good an instance of the *Sortes Virgilianae* as most to quote. But what makes this coincidence very little if at all remarkable to me is the fact of the obviousness of the moral, so that I had, perhaps, *thought* the same thing myself twenty times during the day, and yet had not been *contented* with that account of it, leaving me thus to be amused by the coincidence, rather than impressed as by an intimation out of the deeps. —Journal, December 12, 1851[151]

It would give me such joy to know that a friend had come to see me, and yet that pleasure I seldom if ever experience. —Journal, December 23, 1851[152]

I never realized so distinctly as this moment that I am peacefully parting company with the best friend I ever had, by each pursuing his proper path. I perceive that it is possible that we may have a better *understanding* now than when we were more at one. Not expecting such essential agreement as before. Simply our paths diverge. —Journal, January 21, 1852[153]

My friend invites me to read my papers to him. Gladly would I read, if he would hear. He must not hear coarsely but finely, suffering not the *least* to pass through the sieve of hearing. To associate with one for years with joy who never met your thought with thought! An overflowing sympathy while yet there is no intellectual communion. Could we not meet on higher ground with the same heartiness? It is dull work reading to one who does not apprehend you. How can it go on? I will still abide by the truth in my converse and intercourse with my friends, whether I am so brought nearer to or removed further from them. I shall not be the less your friend for answering you truly though coldly. Even the estrangement of friends is a fact to be serenely contemplated, as in the course of nature. It is of no use to lie either by word or action. Is not the everlasting truth agreeable to you? —Journal, January 22, 1852[154]

We resist no true invitations; they are irresistible. When my friend asks me to stay, and I do not, unless I have another engagement it is because I do not find myself invited. It is not in his will to invite me. We should deal with the real mood of our friends. I visited my friend constantly for many years, and he postponed our friendship to trivial engagements, so that I saw him not at all. When in after years he had leisure to meet me, I did not find myself invited to go to him.   —Journal, January 22, 1852[155]

I feel as if I were gradually parting company with certain friends, just as I perceive familiar objects successively disappear when I am leaving my native town in the cars. . . .

One must not complain that his friend is cold, for heat is generated between them.

I doubt if Emerson could trundle a wheelbarrow through the streets, because it would be out of character. One needs to have a comprehensive character.

—Journal, January 30, 1852[156]

Emerson is too grand for me. He belongs to the nobility and wears their cloak and manners; is attracted to Plato, not to Socrates, I fear partly because the latter's life and associates were too humble. I am a commoner. To me there is something devilish in manners. The best manners is nakedness of manners. I should value Emerson's praise more, which is always so discriminating, if there were not some alloy of patronage and hence of flattery about it. In that respect he is like ——; they flatter you, but themselves more. Praise should be spoken as simply and naturally as a flower emits its fragrance. . . .

I hear my friend say, "I have lost my faith in men; there are none true, magnanimous, holy," etc., etc., meaning, all the while, that I do not possess those unattainable virtues;

but, worm as I am, this is not wise in my friend, and I feel simply discouraged so far as my relation to him is concerned. We must have infinite faith in each other. If we have not, we must never let it leak out that we have not. He erects his want of faith as a barrier between us. When I hear grown man or woman say, "Once I had faith in men; now I have not," I am inclined to ask, "Who are you whom the world has disappointed? Have not you rather disappointed the world? There is the same ground for faith now that ever there was. It needs only a little love in you who complain so to ground it on." For my own part, I am thankful that there are those who come so near being my friends that they can be estranged from me. I had faith before they would destroy the little I have. The mason asks but a narrow shelf to spring his brick from; man requires only an infinitely narrower one to spring the arch of faith from.

What can I do? There is one whom I would fain call my friend. I feel disposed to practice any virtue. I am at liberty to do so. But it chances that at present I feel no sympathy with, no warmth toward, him. I am capable of sympathy and of warmth. What can I do? The universal laws will work; I must condemn what is wrong in him as well as in another. I cannot act a part. I submit myself. Do what you will with us, O ye gods.

See what a swift penalty you have to pay. If you say to your friend that he is less than an angel, he is your friend no longer.

The only ledge I can spring the arch of friendship from is the ground of infinite faith. If you have lost any of your faith in me, you might as well have lost it all. How can you renounce and retain at the same time?

One woman whom I visit sometimes thinks I am conceited, and yet wonders that I do not visit her oftener. If I was sure she was right perhaps I should. Now this is a sad obstacle in the way of hearty communications. As, naturally enough, we are not agreed on that point, our sympathy is lessened. Another with whom I converse a good deal allows that sometimes my actions are better than my principles as expressed in conversation.

I am not sure that I have any right to address to you the words I am about to write. The reason I have not visited you oftener and more earnestly is that I am offended by your pride, your sometime assumption of dignity, your manners, which come over me like waves of Lethe. I know that if I stood in that relation to you which you seem to ask, I should not be met. Perhaps I am wiser than you think. Do you never for an instant treat me as a thing, flatter me? You treat me with politeness, and I make myself scarce. We have not sympathy enough. We not always apprehend each other. You talk to me often as if I were Mr. Tompkins of the firm of ——, retired merchant. If I had never thought of you as a friend, I could make much use of you as an acquaintance.   —Journal, January 31, 1852[157]

When I hear that a Friend on whom I relied has spoken of me, not with cold words perhaps, but even with a cold and indifferent tone, to another, ah! what treachery I feel it to be!—the sum of all crimes against humanity. My friend may cherish a thousand suspicions against me, and they may but represent his faith and expectations, till he cherishes them so heartlessly that he can speak of them.

If I have not succeeded in my friendships, it was because I demanded more of them and did not put up with what I could get; and I got no more partly because I gave so little.

I must be dumb to those who, I have not faith, appreciate my actions, not knowing the springs of them. . . .

My friends! My friends! it does not cheer me to see

them. They but express their want of faith in me or in mankind; their coldest, cruelest thought comes clothed in polite and easy-spoken words at last. I am silent to their invitations, because I do not *feel* invited, and we have no reasons to give for what we do *not* do.

—Journal, February 1, 1852[158]

I hate that my motive for visiting a friend should be that I want society; that it should lie in my poverty and weakness, and not in his and my riches and strength. His friendship should make me strong enough to do without him.

—Journal, February 14, 1852[159]

I have got to that pass with my friend that our words do not pass with each other for what they are worth. We speak in vain; there is none to hear. He finds fault with me that I walk alone, when I pine for want of a companion; that I commit my thoughts to a diary even on my walks, instead of seeking to share them generously with a friend; curses my practice even. Awful as it is to contemplate, I pray that, if I am the cold intellectual skeptic whom he rebukes, his curse may take effect, and wither and dry up those sources of my life, and my journal no longer yield me pleasure nor life.

—Journal, April 4, 1852[160]

Perchance the time will come when we shall not be content to go back and forth upon a raft to some huge Homeric or Shakespearean Indiaman that lies upon the reef, but build a bark out of that wreck and others that are buried in the sands of this desolate island, and such new timber as may be required, in which to sail away to whole new worlds of light and life, where our friends are.

—Thoreau to Harrison Gray Otis Blake,
July 21, 1852[161]

How far we can be apart and yet attract each other! There is one who almost wholly misunderstands me and whom I too probably misunderstand, toward whom, nevertheless, I am distinctly drawn. I have the utmost human good-will toward that one, and yet I know not what mistrust keeps us asunder. I am so much and so exclusively the friend of my friend's virtue that I am compelled to be silent for the most part, because his vice is present. I am made dumb by this third party. I only desire *sincere* relations with the worthiest of my acquaintance, that they may give me an opportunity once in a year to speak the truth. They invite me to see them, and do not show themselves. Who *are* they, pray? I pine and starve near them. The hospitable man will invite me to an atmosphere where truth can be spoken, where a man can live and breathe. Think what crumbs we offer each other,—and think to make up for the deficiency with our *roast meats!* Let us have a human creature's heart and let go the beeve's heart. How happens it that I find myself making such an enormous demand on men and so constantly disappointed? Are my friends aware how disappointed I am? Is it all my fault? Have I no heart? Am I incapable of expansion and generosity? I shall accuse myself of everything else sooner. I have never met with a friend who furnished me sea-room. I have only tacked a few times and come to anchor,—not sailed,—made no voyage, carried no venture. Do they think me eccentric because I refuse this chicken's meat, this babe's food? Would not men have something to communicate if they were sincere? Is not my silent expectation an invitation, an offer, an opportunity offered? My friend has complained of me, cursed me even, but it did not affect me; I did not know the persons he talked about. I have been disappointed from first to last in my friends, but I have never complained of them, nor to them. I would have them know me, guess at me. It is not petty and trivial relations that I seek to establish with them. A world in which there is a demand for ice-creams but not for truth! I leave my friends early; I go away to cherish my idea of friendship. Is not friendship a great relation? My friend so treats me that I feel a thousand miles off; like the greatest possible stranger, speaking a different language; as if it would be the fittest thing in the world for us to be introduced. Persists in thinking me the opposite to what I am, and so shuts my mouth. Intercourse with men! How little it amounts to! How rarely we love them! Do we not meet very much as Yankees meet Arabs? It is remarkable if a man gives us a civil answer about the road. And how far from love still are even pretty intimate friends! How little it is that we can trust each other! It is the bravest thing we do for one moment to put so much confidence in our companion as to treat him for what he aspires to be, a confidence which we retract instantly.

Like cuttlefish we conceal ourselves, we darken the atmosphere in which we move; we are not transparent. I pine for one to whom I can speak my *first thoughts*; thoughts which represent me truly, which are no better and no worse than I; thoughts which have the bloom on them, which alone can be sacred and divine. Our sin and shame prevent our expressing even the innocent thoughts we have. I know of no one to whom I can be transparent instinctively. I live the life of the cuttlefish; another appears, and the element in which I move is tinged and I am concealed. My first thoughts are azure; there is a bloom and a dew on them; they are papillary-feelers which I put out, tender, innocent. Only to a friend can I expose them. To all parties, though they be youth and maiden, if they are transparent to each other, and their thoughts can be expressed, there can be no further nakedness. I cannot be surprised by an intimacy which reveals the outside, when it has shown me the inside. The result of a full communication of our thoughts would be the immediate neglect of those coverings which a false modesty wears.   —Journal, August 24, 1852[162]

P.M.—Talked, or tried to talk, with Emerson. Lost my time—nay, almost my identity. He, assuming a false opposition where there was no difference of opinion, talked to the wind—told me what I knew—and I lost my time trying to imagine myself somebody else to oppose him.
                    —Journal, May 24, 1853[163]

Alcott spent the day with me yesterday. He spent the day before with Emerson. He observed that he had got his wine and now he had come after his venison. Such was the compliment he paid me.   —Journal, August 10, 1853[164]

I was amused by Emerson's telling me that he drove his own calf out of the yard, as it was coming in with the cow, not knowing it to be his own, a drove going by at the time.
                    —Journal, December 8, 1853[165]

Emerson is gone to the Adirondack country with a hunting party. Eddy says he has carried a double-barrelled gun, one side for shot, the other for ball, for Lowell killed a bear there last year. But the story on the Mill-Dam is that he has taken a gun which throws shot from one end and ball from the other!   —Journal, August 6, 1858[166]

Emerson says that he and Agassiz and Company broke some dozens of ale-bottles, one after another, with their bullets, in the Adirondack country, using them for marks! It sounds rather Cockneyish. He says that he shot a peetweet for Agassiz, and this, I think he said, was the first game he ever bagged. He carried a double-barrelled gun,—rifle and shotgun,—which he bought for the purpose, which he says received much commendation,—all parties thought it a very pretty piece. Think of Emerson shooting a peetweet (with shot) for Agassiz, and cracking an ale-bottle (after emptying it) with his rifle at six rods! They cut several pounds of lead out of the tree.   —Journal, August 23, 1858[167]

PART III

Emerson

Friendship[1]

(from *Essays: First Series*)

A ruddy drop of manly blood
The surging sea outweighs;
The world uncertain comes and goes,
The lover rooted stays.
I fancied he was fled,
And, after many a year,
Glowed unexhausted kindliness
Like daily sunrise there.
My careful heart was free again,—
O friend, my bosom said,
Through thee alone the sky is arched,
Through thee the rose is red,
All things through thee take nobler form,
And look beyond the earth,
The mill-round of our fate appears
A sun-path in thy worth.
Me too thy nobleness has taught
To master my despair;
The fountains of my hidden life
Are through thy friendship fair.

We have a great deal more kindness than is ever spoken. Maugre all the selfishness that chills like east winds the world, the whole human family is bathed with an element of love like a fine ether. How many persons we meet in houses, whom we scarcely speak to, whom yet we honor, and who honor us! How many we see in the street, or sit with in church, whom, though silently, we warmly rejoice to be with! Read the language of these wandering eye-beams. The heart knoweth.

The effect of the indulgence of this human affection is a certain cordial exhilaration. In poetry and in common speech the emotions of benevolence and complacency which are felt towards others are likened to the material effects of fire; so swift, or much more swift, more active, more cheering, are these fine inward irradiations. From the highest degree of passionate love, to the lowest degree of good-will, they make the sweetness of life.

Our intellectual and active powers increase with our affection. The scholar sits down to write, and all his years of meditation do not furnish him with one good thought or happy expression; but it is necessary to write a letter to a friend,—and, forthwith, troops of gentle thoughts invest themselves, on every hand, with chosen words. See, in any house where virtue and self-respect abide, the palpitation which the approach of a stranger causes. A commended stranger is expected and announced, and an uneasiness betwixt pleasure and pain invades all the hearts of a household. His arrival almost brings fear to the good hearts that would welcome him. The house is dusted, all things fly into their places, the old coat is exchanged for the new, and they must get up a dinner if they can. Of a commended stranger, only the good report is told by others, only the good and new is heard by us. He stands to us for humanity. He is what we wish. Having imagined and invested him, we ask how we should stand related in conversation and action with such a man, and are uneasy with fear. The same idea exalts conversation with him. We talk better than we are wont. We have the nimblest fancy, a richer memory, and our dumb devil has taken leave for the time. For long hours we can continue a series of sincere, graceful, rich communications, drawn from the oldest, secretest experience, so that they who sit by, of our own kinsfolk and acquaintance, shall feel a lively surprise at our unusual powers. But as soon as the stranger begins to intrude his partialities, his definitions, his defects, into the conversation, it is all over. He has heard the first, the last and best he will ever hear from us. He is no stranger now. Vulgarity, ignorance, misapprehension are old acquaintances. Now, when he comes, he may get the order, the dress, and the dinner,—but the throbbing of the heart, and the communications of the soul, no more.

What is so pleasant as these jets of affection which make a young world for me again? What so delicious as a just and firm encounter of two, in a thought, in a feeling? How beautiful, on their approach to this beating heart, the steps and forms of the gifted and the true! The moment we indulge our affections, the earth is metamorphosed; there is no winter and no night; all tragedies, all ennuis vanish,— all duties even; nothing fills the proceeding eternity but the forms all radiant of beloved persons. Let the soul be assured that somewhere in the universe it should rejoin its friend, and it would be content and cheerful alone for a thousand years.

I awoke this morning with devout thanksgiving for my friends, the old and the new. Shall I not call God the Beautiful, who daily showeth himself so to me in his gifts? I chide society, I embrace solitude, and yet I am not so ungrateful as not to see the wise, the lovely and the noble-minded, as from time to time they pass my gate. Who hears me, who understands me, becomes mine,—a possession for all time. Nor is nature so poor but she gives me this joy several times, and thus we weave social threads of our own, a new web of relations; and, as many thoughts in succession substantiate themselves, we shall by and by stand in a new world of our own creation, and no longer strangers and pilgrims in a traditionary globe. My friends have come to me unsought. The great God gave them to me. By oldest right, by the divine affinity of virtue with itself, I find them, or rather not I, but the Deity in me and in them derides and cancels the thick walls of individual character, relation, age, sex, circumstance, at which he usually connives, and now makes many one. High thanks I owe you, excellent lovers, who carry out the world for me to new and noble depths, and enlarge the meaning of all my thoughts. These are new poetry of the first Bard,—poetry without stop,—hymn, ode and epic, poetry still flowing, Apollo and the Muses chanting still. Will these, too, separate themselves from me again, or some of them? I know not, but I fear it not; for my relation to them is so pure that we hold by simple affinity, and the Genius of my life being thus social, the same affinity will exert its energy on whomsoever is as noble as these men and women, wherever I may be.

I confess to an extreme tenderness of nature on this point. It is almost dangerous to me to "crush the sweet poison of misused wine" of the affections. A new person is to me a great event, and hinders me from sleep. I have often had fine fancies about persons which have given me delicious hours; but the joy ends in the day; it yields no fruit. Thought is not born of it; my action is very little modified. I must feel pride in my friend's accomplishments as if they were mine, and a property in his virtues. I feel as warmly when he is praised, as the lover when he hears applause of his engaged maiden. We over-estimate the conscience of our friend. His goodness seems better than our goodness, his nature finer, his temptations less. Every thing that is his,—his name, his form, his dress, books and instruments,—fancy enhances. Our own thought sounds new and larger from his mouth.

Yet the systole and diastole of the heart are not without their analogy in the ebb and flow of love. Friendship, like the immortality of the soul, is too good to be believed. The lover, beholding his maiden, half knows that she is not verily that which he worships; and in the golden hour of friendship, we are surprised with shades of suspicion and unbelief. We doubt that we bestow on our hero the virtues in which he shines, and afterwards worship the form to which we have ascribed this divine inhabitation. In strictness, the soul does not respect men as it respects itself. In strict science all persons underlie the same condition of an infinite remoteness. Shall we fear to cool our love by mining for the metaphysical foundation of this Elysian temple? Shall I not be as real as the things I see? If I am, I shall not fear to know them for what they are. Their essence is not less beautiful than their appearance, though it needs finer organs for its apprehension. The root of the plant is not unsightly to science, though for chaplets and festoons we cut the stem short. And I must hazard the production of the bald fact amidst these pleasing reveries, though it should prove an Egyptian skull at our banquet. A man who stands united with his thought conceives magnificently of himself. He is conscious of a universal success, even though bought by uniform particular failures. No advantages, no powers, no gold or force, can be any match for him. I cannot choose but rely on my own poverty more than on your wealth. I cannot make your consciousness tantamount to mine. Only the star dazzles; the planet has a faint, moonlike ray. I hear what you say of the admirable parts and tried temper of the party you praise, but I see well that, for all his purple cloaks, I shall not like him, unless he is at least a poor Greek like me. I cannot deny it, O friend, that the vast shadow of the Phenomenal includes thee also in its pied and painted immensity,—thee, also, compared with whom all else is shadow. Thou art not Being, as Truth is, as Justice is,—thou art not my soul, but a picture and effigy of that. Thou hast come to me lately, and already thou art seizing thy hat and cloak. Is it not that the soul puts forth friends as the tree puts forth leaves, and presently, by the germination of new buds, extrudes the old leaf? The law of nature is alternation for evermore. Each electrical state superinduces the opposite. The soul environs itself with friends, that it may enter into a grander self-acquaintance or solitude; and it goes alone for a season, that it may exalt its conversation or society. This method betrays itself along the whole history of our personal relations. The instinct of affection revives the hope of union with our mates, and the returning sense of insulation recalls us from the chase. Thus every man passes his life in the search after friendship, and if he should record his true sentiment, he might write a letter like this to each new candidate for his love:—

DEAR FRIEND,

If I was sure of thee, sure of thy capacity, sure to match my mood with thine, I should never think again of trifles in relation to thy comings and goings. I am not very wise; my moods are quite attainable; and I respect thy genius; it is to me as yet unfathomed; yet dare I not presume in thee a perfect intelligence of me, and so thou art to me a delicious torment. Thine ever, or never.

Yet these uneasy pleasures and fine pains are for curiosity, and not for life. They are not to be indulged. This is to weave cobweb, and not cloth. Our friendships hurry to short and poor conclusions, because we have made them a texture of wine and dreams, instead of the tough fibre of the human heart. The laws of friendship are austere and eternal, of one web with the laws of nature and of morals. But we have aimed at a swift and petty benefit, to suck a sudden sweetness. We snatch at the slowest fruit in the whole garden of God, which many summers and many winters must ripen. We seek our friend not sacredly, but with an adulterate passion which would appropriate him to ourselves. In vain. We are armed all over with subtle antagonisms, which, as soon as we meet, begin to play, and translate all poetry into stale prose. Almost all people descend to meet. All association must be a compromise, and, what is worst, the very flower and aroma of the flower of each of the beautiful natures disappears as they approach each other. What a perpetual disappointment is actual society, even of the virtuous and gifted! After interviews have been compassed with long foresight, we must be tormented presently by baffled blows, by sudden, unseasonable apathies, by epilepsies of wit and of animal spirits, in the heyday of friendship and thought. Our faculties do not play us true, and both parties are relieved by solitude.

I ought to be equal to every relation. It makes no difference how many friends I have, and what content I can find in conversing with each, if there be one to whom I am not equal. If I have shrunk unequal from one contest, the joy I find in all the rest becomes mean and cowardly. I should hate myself, if then I made my other friends my asylum:—

"The valiant warrior famousèd for fight,
After a hundred victories, once foiled,
Is from the book of honor razèd quite,
And all the rest forgot for which he toiled."

Our impatience is thus sharply rebuked. Bashfulness and apathy are a tough husk, in which a delicate organization is protected from premature ripening. It would be lost if it knew itself before any of the best souls were yet ripe enough to know and own it. Respect the *naturlangsamkeit* which hardens the ruby in a million years, and works in duration, in which Alps and Andes come and go as rainbows. The good spirit of our life has no heaven which is the price of rashness. Love, which is the essence of God, is not for levity, but for the total worth of man. Let us not have this childish luxury in our regards, but the austerest worth; let us approach our friend with an audacious trust in the truth of his heart, in the breadth, impossible to be overturned, of his foundations.

The attractions of this subject are not to be resisted, and I leave, for the time, all account of subordinate social benefit, to speak of that select and sacred relation which is a kind of absolute, and which even leaves the language of love suspicious and common, so much is this purer, and nothing is so much divine.

I do not wish to treat friendships daintily, but with roughest courage. When they are real, they are not glass threads or frostwork, but the solidest thing we know. For now, after so many ages of experience, what do we know of nature, or of ourselves? Not one step has man taken toward the solution of the problem of his destiny. In one condemnation of folly stand the whole universe of men. But the sweet sincerity of joy and peace, which I draw from this alliance with my brother's soul is the nut itself whereof all nature and all thought is but the husk and shell. Happy is the house that shelters a friend! It might well be built, like a festal bower or arch, to entertain him a single day. Happier, if he know the solemnity of that relation, and honor its law! He who offers himself a candidate for that covenant comes up, like an Olympian, to the great games, where the first-born of the world are the competitors. He proposes himself for contests where Time, Want, Danger, are in the lists, and he alone is victor who has truth enough in his constitution to preserve the delicacy of his beauty from the wear and tear of all these. The gifts of fortune may be present or absent, but all the speed in that contest depends on intrinsic nobleness, and the contempt of trifles. There are two elements that go to the composition of friendship, each so sovereign that I can detect no superiority in either, no reason why either should be first named. One is Truth. A friend is a person with whom I may be sincere. Before him I may think aloud. I am arrived at last in the presence of a man so real and equal, that I may drop even those undermost garments of dissimulation, courtesy, and second thought, which men never put off, and may deal with him with the simplicity and wholeness with which one chemical atom meets another. Sincerity is the luxury allowed, like diadems and authority, only to the highest rank; *that* being permitted to speak truth, as having none above it to court or conform unto. Every man alone is sincere. At the entrance of a second person, hypocrisy begins. We parry and fend the approach of our fellow-man by compliments, by gossip, by amusements, by affairs. We cover up our thought from him under a hundred folds. I knew a man, who, under a certain religious frenzy, cast off this drapery, and omitting all compliment and commonplace, spoke to the conscience of every person he encountered, and that with great insight and beauty. At first he was resisted, and all men agreed he was mad. But persisting—as indeed he could not help doing—for some time in this course, he attained to the advantage of bringing every man of his acquaintance into true relations with him. No man would think of speaking falsely with him, or of putting him off with any chat of markets or reading-rooms. But every man was constrained by so much sincerity to the like plaindealing, and what love of nature, what poetry, what symbol of truth he had, he did certainly show him. But to most of us society shows not its face and eye, but its side and its back. To stand in true relations with men in a false age is worth a fit of insanity, is it not? We can seldom go erect. Almost every man we meet requires some civility—requires to be humored; he has some fame, some talent, some whim of religion or philanthropy in his head that is not to be questioned, and which spoils all conversation with him. But a friend is a sane man who exercises not my ingenuity, but me. My friend gives me entertainment without requiring any stipulation on my part. A friend, therefore, is a sort of paradox in nature. I who alone am, I who see nothing in nature whose existence I can affirm with equal evidence to my own, behold now the semblance of my being, in all its height, variety, and curiosity, reiterated in a foreign form; so that a friend may well be reckoned the masterpiece of nature.

The other element of friendship is tenderness. We are holden to men by every sort of tie, by blood, by pride, by fear, by hope, by lucre, by lust, by hate, by admiration, by every circumstance and badge and trifle,—but we can scarce believe that so much character can subsist in another as to draw us by love. Can another be so blessed, and we so pure, that we can offer him tenderness? When a man becomes dear to me, I have touched the goal of fortune. I find very little written directly to the heart of this matter in books. And yet I have one text which I cannot choose but remember. My author says,—"I offer myself faintly and bluntly to those whose I effectually am, and tender myself least to him to whom I am the most devoted." I wish that friendship should have feet, as well as eyes and eloquence. It must plant itself on the ground, before it vaults over the moon. I wish it to be a little of a citizen, before it is quite a cherub. We chide the citizen because he makes love a commodity. It is an exchange of gifts, of useful loans; it is good neighborhood; it watches with the sick; it holds the pall at the funeral; and quite loses sight of the delicacies and nobility of the relation. But though we cannot find the god under this disguise of a sutler, yet, on the other hand, we cannot forgive the poet if he spins his thread too fine and does not substantiate his romance by the municipal virtues of justice, punctuality, fidelity, and pity. I hate the prostitution of the name of friendship to signify modish and worldly alliances. I much prefer the company of ploughboys and tin-peddlers, to the silken and perfumed amity which celebrates its days of encounter by a frivolous display, by rides in a curricle, and dinners at the best taverns. The end of friendship is a commerce the most strict and homely that can be joined; more strict than any of which we have experience. It is for aid and comfort through all the relations and passages of life and death. It is fit for serene days, and graceful gifts, and country rambles, but also for rough roads and hard fare, shipwreck, poverty and persecution. It keeps company with the sallies of the wit and the trances of religion. We are to dignify to each other the daily needs and offices of man's life, and embellish it by courage, wisdom and unity. It should never fall into something usual and settled, but should be alert and inventive, and add rhyme and reason to what was drudgery.

Friendship may be said to require natures so rare and costly, each so well tempered and so happily adapted, and withal so circumstanced, (for even in that particular, a poet says, love demands that the parties be altogether paired), that its satisfaction can very seldom be assured. It cannot subsist in its perfection, say some of those who are learned in this warm lore of the heart, betwixt more than two. I am not quite so strict in my terms, perhaps because I have never known so high a fellowship as others. I please my imagination more with a circle of godlike men and women variously related to each other, and between whom subsists a lofty intelligence. But I find this law of *one to one* peremptory for conversation, which is the practice and consummation of friendship. Do not mix waters too much. The best mix as ill as good and bad. You shall have very useful and cheering discourse at several times with two several men, but let all three of you come together, and you shall not have one new and hearty word. Two may talk and one may hear, but three cannot take part in a conversation of the most sincere and searching sort. In good company there is never such discourse between two, across the table, as takes place when you leave them alone. In good company, the individuals merge their egotism into a social soul exactly co-extensive with the several consciousnesses there present. No partialities of friend to friend, no fondnesses of brother to sister, of wife to husband, are there pertinent, but quite otherwise. Only he may then speak who can sail on the common thought of the party, and not poorly limited to his own. Now this convention, which good sense demands, destroys the high freedom of great conversation, which requires an absolute running of two souls into one.

No two men but being left alone with each other enter into simpler relations. Yet it is affinity that determines *which* two shall converse. Unrelated men give little joy to each other, will never suspect the latent powers of each. We talk sometimes of a great talent for conversation, as if it were a permanent property in some individuals. Conversation is an evanescent relation,—no more. A man is reputed to have thought and eloquence; he cannot, for all that, say a word to his cousin or his uncle. They accuse his silence with as much reason as they would blame the insignificance of a dial in the shade. In the sun it will mark the hour. Among those who enjoy his thought he will regain his tongue.

Friendship requires that rare mean betwixt likeness and unlikeness, that piques each with the presence of power and of consent in the other party. Let me be alone to the end of the world, rather than that my friend should overstep, by a word or a look, his real sympathy. I am equally balked by antagonism and by compliance. Let him not cease an instant to be himself. The only joy I have in his being mine, is that the *not mine* is *mine*. I hate, where I looked for a manly furtherance, or at least a manly resistance, to find a mush of concession. Better be a nettle in the side of your friend than his echo. The condition which high friendship demands is ability to do without it. That high office requires great and sublime parts. There must be very two, before there can be very one. Let it be an alliance of two large, formidable natures, mutually beheld, mutually feared, before yet they recognize the deep identity which, beneath these disparities, unites them.

He only is fit for this society who is magnanimous; who is sure that greatness and goodness are always economy; who is not swift to intermeddle with his fortunes. Let him not intermeddle with this. Leave to the diamond its ages to grow, nor expect to accelerate the births of the eternal. Friendship demands a religious treatment. We talk of choosing our friends, but friends are self-elected. Reverence is a great part of it. Treat your friend as a spectacle. Of course he has merits that are not yours, and that you cannot honor, if you must needs hold him close to your person. Stand aside; give those merits room; let them mount and expand. Are you the friend of your friend's buttons, or of his thought? To a great heart he will still be a stranger in a thousand particulars, that he may come near in the holiest ground. Leave it to girls and boys to regard a friend as property, and to suck a short and all-confounding pleasure, instead of the noblest benefit.

Let us buy our entrance to this guild by a long proba-tion. Why should we desecrate noble and beautiful souls by intruding on them? Why insist on rash personal rela-tions with your friend? Why go to his house, or know his mother and brother and sisters? Why be visited by him at your own? Are these things material to our covenant? Leave this touching and clawing. Let him be to me a spirit. A message, a thought, a sincerity, a glance from him, I want, but not news, nor pottage. I can get politics and chat and neighborly conveniences from cheaper companions. Should not the society of my friend be to me poetic, pure, universal and great as nature itself? Ought I to feel that our tie is profane in comparison with yonder bar of cloud that sleeps on the horizon, or that clump of waving grass that divides the brook? Let us not vilify, but raise it to that standard. That great defying eye, that scornful beauty of his mien and action, do not pique yourself on reducing, but rather fortify and enhance. Worship his superiorities; wish him not less by a thought, but hoard and tell them all. Guard him as thy counterpart. Let him be to thee for ever a sort of beautiful enemy, untamable, devoutly revered, and not a trivial con-veniency to be soon outgrown and cast aside. The hues of the opal, the light of diamond, are not to be seen if the eye is too near. To my friend I write a letter, and from him I receive a letter. That seems to you a little. It suffices me. It is a spiritual gift worthy of him to give, and of me to receive. It profanes nobody. In these warm lines the heart will trust itself, as it will not to the tongue, and pour out the prophecy of a godlier existence than all the annals of heroism have yet made good.

Respect so far the holy laws of this fellowship as not to prejudice its perfect flower by your impatience for its opening. We must be our own before we can be another's. There is at least this satisfaction in crime, according to the

Latin proverb;—you can speak to your accomplice on even terms. *Crimen quos inquinat, aequat.* To those whom we admire and love, at first we cannot. Yet the least defect of self-possession vitiates, in my judgment, the entire relation. There can never be deep peace between two spirits, never mutual respect, until, in their dialogue, each stands for the whole world.

What is so great as friendship, let us carry with what grandeur of spirit we can. Let us be silent,—so we may hear the whisper of the gods. Let us not interfere. Who set you to cast about what you should say to the select souls, or how to say any thing to such? No matter how ingenious, no matter how graceful and bland. There are innumerable degrees of folly and wisdom, and for you to say aught is to be frivolous. Wait, and thy heart shall speak. Wait until the necessary and everlasting overpowers you, until day and night avail themselves of your lips. The only reward of virtue is virtue; the only way to have a friend is to be one. You shall not come nearer a man by getting into his house. If unlike, his soul only flees the faster from you, and you shall never catch a true glance of his eye. We see the noble afar off and they repel us; why should we intrude? Late,—very late,—we perceive that no arrangements, no introductions, no consuetudes or habits of society, would be of any avail to establish us in such relations with them as we desire,—but solely the uprise of nature in us to the same degree it is in them; then shall we meet as water with water; and if we should not meet them then, we shall not want them, for we are already they. In the last analysis, love is only the reflection of a man's own worthiness from other men. Men have sometimes exchanged names with their friends, as if they would signify that in their friend each loved his own soul.

The higher the style we demand of friendship, of course the less easy to establish it with flesh and blood. We walk alone in the world. Friends such as we desire are dreams and fables. But a sublime hope cheers ever the faithful heart, that elsewhere, in other regions of the universal power, souls are now acting, enduring, and daring, which can love us, and which we can love. We may congratulate ourselves that the period of nonage, of follies, of blunders and of shame, is passed in solitude, and when we are finished men we shall grasp heroic hands in heroic hands. Only be admonished by what you already see, not to strike leagues of friendship with cheap persons, where no friendship can be. Our impatience betrays us into rash and foolish alliances which no God attends. By persisting in your path, though you forfeit the little you gain the great. You demonstrate yourself, so as to put yourself out of the reach of false relations, and you draw to you the first-born of the world,—those rare pilgrims whereof only one or two wander in nature at once, and before whom the vulgar great show as spectres and shadows merely.

It is foolish to be afraid of making our ties too spiritual, as if so we could lose any genuine love. Whatever correction of our popular views we make from insight, nature will be sure to bear us out in, and though it seem to rob us of some joy, will repay us with a greater. Let us feel if we will the absolute insulation of man. We are sure that we have all in us. We go to Europe, or we pursue persons, or we read books, in the instinctive faith that these will call it out and reveal us to ourselves. Beggars all. The persons are such as we; the Europe, an old faded garment of dead persons; the books, their ghosts. Let us drop this idolatry. Let us give over this mendicancy. Let us even bid our dearest friends farewell, and defy them, saying, "Who are you? Unhand me: I will be dependent no more." Ah! seest thou not, O brother, that thus we part only to meet again on a higher platform, and only be more each other's, because we are more our own? A friend is Janus-faced; he looks to the past and the future. He is the child of all my foregoing hours, the prophet of those to come, and the harbinger of a greater friend.

I do then with my friends as I do with my books. I would have them where I can find them, but I seldom use them. We must have society on our own terms, and admit or exclude it on the slightest cause. I cannot afford to speak much with my friend. If he is great he makes me so great that I cannot descend to converse. In the great days, presentiments hover before me in the firmament. I ought then to dedicate myself to them. I go in that I may seize them, I go out that I may seize them. I fear only that I may lose them receding into the sky in which now they are only a patch of brighter light. Then, though I prize my friends, I cannot afford to talk with them and study their visions, lest I lose my own. It would indeed give me a certain household joy to quit this lofty seeking, this spiritual astronomy or search of stars, and come down to warm sympathies with you; but then I know well I shall mourn always the vanishing of my mighty gods. It is true, next week I shall have languid moods, when I can well afford to occupy myself with foreign objects; then I shall regret the lost literature of your mind, and wish you were by my side again. But if you come, perhaps you will fill my mind only with new visions; not with yourself but with your lustres, and I shall not be able any more than now to converse with you. So I will owe to my friends this evanescent intercourse. I will receive from them not what they have but what they are. They shall give me that which properly they cannot give, but which emanates from them. But they shall not hold me by any relations less subtile and pure. We will meet as though we met not, and part as though we parted not.

It has seemed to me lately more possible than I knew,

to carry a friendship greatly, on one side, without due corre-spondence on the other. Why should I cumber myself with regrets that the receiver is not capacious? It never troubles the sun that some of his rays fall wide and vain into ungrate-ful space, and only a small part on the reflecting planet. Let your greatness educate the crude and cold companion. If he is unequal, he will presently pass away; but thou art en-larged by thy own shining, and, no longer a mate for frogs and worms, dost soar and burn with the gods of the em-pyrean. It is thought a disgrace to love unrequited. But the great will see that true love cannot be unrequited. True love transcends the unworthy object, and dwells and broods on the eternal, and when the poor interposed mask crumbles, it is not sad, but feels rid of so much earth and feels its in-dependency the surer. Yet these things may hardly be said without a sort of treachery to the relation. The essence of friendship is entireness, a total magnanimity and trust. It must not surmise or provide for infirmity. It treats its object as a god, that it may deify both.

Selected Writings on Friendship

The wise man, the true friend, the finished character, we seek everywhere, and only find in fragments. Yet I cannot persuade myself that all the beautiful souls are fled out of the planet, or that always I shall be excluded from good company and yoked with green, dull, pitiful persons. After being cabined up by sea and by land, since I left home, with various little people,—all better to be sure and much wiser than me, but still such persons as did not help me,—how refreshing was it to fall in with two or three sensible persons with whom I could eat my bread and take my walk and feel myself a free man once more of God's universe.

—Emerson to Mary Moody Emerson,
April 22, 1833[2]

It occurs that the distinction should be drawn in treating of Friendship between the *aid of commodity* which our friends yield us, as in hospitality, gifts, sacrifices, etc., and which, as in the old story about the poor man's will in Montaigne, are evidently esteemed by the natural mind (to use such a cant word) the highest manifestations of love; and, secondly, the spiritual aid,—far more precious and leaving the other at infinite distances,—which our friends afford us, of confession, of appeal, of social stimulus, mirroring ourselves.

—Journal, March 23, 1834[3]

If friendship were perfect, there would be no false prayers.

—Journal, June 26, 1834[4]

Who is capable of a manly friendship? Very few.

—Journal, May 13, 1835[5]

Every person who comes to me has two offices,—a present and a prophetical. He is at once a fulfilment and a prediction. He is the long expected son returned, and he is a herald of a coming Friend.   —Journal, 1835[6]

I take the law of hospitality to be this:—I confer on the friend whom I visit the highest compliment, in giving him my time. He gives me shelter and bread. Does he therewith buy my suffrage to his opinions henceforward? No more than by giving him my time, I have bought his. We stand just where we did before. The fact is, before we met he was bound to "speak the truth (of me) in love"; and he is bound to the same now.   —Journal, January16, 1836[7]

Miserable is my own prospect from whom my friend is taken.   —Journal, May 16, 1836[8]

We are associated in adolescent and adult life with some friends, who, like skies and waters, are coextensive with our idea; who, answering each to a certain affection of the soul, satisfy our desire on that side; whom we lack power to put at such focal distance from us, that we can mend or even analyze them. We cannot choose but love them.

—*Nature* (1836)[9]

Last Saturday evening, I had a conversation with Elizabeth Hoar which I cannot recall, but of which the theme was, that when we deal truly and lay judgment to the line and rule, we are no longer permitted to think that the presence or absence of friends is material to our highest states of mind.   —Journal, June 6, 1836[10]

Have you been associated with any friend whose charm over you was coextensive with your idea, that is, was infinite; who filled your thought on that side; and so, as most certainly befals us, you were enamoured of the person? And from that person have you at last, by incessant love and study, acquired a new measure of excellence, also a confidence in the resources of God who thus sends you a real person to outgo your ideal,—you will readily see, when you are separated, as you shortly will be, the bud, flower, and fruit of the whole fact. As soon as your friend has become to you an object of thought, has revealed to you with great prominence a new nature, and has become a measure whereof you are fully possessed to gauge and test more, as his character becomes solid and sweet wisdom, it is already a sign to you that his office to you is closing: expect thenceforward the hour in which he shall be withdrawn from your sight.

—Journal, June 14, 1836[11]

We want but two or three friends, but these we cannot do without, and they serve us in every thought we think.

—Emerson to Thomas Carlyle,
September 17, 1836[12]

The newspapers persecute Alcott. I have never more regretted my inefficiency in practical ends. I was born a seeing eye, not a helping hand. I can only comfort my friends by thought, and not by love or aid. But they naturally look for this other also, and thereby vitiate our relation throughout.　　　　　—Journal, April 16, 1837[13]

A friendship is good which begins on sentiment and proceeds into all mutual convenience, and alternation of great benefits. Less good that which begins in commodity and proceeds to sentiment.　　　—Journal, October 27, 1837[14]

You must love me as I am. Do not tell me how much I should love you. I am content. I find my satisfactions in a calm, considerate reverence, measured by the virtues which provoke it. So love me as I am. When I am virtuous, love me; when I am vicious, hate me; when I am lukewarm, neither good nor bad, care not for me. But do not by your sorrow or your affection solicit me to be somewhat else than I by nature am.   —Journal, February 9–10, 1838[15]

It is one of the blessings of old friends that you can afford to be stupid with them.   —Journal, August 31, 1838[16]

I like the *abandon* of a saunter with my friend. It is a balsam unparalleled.   —Journal, September 5, 1838[17]

If it were possible to speak to the virtue in each of our friends in perfect simplicity, then would society instantly attain its perfection.   —Journal, October 12, 1838[18]

I have no right of nomination in the choice of my friends.
                                        —Journal, August 1, 1839[19]

To be sure, if we outgrow our early friendships there is no help, and undoubtedly where there is inequality in the intellect we must resign them, but true society is so rare that I think I could not afford to spare from my circle a poet as long as he can offer so indisputable a token as a good verse of his relation to what is highest in Being.
                                        —Emerson to Samuel Gray Ward,
                                        October 3, 1839[20]

Fear when you friends say to you what you have done well, and say it through. But when they cannot say it, when they stand beside you with uncertain, timid looks of respect and yet half dislike, inclined to suspend their judgment of you for years to come, then you may begin to hope and to trust.

—Journal, November 9–12, 1839[21]

I dare not look for a friend to me who have never been one.

—Journal, November 13, 1839[22]

In this country we need whatever is generous and beautiful in character more than ever because of the general mediocrity of thought produced by the arts of gain. With a few friends who can yield us the luxury of sincerity and of a manly resistance too, one can face with more courage the battle of every day—and these friends, it is a part of my creed, we always find; the spirit provides for itself. If they come late, they are of a higher class.

—Emerson to Samuel Gray Ward,
November 26, 1839[23]

You would have me at advantage, O friend; you would come to face me by having first wronged me. You would cheat me of the majesty which belongs to every human being.

—Journal, November 15, 1839[24]

When once and again the regard and friendship of the noble-minded is offered me, I am made sensible of my disunion with myself. The head is of gold, the feet are of clay.

—Journal, November 27, 1839[25]

I do not wish to dissect a real rose or a friend.

—Emerson to Margaret Fuller,
December 12, 1839[26]

I am very happy lately in adding one or two new friends to my little circle.... A new person is always to me a great event, and will not let me sleep.

—Emerson to Thomas Carlyle,
December 12, 1839[27]

Certainly we discover our friends by the very highest tokens, and these not describable, often not even intelligible, but not the less sure to that augury which is within the intellect and therefore higher. This is to me the most attractive of all topics, and, I doubt not, whenever I get your full confession of faith, we shall be at one on the matter. Because the subject is so high and sacred, we cannot walk straight up to it; we must saunter if we would find the secret. Nature's roads are not turnpikes but circles, and the instincts are the only sure guides. I am glad if you have so much patience as you say, it is the only sure method that can be trusted. If men are fit for friendship I think they must see their mutual sympathy across the unlikeness and even apathy of to-day. But I see that I am writing sentences and no letter, and as I wish you to like me, I will not add another word.   —Emerson to Samuel Gray Ward,
January 17, 1840[28]

I am a worshipper of Friendship, and cannot find any other good equal to it.   —Emerson to John Sterling,
May 29, 1840[29]

We are never so fit for friendship as when we cease to seek for it, and take ourselves to friend.

—Journal, June 24, 1840[30]

I think we must give up this superstition of company to spend weeks and fortnights. Let my friend come and say that he has to say, and go his way. Otherwise we live for show. That happens continually in my house, that I am expected to play tame lion by readings and talkings to the friends. The rich live for show: I will not.

—Journal, before July 6, 1840[31]

We pretend to our friends that we do not need direct communication—neither actions, nor gifts, nor conversation—to keep their influence whole. But it is a pretence.   —Journal, July 6, 1840[32]

I rode with Margaret Fuller to the plains. She taxed me, as often before, so now more explicitly, with inhospitality of Soul. She and Caroline Sturgis would gladly be my friends, yet our intercourse is not friendship, but literary gossip. I count and weigh, but do not love. They make no progress with me, but however often we have met, we still meet as strangers. They feel wronged in such relation and do not wish to be catechised and criticised. I thought of my experience with several persons which resembled this: and confessed that I would not converse with the divinest person more than one week. Margaret insisted that it was no friendship which was thus so soon exhausted, and that I ought to know how to be silent and companionable at the same moment. She would surprise me,—she would have me say and do what surprised myself. I confess to all this charge with humility unfeigned. I can better converse with George Bradford than with any other. Elizabeth Hoar and I have a beautiful relation, not however quite free from the same hardness and fences. Yet would nothing be so grateful to me as to melt once for all these icy barriers, and unite with these lovers. But great is the law. I must do nothing to court their love which would lose my own. Unless that which I do build up myself, endears me to them, our covenant would be injurious. Yet how joyfully would I form permanent relations with the three or four wise and beautiful whom I hold so dear, and dwell under the same roof or in a strict neighborhood. That would at once ennoble life. And it is practicable. It is easier than things which others do. It is easier than to go to Europe, or to subdue a forest farm in Illinois. But this survey of my experience taught me anew that no friend I have surprises, none exalts me. This then is to be set down, is it not? to the requirements we make of the friend, that he shall constrain us to sincerity, and put under contribution all our faculties.

—Journal, August 16, 1840[33]

A man's growth is seen in the successive choirs of his friends. For every friend whom he loses for truth, he gains a better. —"Circles" (1840)[34]

If we, dear friends, shall arrive at speaking the truth to each other we shall not come away as we went. We shall be able to bring near and give away to each other the love and power of all the friends who encircle each of us, and that society which is the dream of each shall stablish itself in our midst, and the fable of Heaven be the fact of God.

—Journal, September 8, 1840[35]

We dare not trust our wit for making our house pleasant to our friend, and so we buy ice-creams.

—"Man the Reformer" (1841)[36]

But who is fit for friendship? Not one. . . . What we now call friendship, like what we call religion and poetry, is but rudiments and gymnastics.

—Emerson to Caroline Sturgis,
March 15, 1841[37]

His friends were his study, and to see them loosened his talents and his tongue.

—"Ezra Ripley, D.D." (October 1841)[38]

That mood into which a friend can bring us is his dominion over us. —"Spiritual Laws" (1841)[39]

If you visit your friend, why need you apologize for not having visited him, and waste his time and deface your own act? Visit him now. Let him feel that the highest love has come to see him, in thee its lowest organ. Or why need you torment yourself and friend by secret self-reproaches that you have not assisted him or complimented him with gifts and salutations heretofore? Be a gift and a benediction.

—"Spiritual Laws" (1841)[40]

We cannot part with our friends. We cannot let our angels go. We do not see that they only go out that archangels may come in. —"Compensation" (1841)[41]

O, be my friend, and teach me to be thine!

—"Forbearance"[42]

Sometimes it seems as if we used friends as expedients much as we do stoves. We are very cold, miserably cold; we build a fire and get warm; but the heat leaves us where it found us. It has not forwarded our affair a single step; and so the friend when he has come and gone. —"Prospects" (1842)[43]

But in our experience, man is cheap and friendship wants its deep sense. We affect to dwell with our friends in their absence, but we do not; when deed, word, or letter comes not, they let us go. —"The Transcendentalist" (1842)[44]

They feel that they are never so fit for friendship as when they have quitted mankind and taken themselves to friend. A picture, a book, a favorite spot in the hills or the woods which they can people with the fair and worthy creation of the fancy, can give them often forms so vivid that these for the time shall seem real, and society the illusion.

—"The Transcendentalist" (1842)[45]

It is sad to outgrow our preachers, our friends, and our books, and find them no longer potent.

—Journal, July 12, 1842[46]

There is reality, however, in our relations to our friend, is there not?

Yes, and I hail the grander lights and hints that proceed from these, as the worthiest fruits of our being, thus far....

Alas, my friend, you have no generosity; you cannot give yourself away. I see the law of all your friendships. It is a bargain. You tell your things, your friend tells his things, and as soon as the inventory is complete, you take your hats.

—Journal, September 1842[47]

My companion should not be able to paralyze me, nor narrow, nor disturb my temper. When met meet, each should descend like a shower of rockets, like a shower of falling stars so rich with deeds, with thoughts, with so much accomplishment that it should be the festival of nature which all things symbolize; as now love is only the highest symbol of Friendship, as all other things seem lower symbols of it.   —Journal, 1842[48]

I must thank the Quaker City, however, for a new conviction, that this whim called friendship was the brightest thought in what Eden or Olympus it first occurred. I think the two first friends must have been travellers.—I doubt you think my practice of the *finest art* to be bad enough, but friendship does not ever seem to me quite real in the world, but always prophetic; and if I wrote on the Immortality of the Soul, this would be my first topic. Yet is nothing more right than that men should think to address each other with truth and the highest poetry at certain moments, far as their ordinary intercourse is therefrom and buried in trifles. I will try if a man is a man. I will know if he feels that star as I feel it; among trees, does he know them and they him? Is he at the same time both flowing and fixed? Does he feel that Nature proceeds from him, yet can he carry himself as if he were the meanest particle? All and nothing? These things I would know of him, yet without catechism: he shall tell me them in all manner of unexpected ways, in his behavior and in his repose.

—Emerson to Samuel Gray Ward,
January 24, 1843[49]

Strict conversation with a friend is the magazine out of which all good writing is drawn.

—Journal, February 8, 1843[50]

It is very funny to go in to a family where the father and mother are devoted to the children. You flatter yourself for an instant that you have secured your friend's ear, for his countenance brightens; then you discover that he has just caught the eye of his babe over your shoulder, and is chirruping to him.   —Journal, February–March 1843[51]

It is a pathetic thing to meet a friend prepared to love you, to whom yet, from some inaptitude, you cannot communicate yourself with that grace and power which only love will allow.   —Journal, 1843[52]

It is a great joy to find that we have underrated our friend, that he or she is far more excellent than we had thought.

—Journal, March 23, 1843[53]

My friends are leaving the town, and I am sad at heart that they cannot have that love and service from me to which they seem by their aims and the complexion of their minds, and by their unpopularity, to have rich claims.

—Journal, May 1843[54]

Persons are fine things, but they cost so much! for *thee* I must pay *me*.

—Journal, 1843[55]

It is the grace of new friends to be frank, and of old friends to be reticent.

—Journal, 1843[56]

We must not be parties in our dealing with our friends, but the judge.

—Journal, 1844(?)–45[57]

Our friends early appear to us as representatives of certain ideas which they never pass or exceed.

—"Experience" (1844)[58]

New actions are the only apologies and explanations of old ones which the noble can bear to offer or to receive. If your friend has displeased you, you shall not sit down to consider it, for he has already lost all memory of the passage, and has doubled his power to serve you, and ere you can rise up again will burden you with blessings.

—"Character" (1844)[59]

I know nothing which life has to offer so satisfying as the profound good understanding which can subsist, after much exchange of good offices, between two virtuous men, each of whom is sure of himself and sure of his friend. It is a happiness which postpones all other gratifications, and makes politics, and commerce, and churches, cheap. For when men shall meet as they ought, each a benefactor, a shower of stars, clothed with thoughts, with deeds, with accomplishments, it should be the festival of nature which all things announce. Of such friendship, love in the sexes is the first symbol, as all other things are symbols of love. Those relations to the best men, which, at one time, we reckoned the romances of youth, become, in the progress of the character, the most solid enjoyment.   —"Character" (1844)[60]

Could we not pay our friend the compliment of truth, of silence, of forbearing? Need we be so eager to seek him? If we are related, we shall meet.   —"Character" (1844)[61]

A divine person is the prophecy of the mind; a friend is the hope of the heart.   —"Character" (1844)[62]

The service a man renders his friend is trivial and selfish compared with the service he knows his friend stood in readiness to yield him, alike before he had begun to serve his friend, and now also. Compared with that good-will I bear my friend, the benefit it is in my power to render him seems small.   —"Gifts" (1844)[63]

Is there then no friend?   —"Nature" (1844)[64]

Love shows me the opulence of nature, by disclosing to me in my friend a hidden wealth, and I infer an equal depth of good in every other direction.
                    —"Nominalist and Realist" (1844)[65]

Friends to me are frozen wine;
I wait the sun on them should shine.[66]

You shall not love me for what daily spends;
You shall not know me in the noisy street,
Where I, as others, follow petty ends;
Nor when in fair saloons we chance to meet;
Nor when I'm jaded, sick, anxious or mean.
But love me then and only, when you know
Me for the channel of the rivers of God
From deep ideal fontal heavens that flow.[67]

Friends have nothing to give each other; nothing to with-hold; nothing to ask for, or that can be refused: such liberty would infer imperfect affinity. All that behooves them is clearness, or, not to miscall relations, Truth forevermore, and love after that.　　　　—Journal, March–April 1845[68]

When I am in the woods I am warm; when I am cold and wish sticks to burn I have arrived where no trees are. When I am listless, thoughts come crowding on my brain and each hinders the remembrance of the other. So do friends come when I would be alone, and come not when they would refresh me.　　　　　　　　　—Journal, 1845[69]

Dear heart, take it sadly home to thee, that there will and can be no coöperation.　　　　—Journal, after November 5, 1845[70]

The other part of life is self-reliance. Love and it balance up and down, and the beam never rests. Thou wouldst fain not look out of the window, nor waste time in expecting thy friend. Thou wouldst be sought by him. Well, that is also in thy soul, and this is its law. The soul of man must be the servant of another. In its good estate, it is the servant of the

Spirit of Truth. When it is abandoned to that dominion, it is great and sovereign, and draweth friends and lovers. When it is not so, it serveth a friend or lover.

—Journal, after November 5, 1845[71]

Live for friendship, live for love ...

—"Ode Inscribed to W.H. Channing" (June 1846)[72]

Health, south wind, books, old trees, a boat, a friend.

—Journal, 1847[73]

I see that I shall not readily find better or wiser men than my old friends at home.　　　—Journal, October 1847[74]

That which lures a solitary American in the woods with the wish to see England, is the moral peculiarity of the Saxon race,—its commanding sense of right and wrong, the love and devotion to that,—this is the imperial trait, which arms them with the sceptre of the globe. It is this which lies at the foundation of that aristocratic character, which certainly wanders into strange vagaries, so that its origin is often lost sight of, but which, if it should lose this, would find itself paralyzed; and in trade and in the mechanic's shop, gives that honesty in performance, that thoroughness and solidity of work which is a national characteristic. This conscience is one element, and the other is that loyal adhesion, that habit of friendship, that homage of man to man, running through all classes,—the electing of worthy persons to a certain fraternity, to acts of kindness and warm and stanch support, from year to year, from youth to age,—which is alike lovely and honorable to those who render and those who receive it; which stands in strong contrast with the superficial attachments of other races, their excessive courtesy and short-lived connection.　　　—"Speech at Manchester"[75]

What has friendship so signal as its sublime attraction to whatever virtue is in us?　　—"Uses of Great Men" (1850)[76]

A man of 45 does not want to open new accounts of friendship. He has said "kitty kitty" long enough.

—Journal, 1850[77]

A man's fortunes are the fruit of his character. A man's friends are his magnetisms.　　—"Fate" (1851)[78]

Another point of economy is to look for seed of the same kind as you sow, and not to hope to buy one kind with another kind. Friendship buys friendship . . .

—"Wealth" (January 1852)[79]

The belief of some of our friends in their duration suggests one of those musty householders who keep every broomstick and old grate, put in a box every old tooth that falls out of their heads, preserve their ancient frippery of their juvenile wardrobe, and they think God saves all the old souls which he has used up. What does he save them for?

—Journal, June 1, 1852[80]

Would you know a man's thoughts,—look at the circle of his friends, and you know all he likes to think of. Well, is the life of the Boston patrician so desirable, when you see the graceful fools who make all his company?

—Journal, February–March 1854[81]

I remember the maxim which the French stole from our Indians,—and it was worth stealing,—"Let not the grass grow on the path of friendship!"

—Emerson to Thomas Carlyle,
March 11, 1854[82]

Friends do not shake hands. I talk with you, and we have marvelous intimacies, and take all manner of beautiful liberties. After an hour, it is time to go, and straightway I take hold of your hand, and find you a coarse stranger, instead of that musical and permeable angel with whom I have been entertained. —Journal, 1854[83]

Life is not long enough for art, nor long enough for friendship.

—"Address . . . at the Consecration of Sleepy Hollow Cemetery, September 29, 1855"[84]

The child quotes his father, and the man quotes his friend.

—"Quotation and Originality" (March 1859)[85]

The ornament of a house is the friends who frequent it.

—"Domestic Life" (November 1859)[86]

The youth aches for solitude. When he comes to the house he passes through the house. That does not make the deep recess he sought. "Ah! now I perceive," he says, "it must be deep with persons; friends only can give depth." Yes, but there is a great dearth, this year, of friends; hard to find, and hard to have when found: they are just going away; they too are in the whirl of the flitting world, and have engagements and necessities. They are just starting for Wisconsin; have letters from Bremen;—see you again, soon.

—"Considerations by the Way" (1860)[87]

The one prudence in life is concentration; the one evil is dissipation; and it makes no difference whether our dissipations are coarse or fine; property and its cares, friends and a social habit, or politics, or music, or feasting. Everything is good which takes away one plaything and delusion more and drives us home to add one stroke of faithful work. Friends, books, pictures, lower duties, talents, flatteries, hopes,—all are distractions which cause oscillations in our giddy balloon, and make a good poise and a straight course impossible. —"Power" (1860)[88]

When our friends die, we not only lose them, but we lose a great deal of life which in the survivors was related to them.
—Journal, May 1860[89]

Of friendship. There is not only the unspeakable benefit of a reasonable creature to talk to, but also a certain increase of sanity, through testing one's health by the other's, and noting the accords and discords.
—Journal, May 1860[90]

Friendship is an order of nobility; from its revelations we come more worthily into nature. —"Education" (1863)[91]

Friendship requires more time than poor busy men can usually command. —"Behavior" (1860)[92]

'T is a French definition of friendship, *rien que s'entendre*, good understanding. —"Behavior" (1860)[93]

Our chief want in life is somebody who shall makes us do what we can. This is the service of a friend. With him we are easily great. There is a sublime attraction in him to whatever virtue is in us. How he flings wide the doors of existence! What questions we ask of him! what an understanding we have! how few words are needed! It is the only real society.
—"Considerations by the Way" (1860)[94]

There is a pudency about friendship as about love, and though fine souls never lose sight of it, yet they do not name it.   —"Considerations by the Way" (1860)[95]

We take care of our health; we lay up money; we make our roof tight, and our clothing sufficient; but who provides wisely that he shall not be wanting in the best property of all,—friends?   —"Considerations by the Way" (1860)[96]

He basked in friendships all the days of Spring.
                                             —Journal, July 1861[97]

The youth longs for a friend; when he forms a friendship he fills up the unknown parts of his friend's character with all virtues of man.   —Journal, 1863[98]

Friendship a better base for treating of the soul than Immortality. Then it affirms it inclusively.
                                                  —Journal, 1863[99]

Dearest friends will know to-morrow, as the whole earth will know, whether I have kept faith with them.
                                    —Journal, December 1863[100]

Barriers of man impassable. They who should be friends cannot pass into each other. Friends are fictions founded on some single momentary experience.
                                       —Journal, March 1864[101]

We want real relations of the mind and the heart; we want friendship; we want knowledge; we want virtue; a more inward existence to read the history of each other.
                               —"Social Aims" (December 1864)[102]

The true friend must have an attraction to whatever virtue is in us. —"Social Aims" (December 1864)[103]

How the countenance of our friend still left some light after he had gone! —"Clubs"[104]

What is best in the ancient religions was the sacred friendships between heroes ... —"Remarks at the Meeting for Organizing the Free Religious Society" (May 1867)[105]

Many times the reading of a book has made the fortune of the man,—has decided his way of life. It makes friends. 'T is a tie between men to have been delighted with the same book. Every one of us is always in search of his friend, and when unexpectedly he finds a stranger enjoying the rare poet or thinker who is dear to his own solitude,—it is like finding a brother. —"Address at the Opening of the Concord Free Public Library"[106]

There is so much, too, which a book cannot teach which an old friend can. —"Concord Walks" (1876)[107]

Walden

If Thought unlock her mysteries,
    If Friendship on me smile,
I walk in marble galleries,
    I talk with kings the while.[108]

Emerson on Thoreau

Your view concerning Thoreau is entirely in consent with that which I entertain. His general conduct has been very satisfactory, and I was willing and desirous that whatever falling off there had been in his scholarship should be attributable to his sickness. He had, however, imbibed some notions concerning emulation and college rank which had a natural tendency to diminish his zeal, if not his exertions. His instructors were impressed with the conviction that he was indifferent, even to a degree that was faulty, and that they could not recommend him, consistent with the rule by which they are usually governed in relation to beneficiaries. I have always entertained a respect for and interest in him, and was willing to attribute any apparent neglect or indifference to his ill health rather than to wilfulness. I obtained from the instructors the authority to state all the facts to the Corporation, and submit the result to their discretion. This I did, and that body granted *twenty-five dollars*, which was within *ten*, or at most *fifteen*, dollars of any sum he would have received, had no objection been made. There is no doubt that, from some cause, an unfavorable opinion has been entertained, since his return after his sickness, of his disposition to exert himself. To what it has been owing may be doubtful. I appreciate very fully the goodness of his heart and the strictness of his moral principle; and have done as much for him as, under the circumstances, was possible.   —Emerson to Josiah Quincy,
June 25, 1837[109]

At the "teacher's meeting" last night, my good Edmund Hosmer, after disclaiming any wish to difference Jesus from a human mind, suddenly seemed to alter his tone, and said that Jesus made the world and was the Eternal God. Henry Thoreau merely remarked that "Mr. Hosmer had kicked the pail over." I delight much in my young friend, who seems to have as free and erect a mind as any I have ever met. He told as we walked this afternoon a good story about a boy who went to school with him, Wentworth, who resisted the school mistress's command that the children should bow to Dr. Heywood and other gentlemen as they went by, and when Dr. Heywood stood waiting and cleared his throat with a Hem, Wentworth said, "You need n't hem, Doctor. I shan't bow."

—Journal, February 11, 1838[110]

My good Henry Thoreau made this else solitary afternoon sunny with his simplicity and clear perception. How comic is simplicity in this double-dealing, quacking world. Everything that boy says makes merry with society, though nothing can be graver than his meaning. I told him he should write out the history of his college life, as Carlyle has his tutoring. We agreed that the seeing the stars through a telescope would be worth all the astronomical lectures. Then he described Mr. Quimby's electrical lecture here, and the experiment of the shock, and added that "college corporations are very blind to the fact that the twinge in the elbow is worth all the lecturing."

—Journal, February 17, 1838[111]

Montaigne is spiced throughout with rebellion, as much as Alcott or my young Henry Thoreau.

—Journal, March 6, 1838[112]

Yesterday afternoon I went to the Cliff with Henry Thoreau. Warm, pleasant, misty weather, which the great mountain amphitheatre seemed to drink in with gladness. . . .

Have I said it before in these pages? then I will say it again, that it is a curious commentary on society that the expression of a devout sentiment by any young man who lives in society strikes me with surprise and has all the air and effect of genius. —Journal, April 1838[113]

I cordially recommend Mr. Henry D. Thoreau, a graduate of Harvard University in August, 1837, to the confidence of such parents or guardians as may propose to employ him as an instructor. I have the highest confidence in Mr. Thoreau's moral character, and in his intellectual ability. He is an excellent scholar, a man of energy and kindness, and I shall esteem the town fortunate that secures his services.

—Emerson's recommendation for Thoreau, May 2, 1838[114]

Thoreau's poetry; poetry pre-written; mass a compensation for quality. —Notebook, 1838–44[115]

Henry Thoreau has just come, with whom I have promised to make a visit, a brave fine youth he is.

—Emerson to Mary Moody Emerson, September 1, 1838[116]

Henry Thoreau told a good story of Deacon Parkman, who lived in the house he now occupies, and kept a store close by. He hung out a salt fish for a sign, and it hung so long and grew so hard, black and deformed, that the deacon forgot what thing it was, and nobody in town knew, but being examined chemically it proved to be salt fish. But duly every morning the deacon hung it on its peg.

—Journal, September 8, 1838[117]

My brave Henry Thoreau walked with me to Walden this afternoon and complained of the proprietors who compelled him, to whom, as much as to any, the whole world belonged, to walk in a strip of road and crowded him out of all the rest of God's earth. He must not get over the fence: but to the building of that fence he was no party. Suppose, he said, some great proprietor, before he was born, had bought up the whole globe. So he had been hustled out of nature. Not having been privy to any of these arrangements, he does not feel called on to consent to them, and so cuts fishpoles in the woods without asking who has a better title to the wood than he. I defended, of course, the good institution as a scheme, not good, but the best that could be hit on for making the woods and waters and fields available to wit and worth, and for restraining the bold, bad man. At all events, I begged him, having this maggot of Freedom and Humanity in his brain, to write it out into good poetry and so clear himself of it. He replied, that he feared that that was not the best way, that in doing justice to the thought, the man did not always do justice to himself, the poem ought to sing itself: if the man took too much pains with the expression, he was not any longer the Idea himself.

—Journal, November 10, 1838[118]

My Henry Thoreau has broke out into good poetry and better prose; he, my protester.

—Emerson to Margaret Fuller,
February 7, 1839[119]

My brave Henry here who is content to live now, and feels no shame in not studying any profession, for he does not postpone his life, but lives already,—pours contempt on these crybabies of routine and Boston. He has not one chance but a hundred chances. —Journal May 27, 1839[120]

Last night came to me a beautiful poem from Henry Thoreau, "Sympathy." The purest strain, and the loftiest, I think, that has yet pealed from this unpoetic American forest. I hear his verses with as much triumph as I point to my Guido when they praise half-poets and half-painters.
—Journal, August 1, 1839[121]

I have a young poet in this village named Thoreau, who writes the truest verses. —Emerson to Thomas Carlyle,
August 8, 1839[122]

Now here are my wise young neighbors who, instead of getting, like the wordmen, into a railroad-car, where they have not even the activity of holding the reins, have got into a boat which they have built with their own hands, with sails which they have contrived to serve as a tent by night, and gone up the Merrimack to live by their wits on the fish of the stream and the berries of the wood.
—Journal, September 14, 1839[123]

My Henry Thoreau will be a great poet for such a company, and one of these days for all companies.
—Emerson to William Emerson,
September 26, 1839 [124]

I can read Plutarch, and Augustine, and Beaumont and Fletcher, and Landor's *Pericles*, and with no very dissimilar feeling the verses of my young contemporaries Thoreau and Channing.   —Journal, October 1839[125]

Then we have Henry Thoreau here who writes genuine poetry that rarest product of New England wit.
                           —Emerson to Mary Moody Emerson,
                                       December 22, 1839[126]

I will show you Walden Pond, and our Concord poet too, Henry Thoreau.
                     —Emerson to Christopher Pearse Cranch,
                                          March 4, 1840[127]

Ah, Nature! the very look of the woods is heroical and stimulating. This afternoon in a very thick grove where Henry Thoreau showed me the bush of mountain laurel, the first I have seen in Concord, the stems of pine and hemlock and oak almost gleamed like steel upon the excited eye.
                           —Journal, November 20, 1839[128]

I like Henry Thoreau's statement on Diet: "If a man does not believe that he can thrive on board nails, I will not talk with him."   —Journal, June 18, 1840[129]

One reader and friend of yours dwells now in my house, and, as I hope, for a twelvemonth to come,—Henry Thoreau,—a poet whom you may one day be proud of;—a noble, manly youth, full of melodies and inventions. We work together day by day in my garden, and I grow well and strong.
                               —Emerson to Thomas Carlyle,
                                           May 30, 1841[130]

Our household is now enlarged by the presence of . . . Henry Thoreau who may stay with me a year. I do not remember if I have told you about him: but he is to have his board etc. for what labor he chooses to do: and he is thus far a great benefactor and physician to me for he is an indefatigable and a very skilful laborer and I work with him as I should not without him, and expect now to be suddenly well and strong though I have been a skeleton all the spring until I am ashamed. Thoreau is a scholar and a poet and as full of buds of promise as a young apple tree.

—Emerson to William Emerson,
June 1, 1841[131]

I am sometimes discontented with my house because it lies on a dusty road, and with its sills and cellar almost in the water of the meadow. But when I creep out of it into the Night or the Morning and see what majestic and what tender beauties daily wrap me in their bosom, how near to me is every transcendent secret of Nature's love and religion, I see how indifferent it is where I eat and sleep. This very street of hucksters and taverns the moon will transform to a Palmyra, for she is the apologist of all apologists, and will kiss the elm trees alone and hides every meanness in a silver-edged darkness. Then the good river-god has taken the form of my valiant Henry Thoreau here and introduced me to the riches of his shadowy, starlit, moonlit stream, a lovely new world lying as close and yet as unknown to this vulgar trite one of the streets and shops as death to life, or poetry to prose. Through one field only we went to the boat and then left all time, all science, all history, behind us, and entered into Nature with one stroke of a paddle. Take care, good friend! I said, as I looked west into the sunset overhead and underneath, and he with his face toward me rowed towards it,—take care; you know not what you do, dipping your wooden oar into this enchanted liquid, painted with all reds and purples and yellows, which glows under and behind you. Presently this glory faded, and the stars came and said, "Here we are"; began to cast such private and ineffable beams as to stop all conversation. A holiday *villeggiatura*, a royal revel, the proudest, most magnificent, most heart-rejoicing festival that valor and beauty, power and poetry ever decked and enjoyed—it is here, it is this.

—Journal, June 6, 1841[132]

I told Henry Thoreau that his freedom is in the form, but he does not disclose new matter. I am very familiar with all his thoughts,—they are my own quite originally drest. But if the question be, what new ideas has he thrown into circulation, he has not yet told what that is which he was created to say. I said to him what I often feel, I only know three persons who seems to me fully to see this law of reciprocity or compensation,—himself, Alcott, and myself: and 't is odd that we should all be neighbors, for in the wide land or the wide earth I do not know another who seems to have it as deeply and originally as these three Gothamites.

—Journal, September 1841[133]

Henry Thoreau is full of noble madness lately, and I hope more highly of him than ever. I know that nearly all the fine souls have a flaw which defeats every expectation they excite but I must trust these large frames as of less fragility—than the others. Besides to have awakened a great hope in another, is already some fruit is it not?

—Emerson to Margaret Fuller,
September 13, 1841[134]

Henry is a person of extraordinary health and vigor, of unerring perception, and equal expression; and yet he is impracticable, and does not flow through his pen or (in any of our legitimate aqueducts) through his tongue.

—Journal, October 1841[135]

I am sorry that you, and the world after you, do not like my brave Henry any better. I do not like his piece very well, but I admire this perennial threatening attitude, just as we like to go under an overhanging precipice. It is wholly his natural relation and no assumption at all.

—Emerson to Margaret Fuller,
July 19, 1842[136]

Henry Thoreau had been one of the family for the last year, and charmed Waldo by the variety of toys,—whistles, boats, popguns,—and all kinds of instruments which he could make and mend; and possessed his love and respect by the gentle firmness with which he always treated him. . . .

Henry Thoreau well said, in allusion to his large way of speech, that "his questions did not admit of an answer; they were the same which you would ask yourself."

—Journal, January 30, 1842[137]

I have sometimes fancied my friend's wisdom rather corrective than initiative, an excellent element in conversation to counteract the common exaggerations and preserve the sanity, but chiefly valuable so, and not for its adventure and exploration or for its satisfying peace.

—Journal, April 13, 1842[138]

Henry Thoreau made, last night, the fine remark that, as long as a man stands in his own way, everything seems to be in his way, governments, society, and even the sun and moon and stars, as astrology may testify.

—Journal, October–November 1842[139]

Last night Henry Thoreau read me verses which pleased, if not by beauty of particular lines, yet by the honest truth, and by the length of flight and strength of wing; for most of our poets are only writers of lines or of epigrams. These of Henry's at least have rude strength, and we do not come to the bottom of the mine. Their fault is, that the gold does not yet flow pure, but is drossy and crude. The thyme and marjoram are not yet made into honey; the assimilation is imperfect. —Journal, November 1842[140]

Elizabeth Hoar says, "I love Henry, but do not like him." Young men, like Henry Thoreau, owe us a new world, and they have not acquitted the debt. For the most part, such die young, and so dodge the fulfilment. One of our girls said, that Henry never went through the kitchen without coloring. —Journal, March–April 1843[141]

And now goes our brave youth into the new house, the new connexion, the new City. I am sure no truer and no purer person lives in wide New York; and he is a bold and a profound thinker though he may easily chance to pester you with some accidental crotchets and perhaps a village exaggeration of the value of facts.

—Emerson to William Emerson,
May 6, 1843[142]

Henry Thoreau sends me a paper with the old fault of unlimited contradiction. The trick of his rhetoric is soon learned: it consists in substituting for the obvious word and thought its diametrical antagonist. He praises wild mountains and winter forests for their domestic air; snow and ice for their warmth; villagers and wood-choppers for their urbanity, and the wilderness for resembling Rome and Paris. With the constant inclination to dispraise cities and civilization, he yet can find no way to know woods and woodmen except by paralleling them with towns and townsmen.

Channing declares the piece is excellent: but it makes me nervous and wretched to read it, with all its merits.

—Journal, August–September 1843[143]

Ellery Channing says, that writers never do anything: they are passive observers. Some of them seem to do, but they do not; Henry will never be a writer; he is as active as a shoemaker.

—Journal, 1843[144]

Precisely what the painter or the sculptor or the epic rhapsodist feels, I feel in the presence of this house, which stands to me for the human race, the desire, namely, to express myself fully, symmetrically, gigantically to them, not dwarfishly and fragmentarily. Henry David Thoreau, with whom I talked of this last night, does not or will not perceive how natural is this, and only hears the word Art in a sinister sense.

—Journal, February 1844[145]

Henry Thoreau said, he knew but one secret, which was to do one thing at a time, and though he has his evenings for study, if he was in the day inventing machines for sawing his plumbago, he invents wheels all the evening and night also; and if this week he has some good reading and thoughts before him, his brain runs on that all day, whilst pencils pass through his hands. I find in me an opposite facility or perversity, that I never seem well to do a particular work until another is due. I cannot write the poem, though you give me a week, but if I promise to read a lecture the day after to-morrow, at once the poem comes into my head and now the rhymes will flow. And let the proofs of the *Dial* be crowding on me from the printer, and I am full of faculty how to make the lecture.

—Journal, February 1844[146]

Henry Thoreau's conversation consisted of a continual coining of the present moment into a sentence and offering it to me. I compared it to a boy, who, from the universal snow lying on the earth, gathers up a little in his hand, rolls it into a ball, and flings it at me.   —Journal, May 1844[147]

Henry said that the other world was all his art; that his pencils would draw no other; that his jackknife would cut nothing else. He does not use it as a means. Henry is a good substantial Childe, not encumbered with himself. He has not troublesome memory, no wake, but lives *ex tempore*, and brings to-day a new proposition as radical and revolutionary as that of yesterday, but different. The only man of leisure in the town. He is a good Abbot Samson: and carries counsel in his breast. If I cannot show his performance much more manifest that that of the other grand promisers, at least I can see that, with his practical faculty, he has declined all the kingdoms of this world. Satan has no bribe for him.
                                                —Journal, May 1844[148]

Henry Thoreau said that the Fourierists had a sense of duty which led them to devote themselves to their second best.
                                                —Journal, 1845[149]

Henry Thoreau complained that when he came out of the garden, he remembered his work.   —Journal, 1845[150]

A cat falls on its feet; shall not a man? You think he has character; have you kicked him? Talleyrand would not change countenance; Edward Taylor, Henry Thoreau, would put the assailant out of countenance.   —Journal, 1845[151]

Henry Thoreau says "that philosophers are broken-down poets"; and "that universal assertions should never allow any remarks of the individual to stand in their neighbor-hood, for the broadest philosophy is narrower than the worst poetry."   —Journal, 1845[152]

Henry Thoreau objected to my "Shakespeare," that the eulogy impoverished the race. Shakespeare ought to be praised, as the sun is, so that all shall be rejoiced.
                    —Journal, April 1846[153]

Queenie [Lidian Emerson] came it over Henry last night when he taxed the new astronomers with the poverty of their discoveries and showings—not strange enough. Queenie wished to see with eyes some of those strange things which the telescope reveals, the satellites of Saturn, etc. Henry said that stranger things might be seen with the naked eye. "Yes," said Queenie "but I wish to see some of those things that are not quite so strange."
                    —Journal, April 1846[154]

The teamster, the farmer, are jocund and hearty, and stand on their legs: but the women are demure and subdued as Shaker women, and, if you see them out of doors, look, as Henry Thoreau said, "as if they were going for the Doctor."
                    —Journal, 1846[155]

Henry Thoreau seems to think that society suffers for want of war, or some good excitant. But how partial that is!
                    —Journal, June 1846[156]

Society is a curiosity-shop full of odd excellences, a Brah-min, a Fakeer, a giraffe, an alligator, Colonel Bowie, Alvah Crocker, Bronson Alcott, Henry Thoreau; a world that can-not keep step, admirable melodies, but no chorus, for there is no accord.   —Journal, June 1846[157]

In a short time, if Wiley & Putnam smile, you shall have Henry Thoreau's "Excursion on Concord and Merrimack rivers," a seven days' voyage in as many chapters, pastoral as Isaak Walton, spicy as flagroot, broad and deep as Menu. He read me some of it under an oak on the river bank the other afternoon, and invigorated me.

—Emerson to Charles King Newcomb,
July 16, 1846[158]

These—rabble—at Washington are really better than the sniveling opposition. They have a sort of genius of a bold and manly cast, though Satanic. They see, against the unanimous expression of the people, how much a little well-directed effrontery can achieve, how much crime the people will bear, and they proceed from step to step, and it seems they have calculated but too justly upon your Excellency, O Governor Briggs. Mr. Webster told them how much the war cost, that was his protest, but voted the war, and sends his son to it. They calculated rightly on Mr. Webster. My friend Mr. Thoreau has gone to jail rather than pay his tax. On him they could not calculate. The Abolitionists denounce the war and give much time to it, but they pay the tax.   —Journal, July 1846[159]

Henry Thoreau wants to go to Oregon, not to London. Yes, surely; but what seeks he but the most energetic Nature? And, seeking that, he will find Oregon indifferently in all places; for it snows and blows and melts and adheres and repels all the world over.   —Journal, 1847[160]

My friend Thoreau has written and printed in "Graham's Magazine" here an Article on Carlyle which he will send to you as soon as the second part appears in a next number, and which you must not fail to read. You are yet to read a

good American book made by this Thoreau, and which is
shortly to be printed, he says.

—Emerson to Thomas Carlyle,
February 27, 1847[161]

Henry Thoreau's paper on Carlyle is printed in Graham's
Magazine: and his Book, "Excursion on Concord and Merrimack rivers" will soon be ready. Admirable, though Ellery
Channing rejects it altogether. Mrs. Ripley and other members of the opposition came down the other night to hear
Henry's Account of his housekeeping at Walden Pond,
which he read as a lecture, and were charmed with the
witty wisdom which ran through it all.

—Emerson to Margaret Fuller,
February 28, 1847[162]

Novels, Poetry, Mythology must be well allowed for an
imaginative being. You do us great wrong, Henry Thoreau,
in railing at the novel reading.

—Journal, May–June 1847[163]

Mr. Henry D. Thoreau of this town has just completed
a book of extraordinary merit, which he wishes to
publish....

This book has many merits. It will be as attractive to
lovers of nature, in every sense, that is, to naturalists, and
to poets, as Isaak Walton. It will be attractive to scholars
for its excellent literature, and to all thoughtful persons for
its originality and profoundness. The narrative of the little
voyage, though faithful, is a very slender thread for such big
beads and ingots as are strung on it. It is really a book of the
results of the studies of years.

—Emerson to Evert Duyckinck,
March 12, 1847[164]

Thoreau sometimes appears only as a *gendarme*, good to knock down a cockney with, but without that power to cheer and establish which makes the value of a friend.

—Journal, July 10, 1847[165]

Henry Thoreau says that twelve pounds of Indian meal, which one can easily carry on his back, will be food for a fortnight. Of course, one need not be in want of a living wherever corn grows, and where it does not, rice is as good.

Henry, when you talked of art, blotted a paper with ink, then doubled it over, and safely defied the artist to surpass his effect. —Journal, July 1847[166]

Henry D. Thoreau is a great man in Concord, a man of original genius and character, who knows Greek, and knows Indian also,—not the language quite as well as John Eliot—but the history monuments and genius of the Sachems, being a pretty good Sachem himself, master of all woodcraft, and an intimate associate of the birds, beasts, and fishes, of this region. I could tell you many a good story of his forest life.—He has written what he calls "A Week on the Concord and Merrimack Rivers," which is an account of an excursion made by himself and his brother (in a boat which he built) some time ago, from Concord, Mass., down the Concord river and up the Merrimack, to Concord, N.H.—I think it a book of wonderful merit, which is to go far and last long. It will remind you of Izaak Walton, and, if it have not all his sweetness, it is rich, as he is not, in profound thought.

—Emerson to William H. Furness,
August 6, 1847[167]

I have to thank you for your letter which was a true refreshment. Let who or what pass, there stands the dear

Henry,—if indeed any body had a right to call him so,—erect, serene, & undeceivable. So let it ever be! I should quite subside into idolatry of some of my friends, if I were not every now and then apprised that the world is wiser than any one of its boys, and penetrates us with its sense, to the disparagement of the subtleties of private gentlemen.
—Emerson to Thoreau, January 28, 1848[168]

Charles Newcomb remarked, as Ellery Channing had done, the French trait in Henry Thoreau and in his family. Here is the precise *voyageur* of Canada sublimed, or carried up to the seventh power. In the family the brother and one sister preserved the French character of face.
—Journal, January–February 1848[169]

Henry Thoreau thought what we reckon a good Englishman is in this country a stage-proprietor.
—Journal, March 1848[170]

Henry Thoreau is like the wood-god who solicits the wandering poet and draws him into "antres vast and desarts idle," and bereaves him of his memory, and leaves him naked, plaiting vines and with twigs in his hand. Very seductive are the first steps from the town to the woods, but the end is want and madness.   —Journal, August 1848[171]

I spoke of friendship, but my friends and I are fishes in our habit. As for taking Thoreau's arm, I should as soon take the arm of an elm tree.   —Journal, August 1848[172]

Henry Thoreau, working with Alcott on the summer house, said, he was nowhere, doing nothing.
—Journal, Summer 1848[173]

We have not had since ten years a pamphlet which I have saved to bind! and here at last is Bushnell's; and now, Henry Thoreau's *Ascent of Katahdin*.

—Journal, October 1848[174]

Henry Thoreau sports the doctrines of activity: but I say, What do *we*? We want a sally into the regions of wisdom, and do we go out and lay stone wall or dig a well or turnips? No, we leave the children, sit down by a fire, compose our bodies to corpses, shut our hands, shut our eyes, that we may be entranced and see truly.   —Journal, October 1848[175]

My friends begin to value each other, now that Alcott is to go; and Ellery Channing declares, "that he never saw that man without being cheered," and Henry says, "He is the best natured man I ever met. The rats and mice make their nests in him."   —Journal, November 1848[176]

Henry Thoreau is still falling on some bold volunteer like his Dr. Heaton who discredits the regulars; but Thoreau like all the rest of sensible men, when he is sick, will go to Jackson and Warren.   —Journal, December 10, 1848[177]

Thoreau can pace 16 rods accurately.   —Journal, 1849[178]

Big-endians	Little-endians
Plato	Alcott
Swedenborg	Very
Shakspeare	Newcomb
Montaigne	Channing
Goethe	Emerson
Napoleon	Thoreau

—Journal, 1849[179]

It is well worth thinking on. Thus, if Thoreau, Ellery Channing, and I could (which is perhaps impossible) combine works heartily (being fired by such a desire to carry one point as to fuse all our repulsions and incompatibilities), I doubt not we could engender something far superior for quality and for effect to any of the thin, cold-blooded creatures we have hitherto flung into the light.

—Journal, February 1850[180]

In Natural History of Intellect Goethe becomes a sample of an eye, for he sees the site of Rome, its unfitness, he sees the difference between Palermo and Naples; he sees rivers, and which way they run. Henry Thoreau, too. An advancing eye, that like the heavens journeys too and sojourns not.

—Journal, 1850[181]

Nature, Ellery Channing thought, is less interesting. Yesterday Thoreau told me it was more so, and persons less. I think it must always combine with man. Life is ecstatical, and we radiate joy and honor and gloom on the days and landscapes we converse with.   —Journal, September 1, 1850[182]

Practical naturalist. Now that the civil engineer is fairly established, I think we must have one day a naturalist in each village as invariably as a lawyer or doctor. It will be a new subdivision of the medical profession. . . .

The universal impulse toward natural science in the last twenty years promises this practical issue. And how beautiful would be the profession. C.T. Jackson, John L. Russell, Henry Thoreau, George Bradford, and John Lesley would find their employment. All questions answered for stipulated fees; and, on the other hand, new information paid for, as a newspaper office pays for news.

—Journal, October 1850[183]

Rambling talk with Henry Thoreau last night, in accordance with my proposal to hold a session, the first for a long time, with malice prepense, and take the bull by the horns. We disposed pretty fast of America and England, I maintaining that our people did not get ripened, but, like the peaches and grapes of this season, wanted a fortnight's more sun and remained green, whilst in England, because of the density, perhaps, of cultivated population, more caloric was generated and more completeness obtained. Layard is good example, both of the efficiency as measured by effect on the Arab, and in its reaction of his enterprise on him; for his enterprise proved a better university to him than Oxford or Sorbonne.

Henry thought "the English all train," are mere soldiers, as it were, in the world. And that their business is winding up, whilst our pioneer is unwinding his lines.

I like the English better than our people, just as I like merchants better than scholars; for, though on a lower platform, yet there is no cant, there is great directness, comprehension, health, and success. So with English.

Then came the difference between American and English scholars. Henry said, the English were all bred in one way, to one thing; he had read many lives lately, and they were all one life, Southey, Campbell, Leigh Hunt, or whosoever; they went to Eton, they went to College, they went to London, they all knew each other, and never did not feel the ability of each. But here, Channing is obscure, Newcomb is obscure, and so all the scholars are in a more natural, healthful, and independent condition.

My own quarrel with America, of course, was that the geography is sublime, but the men are not. . . .

It was agreed, however, that what is called success in America or in England is none; that their book or man or law had no root in nature, of course!

—Journal, October 27, 1850[184]

Nothing so marks a man as bold imaginative expressions. Henry Thoreau promised to make as good sentences of that kind as anybody.   —Journal, 1850[185]

Is it not a convenience to have a person in town who knows where pennyroyal grows, or sassafras, or punk for a slow-match; or Celtis,—the false elm; or cats-o'-nine-tails; or wild cherries; or wild pears; where is the best apple tree, where is the Norway pine, where the beech, . . . where are trout, where woodcocks, where wild bees, where pigeons; or who can tell where the stake-driver (bittern) can be heard; who has seen and can show you the Wilson's plover?

Thoreau wants a little ambition in his mixture. Fault of this, instead of being the head of American engineers, he is captain of a huckleberry party.   —Journal, July 1851[186]

Henry Thoreau will not stick, he is not practically renovator. He is a boy, and will be an old boy. Pounding beans is good to the end of pounding Empires, but not, if at the end of years, it is only beans.

I fancy it an inexcusable fault in him that he is insignificant here in the town. He speaks at Lyceum or other meeting but somebody else speaks and his speech falls dead and is forgotten. He rails at the town doings and ought to correct and inspire them.   —Journal, 1851[187]

It would be hard to recall the rambles of last night's talk with Henry Thoreau. But we stated over again, to sadness almost, the eternal loneliness. I found that though the stuff of Tragedy and of Romances is in a moral union of two superior persons, and the confidence of each in the other, for long years, out of sight and in sight, and against all appearances, is at last justified by victorious proof of probity to gods and men, causing a gush of joyful emotion, tears, glory, or what-not,—though there be for heroes this *moral union*, yet they, too, are still as far off as ever from an intellectual union, and this moral union is for comparatively low and external purposes, like the coöperation of a ship's crew or of a fire-club. But how insular and pathetically solitary are all the people we know!

—Journal, October 27, 1851[188]

"You may be sure Kossuth is an old woman, he speaks so well." Said H.D.T. —Journal, 1851[189]

Of Henry Thoreau. He who sees the horizon may securely say what he pleases of any tree or twig between him and it.

—Journal, 1852[190]

Observe, that the whole history of the intellect is expansions and concentrations. . . .

But all this old song I have trolled a hundred times already, in better ways, only, last night, Henry Thoreau insisted much on "expansions," and it sounded new.

—Journal, May 1852[191]

I find in my platoon contrasted figures; as, my brothers, and Everett, and Caroline, and Margaret, and Elizabeth, and Jones Very, and Sam Ward, and Henry Thoreau, and Alcott, and Channing. Needs all these and many more to represent my relations.

—Journal, June 1, 1852[192]

Henry Thoreau's idea of the men he meets is, that they are his old thoughts walking. It is all affectation to make much of them, as if he did not long since know them thoroughly.
—Journal, June 1, 1852[193]

Henry Thoreau rightly said, the other evening, talking of lightning-rods, that the only rod of safety was in the vertebræ of his own spine. —Journal, July 1852[194]

Thoreau gives me, in flesh and blood and pertinacious Saxon belief, my own ethics. He is far more real, and daily practically obeying them, than I; and fortifies my memory at all times with an affirmative experience which refuses to be set aside. —Journal, July 1852[195]

Lovejoy, the preacher, came to Concord, and hoped Henry Thoreau would go to hear him. "I have got a sermon on purpose for him." "No," the aunts said, "we are afraid not." Then he wished to be introduced to him at the house. So he was confronted. Then he put his hand from behind on Henry, tapping his back, and said, "Here's the chap who camped in the woods." Henry looked round, and said, "And here's the chap who camps in a pulpit." Lovejoy looked disconcerted, and said no more. —Journal, July 1852[196]

Henry Thoreau makes himself characteristically the admirer of the common weeds which have been hoed at by a million farmers all spring and summer and yet have prevailed, and just now come out triumphant over all lands, lanes, pastures, fields, and gardens, such is their pluck and vigor. We have insulted them with low names, too, pigweed, smart-weed, red-root, lousewort, chickweed. He says that they have fine names,—amaranth, ambrosia.
—Journal, July 18, 1852[197]

Thoreau read me a letter from Harrison Gray Otis Blake to himself, yesterday, by which it appears that Blake writes to ask his husband for leave to marry a wife.

—Journal, October 1852[198]

Thoreau remarks that the cause of Freedom advances, for all the able debaters now are freesoilers, Sumner, Mann, Giddings, Hale, Seward, Burlingame. —Journal, 1852[199]

Thoreau is at home; why, he has got to maximize the minimum; that will take him some days.

—Journal, December 1852[200]

At home, I found Henry himself, who complained of Clough or somebody that he or they recited to every one at table the paragraph just read by him and by them in the last newspaper and studiously avoided everything private. I should think he was complaining of one H.D.T.

—Journal, December 1852[201]

Henry is military. He seemed stubborn and implacable; always manly and wise, but rarely sweet. One would say that, as Webster could never speak without an antagonist, so Henry does not feel himself except in opposition. He wants a fallacy to expose, a blunder to pillory, requires a little sense of victory, a roll of the drums, to call his powers into full exercise. —Journal, June 1853[202]

Henry Thoreau sturdily pushes his economy into houses and thinks it the false mark of the gentleman that he is to pay much for his food. He ought to pay little for his food. Ice,—he must have ice! And it is true, that, for each artificial want that can be invented and added to the ponderous expense, there is new clapping of hands of newspaper editors and the donkey public. To put one more rock to be lifted betwixt a man and his true ends. If Socrates were here, we could go and talk with him; but Longfellow, we cannot go and talk with; there is a palace, and servants, and a row of bottles of different coloured wines, and wine glasses, and fine coats. —Journal, August 1853[203]

Sylvan [Henry Thoreau] could go wherever woods and waters were, and no man was asked for leave—once or twice the farmer withstood, but it was to no purpose,—he could as easily prevent the sparrows or tortoises. It was their land before it was his, and their title was precedent. Sylvan knew what was on their land, and they did not; and he sometimes brought them ostentatious gifts of flowers or fruits or shrubs which they would gladly have paid great prices for, and did not tell them that he took them from their own woods.

Moreover the very time at which he used their land and water (for his boat glided like a trout everywhere unseen,) was in hours when they were sound asleep. Long before they were awake he went up and down to survey like a sovereign his possessions, and he passed onward, and left them before the farmer came out of doors. Indeed, it was the common opinion of the boys that Mr. Thoreau made Concord. —Journal, 1853[204]

Mother wit. Dr Johnson, Milton, Chaucer, and Burns had it....
Henry Thoreau has it. —Journal 1853[205]

Henry Thoreau says he values only the man who goes directly to his needs; who, wanting wood, goes to the woods and brings it home; or to the river, and collects the drift, and brings it in his boat to his door, and burns it: not him who keeps shop, that he may buy wood. One is pleasing to reason and imagination; the other not.

—Journal, September 1853[206]

My two plants, the deerberry vaccinium stamineum and the golden flowers Chrysopsis ——, were eagerly greeted here. Henry Thoreau could hardly suppress his indignation that I should bring him a berry he had not seen.

—Emerson to William Emerson,
September 28, 1853[207]

The other day, Henry Thoreau was speaking to me about my lecture on the Anglo-American, and regretting that whatever was written for a lecture, or whatever succeeded with the audience was bad, etc. I said, I am ambitious to write something which all can read, like *Robinson Crusoe*. And when I have written a paper or a book, I see with regret that it is not solid, with a right materialistic treatment, which delights everybody. Henry objected, of course, and vaunted the better lectures which only reached a few persons. Well, yesterday, he came here, and at supper Edith, understanding that he was to lecture at the Lyceum, sharply asked him, "Whether his lecture would be a nice interesting story, such as she wanted to hear, or whether it was one of those old philosophical things that she did not care about?" Henry instantly turned to her, and bethought himself, and I saw was trying to believe that he had matter that might fit Edith and Edward, who were to sit up and go to the lecture, if it was a good one for them.

—Journal, December 1853[208]

Henry Thoreau charged Blake, if he could not do hard tasks, to take the soft ones, and when he liked anything, if it was only a picture or a tune, to stay by it, find out what he liked, and draw that sense or meaning out of it, and do *that*: harden it, somehow, and make it his own. Blake thought and thought on this, and wrote afterwards to Henry, that he had got his first glimpse of heaven. Henry was a good physician. —Journal, March 1854[209]

Mr. Thoreau is a man of rare ability: he is a good scholar, and a good naturalist, and he is a man of genius, and writes always with force, and sometimes with wonderful depth and beauty.

—Emerson to Richard Bentley,
March 20, 1854[210]

All American kind are delighted with "Walden" as far as they have dared say. The little pond sinks in these very days as tremulous at its human fame. I do not know if the book has come to you yet;—but it is cheerful, sparkling, readable, with all kinds of merits, and rising sometimes to very great heights. We account Henry the undoubted King of all American lions. He is walking up and down Concord, firm-looking, but in a tremble of great expectation.

—Emerson to George Bradford,
August 28, 1854[211]

Thoreau thinks 't is immoral to dig gold in California; immoral to leave creating value, and go to augmenting the representative of value, and so altering and diminishing real value, and, that, of course, the fraud will appear.

—Journal, 1857[212]

Henry Thoreau asks, fairly enough, when is it that the man is to begin to provide for himself? —Journal, 1855[213]

It is true—is it not?—that the intellectual man is stronger than the robust animal man; for he husbands his strength, and endures. . . .

Henry Thoreau notices that Franklin and Richardson of Arctic expeditions outlived their robuster comrades by more intellect. Frémont did the same.   —Journal, 1855[214]

If I knew only Thoreau, I should think coöperation of good men impossible. Must we always talk for victory, and never once for truth, for comfort, and joy? Centrality he has, and penetration, strong understanding, and the higher gifts,— the insight of the real, or from the real, and the moral rectitude that belongs to it; but all this and all his resources of wit and invention are lost to me, in every experiment, year after year, that I make, to hold intercourse with his mind. Always some weary captious paradox to fight you with, and the time and temper wasted.   —Journal, February 1856[215]

It is curious that Thoreau goes to a house to say with little preface what he has just read or observed, delivers it in lump, is quite inattentive to any comment or thought which any of the company offer on the matter, nay, is merely interrupted by it, and when he has finished his report departs with precipitation.   —Journal, April 1856[216]

Yesterday to the Sawmill Brook with Henry. He was in search of yellow violet (*pubescens*) and *menyanthes* which he waded into the water for; and which he concluded, on examination, had been out five days. Having found his flowers, he drew out of his breast pocket his diary and read the names of all the plants that should bloom this day, May 20; whereof he keeps account as a banker when his notes fall due; *Rubus triflora, Quercus, Vaccinium*, etc. The *Cypripedium* not due till to-morrow. Then we diverged to the brook, where was

Viburnum dentatum, Arrow-wood. But his attention was drawn to the redstart which flew about with its *cheap, cheap chevet*, and presently to two fine grosbeaks, rose-breasted, whose brilliant scarlet "bids the rash gazer wipe his eye," and which he brought nearer with his spyglass, and whose fine, clear note he compares to that of a "tanager who has got rid of his hoarseness." Then he heard a note which he calls that of the night-warbler, a bird he has never identified, has been in search of for twelve years, which, always, when he sees it, is in the act of diving down into a tree or bush, and which 't is vain to seek; the only bird that sings indifferently by night and by day. I told him, he must beware of finding and booking him, lest life should have nothing more to show him. He said, "What you seek in vain for half your life, one day you come full upon—all the family at dinner. You seek him like a dream, and as soon as you find him, you become his prey." He thinks he could tell by the flowers what day of the month it is, within two days. . . .

Water is the first gardener: he always plants grasses and flowers about his dwelling. There came Henry with music-book under his arm, to press flowers in; with telescope in his pocket, to see the birds, and microscope to count stamens; with a diary, jack-knife, and twine; in stout shoes, and strong grey trousers, ready to brave the shrub-oaks and smilax, and to climb the tree for a hawk's nest. His strong legs, when he wades, were no insignificant part of his armour. —Journal, May 21, 1856[217]

The finest day, the high noon of the year, went with Thoreau in a wagon to Perez Blood's auction. . . .

Henry told his story of the *Ephemera*, the manna of the fishes, which falls like a snowstorm one day in the year, only on this river [the Assabet], not on the Concord, high up in the air as he can see, and blundering down to the river (the shad-fly), the true angler's fly; the fish die of repletion when it comes, the kingfishers wait for their prey.

—Journal, June 2, 1856[218]

I go for those who have received a retaining fee to this party of Freedom, before they came into this world. I would trust Garrison, I would trust Henry Thoreau, that they would make no compromises.

—Journal, June 1856[219]

A walk around Conantum with Henry Thoreau. . . .
Henry expiated on the omniscience of the Indians.

—Journal, August 8, 1856[220]

If you talk with J.K. Mills, or J.M. Forbes, or any other State Street man, you find that you are talking with all State Street, and if you are impressionable to that force, why, they have great advantage, are very strong men. But if you talk with Thoreau or Newcomb, or Alcott, you talk with only one man; he brings only his own force.

—Journal, September 1856[221]

Thoreau says, that when he wakes in the morning, he finds a thought already in his mind, waiting for him. The ground is preoccupied.   —Notebook[222]

Walk yesterday, first day of May, with Henry Thoreau to Goose Pond, and to the "Red chokeberry Lane." . . . From a white birch, Henry cut a strip of bark to show how a naturalist would make the best box to carry a plant or other specimen requiring care, and thought the woodman would make a better hat of birch-bark than of felt,—hat, with cockade of lichens thrown in. I told him the Birkebeiners of the Heimskringla had been before him.

We will make a book on walking, 't is certain, and have easy lessons for beginners. "Walking in ten Lessons."

—Journal, May 2, 1857[223]

Henry thinks that planting acres of barren land by running a furrow every four feet across the field, with a plough, and following it with a planter, supplied with pine seed, would be lucrative. He proposes to plant my Wyman lot so. Go in September, and gather white-pine cones with a hook at the end of a long pole, and let them dry and open in a chamber at home. Add acorns, and birch-seed, and pitch-pines. He thinks it would be profitable to buy cheap land, and plant it so.　　　—Journal, May 30, 1857[224]

Henry praises Bigelow's description of plants: but knows sixty plants not recorded in his edition of Bigelow (1840).

—Journal, June 9, 1857[225]

On Sunday (June 6) on our walk along the river-bank, the air was full of the ephemerides, which Henry celebrates as the manna of the fishes.　　　—Journal, June 9, 1857[226]

On my return from England in 1848 he [Charles Bartlett] had bought some grass in my meadow of Henry D. Thoreau and had got it away contrary to agreement without paying. Henry Thoreau was vexed at this and I went to Mr. Hoar senior and asked him to collect the money which I think was $20. George Heywood was then in Mr. Hoar's office, and did soon after collect it and pay me.

One day, I met Bartlett and told him we would, if he liked, go over the bounds, and mark them anew at our common expense. He agreed to it. I was going one day with Thoreau to the lot, for the purpose of marking the Lincoln line through my lot. We stopped at Bartlett's house, and proposed to him to go now with us, and let Mr. Thoreau as surveyor, find or refind and mark anew the old bounds between us. He consented. Then Thoreau said, he would not go (if it were a joint expense) until Bartlett should pay his part, since Bartlett had cheated him in the matter of the grass. Bartlett then said, he would never pay for any work until it was done. So we left him at home, and Thoreau went with me and surveyed the Lincoln line through my lot.

—Journal, June 17, 1857[227]

Henry said of the railroad whistle, that Nature had made up her mind not to hear it, she knew better than to wake up: and, "The fact you tell is of no value, 't is only the impression."   —Journal, September 4, 1857[228]

Henry avoids commonplace, and talks birch bark to all comers, reduces them all to the same insignificance.

—Journal, Fall 1857[229]

Wonders of arnica. I must surely see the plant growing. Where's Henry?   —Journal, Fall 1857[230]

Mr. Thoreau met your New Bedford Rev. Mr. Thomas, at my house, last evening. The naturalist was in the perfect spirits habitual to him, and the minister courteous as ever, and, as it happened, cognisant of the Cape, and of Henry's travels thereon. I am bound to be specially sensible of Henry Thoreau's merits, as he has just now by better surveying quite innocently made 60 rods of woodland for me, and left the adjacent lot, which he was measuring, larger than the deed gave it. There's a surveyor for you!

—Emerson to Daniel Ricketson,
January 10, 1858[231]

The question is,—Have you got the interesting facts? That yours have cost you time and labor, and that you are a person of wonderful parts, and of wonderful fame, in the society or town in which you live, is nothing to the purpose. Society is a respecter of persons, but Nature is not. 'T is fatal that I do not care a rush for all you have recorded, cannot read it, if I should try. Henry Thoreau says, "The Indians know better natural history than you, they with their type fish, and fingers the sons of hands."

—Journal, January 1858[232]

I found Henry yesterday in my woods. He thought nothing to be hoped from you, if this bit of mould under your feet was not sweeter to you to eat than any other in this world, or in any world. We talked of the willows. He says, 't is impossible to tell when they push the bud (which so marks the arrival of spring) out of its dark scales. It is done and doing all winter. It is begun in the previous autumn. It seems one steady push from autumn to spring.

I say, how divine these studies! Here there is no taint of mortality. How aristocratic, and of how defiant a beauty! This is the garden of Edelweissen.

—Journal, January, 1858[233]

Yesterday with Henry Thoreau at the Pond....

I hear the account of a man who lives in the wilderness of Maine with respect, but with despair. It needs the doing hand to make the seeing eye, and my imbecile hands leave me always helpless and ignorant, after so many years in the country. The beauty of the spectacle I fully feel, but 't is strange that, more than the miracle of the plant and animal, is the impression of mere mass of broken land and water, say a mountain, precipices, and waterfalls, or the ocean-side, and stars. These affect us more than anything except men and women. But neither is Henry's hermit, forty-five miles from the nearest house, important, until we know what he is now, what he thinks of it on his return, and after a year. Perhaps he has found it foolish and wasteful to spend a tenth or twentieth of his active life with a muskrat and fried fishes. I tell him that a man was not made to live in a swamp, but a frog. If God meant him to live in a swamp, he would have made him a frog.

The charm which Henry uses for bird and frog and mink, is Patience. They will not come to him, or show him aught, until he becomes a log among the logs, sitting still for hours in the same place; then they come around him and to him, and show themselves at home.

—Journal, May 11, 1858[234]

John Brown shows us, said Henry Thoreau, another school to send our boys to,—that the best lesson of oratory is to speak the truth. A lesson rarely learned—to stand by the truth. —Journal, Fall 1859[235]

I understand that there is some doubt about Mr. Douglass's keeping his engagement for Tuesday next. If there is a vacancy, I think you cannot do a greater public good than to send for Mr. Thoreau, who has read last night here a discourse on the history and character of Captain John Brown, which ought to be heard or read by every man in the Republic.

—Emerson to Charles W. Slack,
October 31, 1859[236]

Agassiz says, "There are no varieties in nature. All are species." Thoreau says, "If Agassiz sees two thrushes so alike that they bother the ornithologist to discriminate them, he insists they are two species; but if he see Humboldt and Fred Cogswell, he insists they come from one ancestor."

—Journal, April 1860[237]

Came out at Captain Barrett's and through the fields again out at Flint's.

A cornucopia of golden joys. Ellery Channing says that he and Henry Thoreau have agreed that the only reason of turning out of the mowing is not to hurt the feelings of the farmers; but it never does, if they are out of sight. For the farmers have no imagination. And it does n't do a bit of hurt. Thoreau says that when he goes surveying, the farmer leads him straight through the grass.

—Journal, September 11, 1860[238]

Thoreau's page remind me of Farley, who went early into the wilderness in Illinois, lived alone, and hewed down trees, and tilled the land, but retired again into newer country when the population came up with him. Yet, on being asked what he was doing, he pleased himself that he was preparing the land for civilization.

—Journal, January 1861[239]

Thoreau forgot himself once.   —Journal, January 1861[240]

All the music, Henry Thoreau says, is in the strain; the tune don't signify, 't is all one vibration of the string. He says, people sing a song, or play a tune, only for one strain that is in it. I don't understand this, and remind him that collocation makes the force of a word, and that Wren's rule, "*Position essential to beauty*," is universally true, but accept what I know of the doctrine of leasts.   —Journal, 1861[241]

I often say to young writers and speakers that their best masters are their fault-finding brothers and sisters at home, who will not spare them, but be sure to pick and cavil, and tell the odious truth. It is smooth mediocrity, weary elegance, surface finish of our voluminous stock-writers, or respectable artists, which easy times and a dull public call out, without any salient genius, with an indigence of all grand design, of all direct power. A hundred statesmen, historians, painters, and small poets are thus made: but Burns, and Carlyle, and Bettine, and Michel Angelo, and Thoreau were pupils in a rougher school.

—Journal, February 1861[242]

Lately I find myself oft recurring to the experience of the partiality of each mind I know. I so readily imputed symmetry to my fine geniuses, or perceiving their excellence in some insight. How could I doubt that Thoreau, that Charles Newcomb, that Alcott, or that Henry James, as I successively met them, was the master-mind, which, in some act, he appeared. No, he was only master-mind in that particular act. He could repeat the like stroke a million times, but, in new conditions, he was inexpert, and in new company, he was dumb.   —Journal, October 1861[243]

As we live longer, it looks as if our company were picked out to die first, and we live on in a lessening minority. . . . I am ever threatened by the decay of Henry Thoreau.

—Journal, January 1862[244]

Thoreau. Perhaps his fancy for Walt Whitman grew out of his taste for wild nature, for an otter, a woodchuck, or a loon. He loved sufficiency, hate a sum that would not prove; loved Walt and hated Alcott.

—Journal, February 1862[245]

Alek Therien came to see Thoreau on business, but Thoreau at once perceived that he had been drinking, and advised him to go home and cut his throat, and that speedily. Therien did not well know what to make of it, but went away, and Thoreau said he learned that he had been repeating it about town, which he was glad to hear, and hoped that by this time he had begun to understand what it meant.

—Journal, February 1862[246]

Oliver Wendell Holmes came out late in life with a strong sustained growth for two or three years, like old pear trees which have done nothing for ten years, and at last begin and grow great. The Lowells came forward slowly, and Henry Thoreau remarks that men may have two growths like pears. —Journal, March 1862[247]

The snow lies even with the tops of the walls across the Walden road, and, this afternoon, I waded through the woods to my grove. A chickadee came out to greet me. . . . Thoreau tells me that they are very sociable with wood-choppers, and will take crumbs from their hands.

—Journal, March 3, 1862[248]

Sam Staples yesterday had been to see Henry Thoreau. Never spent an hour with more satisfaction. Never saw a man dying with so much pleasure and peace. Thinks that very few men in Concord know Mr. Thoreau; finds him serene and happy.

Henry praised to me lately the manners of an old, established, calm, well-behaved river, as perfectly distinguished from those of a new river. A new river is a torrent; an old one slow and steadily supplied. What happens in any part of the old river relates to what befals in every other part of it. 'T is full of compensations, resources, and reserved funds. —Journal, March 24, 1862[249]

Yesterday I walked across Walden Pond. To-day I walked across it again. I fancied it was late in the season to do thus; but Mr. Thoreau told me, this afternoon, that he has known the ice hold to the 18th of April.

—Journal, April 2, 1862[250]

Heard the purple finch this morning, for the first time this season. Henry Thoreau told me he found the Blue Snowbird (*Fringilla hiemalis*) on Monadnoc, where it breeds.

—Journal, April 16, 1862[251]

Henry Thoreau remains erect, calm, self-subsistent, before me, and I read him not only truly in his Journal, but he is not long out of mind when I walk, and, as to-day, row upon the pond. He chose wisely no doubt for himself to be the bachelor of thought and nature that he was,—how near to the old monks in their ascetic religion! He had no talent for wealth, and knew how to be poor without the least hint of squalor or inelegance. Perhaps he fell—all of us do—into his way of living, without forecasting it much, but approved and confirmed it with later wisdom.

—Journal, June 1862[252]

He loved the sweet fragrance of Melilot.

—Journal, June 1862[253]

He is very sensible of the odor of waterlilies.

—Journal, June 1862[254]

If there is a little strut in the style, it is only from a vigor in excess of the size of his body.   —Journal, June 1862[255]

I see many generals without a command, besides Henry.

—Journal, June 1862[256]

Henry Thoreau fell in Tuckerman's Ravine, at Mount Washington, and sprained his foot. As he was in the act of getting up from his fall, he saw for the first time the leaves of the *Arnica Mollis!* the exact balm for his wound.

—Journal, June 1862[257]

By what direction did Henry entirely escape any influence of Swedenborg? I do not remember ever hearing him name Swedenborg. —Journal, June 1862[258]

If we should ever print Henry's journals, you may look for a plentiful crop of naturalists. Young men of sensibility must fall an easy prey to the charming of Pan's pipe.

—Journal, June 1862[259]

I wish Thoreau had not died before you came. He was an interesting study. . . . Henry often reminded me of an animal in human form. He had the eye of a bird, the scent of a dog, the most acute, delicate intelligence—but no soul. No . . . Henry could not have had a human soul.

—Emerson to Rebecca Harding Davis[260]

I have never recorded a fact, which perhaps ought to have gone into my sketch of "Thoreau," that, on the 1st August, 1844, when I read my Discourse on Emancipation [in the British West Indies], in the Town Hall, in Concord, and the selectmen would not direct the sexton to ring the meeting-house bell, Henry went himself, and rung the bell at the appointed hour. —Journal, April–May 1863[261]

In reading Henry Thoreau's Journal, I am very sensible of the vigor of his constitution. That oaken strength which I noted whenever he walked, or worked, or surveyed wood-lots, the same unhesitating hand with which a field-laborer accosts a piece of work, which I should shun as a waste of strength, Henry shows in his literary task. He has muscle, and ventures on and performs feats which I am forced to decline. In reading him, I find the same thought, the same spirit that is in me, but he takes a step beyond, and illustrates by excellent images that which I should have conveyed in a sleepy generality. 'T is as if I went into a gymnasium, and saw youths leap, climb, and swing with a force unapproachable,— though their feats are only continuations of my initial grapplings and jumps. —Journal, June 1863[262]

See in politics the importance of minorities of one.... Silent minorities of one also, Thoreau, Very, Newcomb, Alcott.... Christianity existed in one child. —Journal, July 1863[263]

State your opinion affirmatively and without apology. Why need you, who are not a gossip, talk as a gossip, and tell eagerly what the Journals, or Mr. Sumner, or Mr. Stanton, say? The attitude is the main thing. John Bradshaw was all his life a consul sitting in judgment on kings. Carlyle has, best of all men in England, kept the manly attitude in his time. His errors of opinion are as nothing in comparison with this merit, in my opinion. And, if I look for a counterpart in my neighbourhood, Thoreau and Alcott are the best, and in majesty Alcott exceeds. This *aplomb* cannot be mimicked. It is the speaking to the heart of the thing.
—Journal, October 1863[264]

Thoreau thought none of his acquaintances dare walk with a patch on the knee of his trousers to the Concord Post-Office. —Journal, 1863[265]

And I remember that Thoreau, with his robust will, yet found certain trifles disturbing the delicacy of that health which composition exacted,—namely, the slightest irregularity, even to the drinking too much water on the preceding day.   —"Inspiration"[266]

I see the Thoreau poison working today in many valuable lives, in some for good, in some for harm.
                                                —Journal, 1864[267]

Among "Resources," too, might be set down that rule of my travelling friend, "When I estimated the costs of my tour in Europe, I added a couple of hundreds to the amount, to be cheated of, and gave myself no more uneasiness when I was overcharged here or there."

So Thoreau's practice to put a hundred seeds into every melon hill, instead of eight or ten.
                                    —Journal, September 1864[268]

Thoreau was with difficulty sweet.
                                    —Journal, September 1864[269]

I am sure he is entitled to stand quite alone on his proper merits. There might easily have been a little influence from his neighbors on his first writings: He was not quite out of college, I believe, when I first saw him: but it is long since I, and I think all who knew him, felt that he was the most independent of men in thought and in action.
                                —Emerson to James Bradley Thayer,
                                                August 25, 1865[270]

When Henry Thoreau in his tramp with his companion came to a field of good grass, and his companion hesitated about crossing it, Henry said, "You may cross it, if the farmer is not in sight: it does not hurt the grass, but only the farmer's feelings."   —Journal, 1868[271]

How dangerous is criticism. My brilliant friend cannot see any healthy power in Thoreau's thoughts. At first I suspect, of course, that he oversees me, who admire Thoreau's power. But when I meet again fine perceptions in Thoreau's papers, I see that there is defect in his critic that he should undervalue them. Thoreau writes, in his *Field Notes*, "I look back for the era of this creation not into the night, but to a dawn for which no man ever rose early enough." A fine example of his affirmative genius.   —Journal, February 1870[272]

Henry Thoreau was well aware of his stubborn contradictory attitude into which almost any conversation threw him, and said in the woods, "When I die, you will find swamp oak written on my heart." I got his words from Ellery Channing today.   —Journal, April–June 1870[273]

Plutarch loves apples like our Thoreau, and well praises them.   —Journal, 1870[274]

I delight ever in having to do with the drastic class, the men who can do things. . . . Such was Thoreau.
                    —Journal, November 30, 1870[275]

I think highly of Thoreau. He is now read by a limited number of men and women, but by very ardent ones. They were dissatisfied with my notice of him in the *Atlantic* after his death: they did not want me to place any bounds to his genius. He came to me a young man, but was so popular with young people that he quite superseded his old master. But now and then I come across a man that scoffs at Thoreau and thinks he is affected. For example, Mr. James Russell Lowell is constantly making flings at him. I have tried to show him that Thoreau did things that no one could have done without high powers; but to no purpose. I am surprised to hear that you have read Thoreau. Neither his books nor mine are much read in the South, I suppose. . . .

Thoreau was unacquainted with the technical names of plants when I first knew him. On my telling him the name of a flower, he remarked that he should never see the *flower* again, for if he met it he would be able only to see the *name*. He, however, afterward became quite accurate in botany. His cabin, or hut, stood on this very spot. There is a pious mark (a cross) on that tree which indicates the place. I don't know who made the mark: I did not. Daily before taking his walk he would examine his diary to see what flowers should be out. His hut was in full view of Walden Pond: these trees here have grown up since then. He could run out on awaking and leap right into the water, which he did every morning. —Emerson to Pendleton King,

June 1870[276]

How vain to praise our literature, when its really superior minds are quite omitted, and utterly unknown to the public. . . . Thoreau quite unappreciated, though his books have been opened and superficially read.

—Journal, October–November 1871[277]

Henry Thoreau we all remember as a man of genius, and of marked character, known to our farmers as the most skilfull of surveyors, and indeed better acquainted with their forests and meadows and trees than themselves, but more widely known as the writer of some of the best books which have been written in this country, and which, I am persuaded, have not yet gathered half their fame. He, too, was an excellent reader. No man would have rejoiced more than he in the event of this day.

—"Address at the Opening of the
Concord Free Public Library"[278]

There was something fine in Thoreau. I have tried to convince Lowell, Longfellow, and Judge Hoar of this. . . . He has left behind him much manuscript on natural history, beautiful and as fine as Linnæus; but I get no encouragement from the publishers to bring it out. From Thoreau might be collected a book of proverbs or sentences that would charm the Hindoos. . . .

Thoreau once took charge of my garden, and on the occasion of a visit from Theodore Parker I sent Thoreau to the station for him, hoping that he would like Parker; but he did not, and expressed a contempt for the man. Haughtiness of manner was frequently a characteristic of Thoreau.

—Emerson to Pendleton King,
Spring 1875[279]

I can well understand that he should vex tender persons by his conversation, but his books, I confide, must and will find a multitude of readers.

—Emerson to Harrison Gray Otis Blake,
December 7, 1876[280]

I have to thank you for the very friendly notice of myself which I find in your monthly magazine, which I ought to have acknowledged some days ago. The tone of it is courtly and kind, and suggests that the writer is no stranger to Boston and its scholars. In one or two hints, he seems to me to have been misinformed. The only pain he gives me is in his estimate of Thoreau, whom he underrates. Thoreau was a superior genius. I read his books and manuscripts always with new surprise at the range of his topics and the novelty and depth of his thought. A man of large reading, of quick perception, of great practical courage and ability,—who grew greater every day, and, had his short life been prolonged, would have found few equals to the power and wealth of his mind.

—Emerson to George Stewart, Jr.,
January 22, 1877[281]

Thoreau[282]

Henry David Thoreau was the last male descendant of a French ancestor who came to this country from the Isle of Guernsey. His character exhibited occasional traits drawn from this blood, in singular combination with a very strong Saxon genius.

He was born in Concord, Massachusetts, on the 12th of July, 1817. He was graduated at Harvard College in 1837, but without any literary distinction. An iconoclast in literature, he seldom thanked colleges for their service to him, holding them in small esteem, whilst yet his debt to them was important. After leaving the University, he joined his brother in teaching a private school, which he soon renounced. His father was a manufacturer of lead-pencils, and Henry applied himself for a time to this craft, believing he could make a better pencil than was then in use. After completing his experiments, he exhibited his work to chemists and artists in Boston, and having obtained their certificates to its excellence and to its equality with the best London manufacture, he returned home contented. His friends congratulated him that he had now opened his way to fortune. But he replied that he should never make another pencil. "Why should I? I would not do again what I have done once." He resumed his endless walks and miscellaneous studies, making every day some new acquaintance with Nature, though as yet never speaking of zoölogy or botany, since, though very studious of natural facts, he was incurious of technical and textual science.

At this time, a strong, healthy youth, fresh from college, whilst all his companions were choosing their profession, or eager to begin some lucrative employment, it was inevitable that his thoughts should be exercised on the same question, and it required a rare decision to refuse all the accustomed paths and keep his solitary freedom at the cost of disappointing the natural expectations of his family and friends: all the more difficult that he had a perfect probity, was exact in securing his own independence, and in holding every man to the like duty. But Thoreau never faltered. He was a born protestant. He declined to give up his large ambition of knowledge and action for any narrow craft or profession, aiming at a much more comprehensive calling, the art of living well. If he slighted and defied the opinions of others, it was only that he was more intent to reconcile his practice with his own belief. Never idle or self-indulgent, he preferred, when he wanted money, earning it by some piece of manual labor agreeable to him, as building a boat or a fence, planting, grafting, surveying or other short work, to any long engagements. With his hardy habits and few wants, his skill in wood-craft, and his powerful arithmetic, he was very competent to live in any part of the world. It would cost him less to supply his wants than another. He was therefore secure of his leisure.

A natural skill for mensuration, growing out of his mathematical knowledge and his habit of ascertaining the measures and distances of objects which interested him, the size of trees, the depth and extent of ponds and rivers, the height of mountains and the air-line distance of his favorite summits,—this, and his intimate knowledge of the territory about Concord, made him drift into the profession of land-surveyor. It had the advantage for him that it led him continually into new and secluded grounds, and helped his studies of Nature. His accuracy and skill in his work were readily appreciated, and he found all the employment he wanted.

He could easily solve the problems of the surveyor, but he was daily beset with graver questions, which he manfully confronted. He interrogated every custom, and wished to settle all his practice on an ideal foundation. He was a protestant *à l'outrance*, and few lives contain so many renunciations. He was bred to no profession; he never married; he lived alone; he never went to church; he never voted; he refused to pay a tax to the State; he ate no flesh; he drank no wine; he never knew the use of tobacco; and though a naturalist, he used neither trap nor gun. He chose, wisely no doubt for himself, to be the bachelor of thought and Nature. He had no talent for wealth, and knew how to be poor without the least hint of squalor or inelegance. Perhaps he fell into his way of living without forecasting it much, but approved it with later wisdom. "I am often reminded," he wrote in his journal, "that if I had bestowed on me the wealth of Crœsus, my aims must be still the same." He had no temptations to fight against,—no appetites, no passions, no taste for elegant trifles. A fine house, dress, the manners and talk of highly cultivated people were all thrown away on him. He much preferred a good Indian, and considered these refinements as impediments to conversation, wishing to meet his companion on the simplest terms. He declined invitations to dinner-parties, because there each was in every one's way, and he could not meet the individuals to any purpose. "They make their pride," he said, "in making their dinner cost much; I make my pride in making my dinner cost little." When asked at table what dish he preferred, he answered, "The nearest." He did not like the taste of wine, and never had a vice in his life. He said,—"I have a faint recollection of pleasure derived from smoking dried lily-stems, before I was a man. I had commonly a supply of these. I have never smoked anything more noxious."

He chose to be rich by making his wants few, and supplying them himself. In his travels, he used the railroad only to get over so much country as was unimportant to the present purpose, walking hundreds of miles, avoiding taverns, buying a lodging in farmers' and fishermen's houses, as cheaper, and more agreeable to him, and because there he could better find the men and the information he wanted.

There was somewhat military in his nature, not to be subdued, always manly and able, but rarely tender, as if he did not feel himself except in opposition. He wanted a fallacy to expose, a blunder to pillory, I may say required a little sense of victory, a roll of the drum, to call his powers into full exercise. It cost him nothing to say No; indeed he found it much easier than to say Yes. It seemed as if his first instinct on hearing a proposition was to controvert it, so impatient was he of the limitations of our daily thought. This habit, of course, is a little chilling to the social affections; and though the companion would in the end acquit him of any malice or untruth, yet it mars conversation. Hence, no equal companion stood in affectionate relations with one so pure and guileless. "I love Henry," said one of his friends, "but I cannot like him; and as for taking his arm, I should as soon think of taking the arm of an elm-tree."

Yet, hermit and stoic as he was, he was really fond of sympathy, and threw himself heartily and childlike into the company of young people whom he loved, and whom he delighted to entertain, as he only could, with the varied and endless anecdotes of his experiences by field and river: and he was always ready to lead a huckleberry-party or a search for chestnuts or grapes. Talking, one day, of a public discourse, Henry remarked that whatever succeeded with the audience was bad. I said, "Who would not like to write something which all can read, like 'Robinson Crusoe?' and who does not see with regret that his page is not solid with a right materialistic treatment, which delights everybody?" Henry objected, of course, and vaunted the better lectures which reached only a few persons. But, at supper, a young girl, understanding that he was to lecture at the Lyceum, sharply asked him, "Whether his lecture would be a nice, interesting story, such as she wished to hear, or whether it was one of those old philosophical things that she did not care about." Henry turned to her, and bethought himself, and, I saw, was trying to believe that he had matter that might fit her and her brother, who were to sit up and go to the lecture, if it was a good one for them.

He was a speaker and actor of the truth,—born such,—and was ever running into dramatic situations from this cause. In any circumstance it interested all bystanders to know what part Henry would take, and what he would say; and he did not disappoint expectation, but used an original judgment on each emergency. In 1845 he built himself a small framed house on the shores of Walden Pond, and lived there two years alone, a life of labor and study. This action was quite native and fit for him. No one who knew him would tax him with affectation. He was more unlike his neighbors in his thought than in his action. As soon as he had exhausted the advantages of that solitude, he abandoned it. In 1847, not approving some uses to which the public expenditure was applied, he refused to pay his town tax, and was put in jail. A friend paid the tax for him, and he was released. The like annoyance was threatened the next year. But as his friends paid the tax, notwithstanding his protest, I believe he ceased to resist. No opposition or ridicule had any weight with him. He coldly and fully stated his opinion without affecting to believe that it was the opinion of the company. It was of no consequence if every one present held the opposite opinion. On one occasion he went to the University Library to procure some books. The librarian refused to lend them. Mr. Thoreau repaired to the President, who stated to him the rules and usages, which permitted the loan of books to resident graduates, to clergymen who were alumni, and to some others resident within a circle of ten miles' radius from the College. Mr. Thoreau explained to the President that the railroad had destroyed the old scale of distances,—that the library was useless, yes, and President and College useless, on the terms of his rules,—that the one benefit he owed to the College was its library,—that, at this moment, not only his want of books was imperative, but he wanted a large number of books, and assured him that he, Thoreau, and not the librarian, was the proper custodian of these. In short, the President found the petitioner so formidable, and the rules getting to look so ridiculous, that he ended by giving him a privilege which in his hands proved unlimited thereafter.

No truer American existed than Thoreau. His preference of his country and condition was genuine, and his aversion from English and European manners and tastes almost reached contempt. He listened impatiently to news or *bonmots* gleaned from London circles; and though he tried to be civil, these anecdotes fatigued him. The men were all imitating each other, and on a small mould. Why can they not live as far apart as possible, and each be a man by himself? What he sought was the most energetic nature; and he wished to go to Oregon, not to London. "In every part of Great Britain," he wrote in his diary, "are discovered traces of the Romans, their funereal urns, their camps, their roads, their dwellings. But New England, at least, is not based on any Roman ruins. We have not to lay the foundations of our houses on the ashes of a former civilization."

But idealist as he was, standing for abolition of slavery, abolition of tariffs, almost for abolition of government, it is needless to say he found himself not only unrepresented in actual politics, but almost equally opposed to every class of reformers. Yet he paid the tribute of his uniform respect to the Anti-Slavery party. One man, whose personal acquaintance he had formed, he honored with exceptional regard. Before the first friendly word had been spoken for Captain John Brown, he sent notices to most houses in Concord that he would speak in a public hall on the condition and character of John Brown, on Sunday evening, and invited all people to come. The Republican Committee, the Abolitionist Committee, sent him word that it was premature and not advisable. He replied, "I did not send to you for advice, but to announce that I am to speak." The hall was filled at an early hour by people of all parties, and his earnest eulogy of the hero was heard by all respectfully, by many with a sympathy that surprised themselves.

It was said of Plotinus that he was ashamed of his body, and 't is very likely he had good reason for it,—that his body was a bad servant, and he had not skill in dealing with the material world, as happens often to men of abstract intellect. But Mr. Thoreau was equipped with a most adapted and serviceable body. He was of short stature, firmly built, of light complexion, with strong, serious blue eyes, and a grave aspect,—his face covered in the late years with a becoming beard. His senses were acute, his frame well-knit and hardy, his hands strong and skilful in the use of tools. And there was a wonderful fitness of body and mind. He could pace sixteen rods more accurately than another man could measure them with rod and chain. He could find his path in the woods at night, he said, better by his feet than his eyes. He could estimate the measure of a tree very well by his eye; he could estimate the weight of a calf or a pig, like a dealer. From a box containing a bushel or more of loose pencils, he could take up with his hands fast enough just a dozen pencils at every grasp. He was a good swimmer, runner, skater, boatman, and would probably outwalk most countrymen in a day's journey. And the relation of body to mind was still finer than we have indicated. He said he wanted every stride his legs made. The length of his walk uniformly made the length of his writing. If shut up in the house he did not write at all.

He has a strong common sense, like that which Rose Flammock, the weaver's daughter in Scott's romance, commends in her father, as resembling a yardstick, which, whilst it measures dowlas and diaper, can equally well measure tapestry and cloth of gold. He had always a new resource. When I was planting forest trees, and had procured half a peck of acorns, he said that only a small portion of them would be sound, and proceeded to examine them and select the sound ones. But finding this took time, he said, "I think if you put them all into water the good ones will sink;" which experiment we tried with success. He could plan a garden or a house or a barn; would have been competent to lead a "Pacific Exploring Expedition;" could give judicious counsel in the gravest private or public affairs. He lived for the day, not cumbered and mortified by his memory. If he brought you yesterday a new proposition, he would bring you to-day another not less revolutionary. A very industrious man, and setting, like all highly organized men, a high value on his time, he seemed the only man of leisure in town, always ready for any excursion that promised well, or for conversation prolonged into late hours. His trenchant sense was never stopped by his rules of daily prudence, but was always up to the new occasion. He liked and used the simplest food, yet, when some one urged a vegetable diet, Thoreau thought all diets a very small matter, saying that "the man who shoots the buffalo lives better than the man who boards at the Graham House." He said,—"You can sleep near the railroad, and never be disturbed: Nature knows very well what sounds are worth attending to, and has made up her mind not to hear the railroad-whistle. But things respect the devout mind, and a mental ecstasy was never interrupted." He noted what repeatedly befell him, that, after receiving from a distance a rare plant, he would presently find the same in his own haunts. And those pieces of luck which happen only to good players happened to him. One day, walking with a stranger, who inquired where Indian arrowheads could be found, he replied, "Everywhere," and, stooping forward, picked one on the instant from the ground. At Mount Washington, in Tuckerman's Ravine, Thoreau had a bad fall, and sprained his foot. As he was in the act of getting up from his fall, he saw for the first time the leaves of the *Arnica mollis*.

His robust common sense, armed with stout hands, keen perceptions and strong will, cannot yet account for the superiority which shone in his simple and hidden life. I must add the cardinal fact, that there was an excellent wisdom in him, proper to a rare class of men, which showed him the material world as a means and symbol. This discovery, which sometimes yields to poets a certain casual and interrupted light, serving for the ornament of their writing, was in him an unsleeping insight; and whatever faults or obstructions of temperament might cloud it, he was not disobedient to the heavenly vision. In his youth, he said, one day, "The other world is all my art; my pencils will draw no other; my jack-knife will cut nothing else; I do not use it as a means." This was the muse and genius that ruled his opinions, conversation, studies, work and course of life. This made him a searching judge of men. At first glance he measured his companion, and, though insensible to some fine traits of culture, could very well report his weight and caliber. And this made the impression of genius which his conversation sometimes gave.

He understood the matter in hand at a glance, and saw the limitations and poverty of those he talked with, so that nothing seemed concealed from such terrible eyes. I have repeatedly known young men of sensibility converted in a moment to the belief that this was the man they were in search of, the man of men, who could tell them all they should do. His own dealing with them was never affectionate, but superior, didactic, scorning their petty ways,—very slowly conceding, or not conceding at all, the promise of his society at their houses, or even at his own. "Would he not walk with them?" "He did not know. There was nothing so important to him as his walk; he had no walks to throw away on company." Visits were offered him from respectful parties, but he declined them. Admiring friends offered to carry him at their own cost to the Yellowstone River,—to the West Indies,—to South America. But though nothing could be more grave or considered than his refusals, they remind one, in quite new relations, of that fop Brummel's reply to the gentleman who offered him his carriage in a shower, "But where will *you* ride, then?"—and what accusing silences, and what searching and irresistible speeches, battering down all defences, his companions can remember!

Mr. Thoreau dedicated his genius with such entire love to the fields, hills and waters of his native town, that he made them known and interesting to all reading Americans, and to people over the sea. The river on whose banks he was born and died he knew from its springs to its confluence with the Merrimack. He had made summer and winter observations on it for many years, and at every hour of the day and night. The result of the recent survey of the Water Commissioners appointed by the State of Massachusetts he had reached by his private experiments, several years earlier. Every fact which occurs in the bed, on the banks or in the air over it; the fishes, and their spawning and nests, their manners, their food; the shad-flies which fill the air on a certain evening once a year, and which are snapped at by the fishes so ravenously that many of these die of repletion; the conical heaps of small stones on the river-shallows, the huge nests of small fishes, one of which will sometimes overfill a cart; the birds which frequent the stream, heron, duck, sheldrake, loon, osprey; the snake, muskrat, otter, woodchuck and fox, on the banks; the turtle, frog, hyla and cricket, which make the banks vocal,—were all known to him, and, as it were, townsmen and fellow creatures; so that he felt an absurdity or violence in any narrative of one of these by itself apart, and still more of its dimensions on an inch-rule, or in the exhibition of its skeleton, or the specimen of a squirrel or a bird in brandy. He liked to speak of the manners of the river, as itself a lawful creature, yet with exactness, and always to an observed fact. As he knew the river, so the ponds in this region.

One of the weapons he used, more important to him than microscope or alcohol-receiver, to other investigators, was a whim which grew on him by indulgence, yet appeared in gravest statement, namely, of extolling his own town and neighborhood as the most favored center for natural observation. He remarked that the Flora of Massachusetts embraced almost all the important plants of America,—most of the oaks, most of the willows, the best pines, the ash, the maple, the beech, the nuts. He returned Kane's "Arctic Voyage" to a friend of whom he had borrowed it, with the remark, that "Most of the phenomena noted might be observed in Concord." He seemed a little envious of the Pole, for the coincident sunrise and sunset, or five minutes' day after six months: a splendid fact, which Annursnac had never afforded him. He found red snow in one of his walks, and told me that he expected to find yet the *Victoria regia* in Concord. He was the attorney of the indigenous plants, and owned to a preference of the weeds to the imported plants, as of the Indian to the civilized man, and noticed, with pleasure, that the willow-bean poles of his neighbor had grown more than his beans. "See these weeds," he said, "which have been hoed at by a million farmers all spring and summer, and yet have prevailed, and just now come out triumphant over all lanes, pastures, fields and gardens, such is their vigor. We have insulted them with low names, too,— as Pigweed, Wormwood, Chickweed, Shad-blossom." He says, "They have brave names, too,—Ambrosia, Stellaria, Amelanchier, Amaranth, etc."

I think his fancy for referring everything to the meridian of Concord did not grow out of any ignorance or depreciation of other longitudes or latitudes, but was rather a playful expression of his conviction of the indifferency of all places, and that the best place for each is where he stands. He expressed it once in this wise: "I think nothing is to be hoped from you, if this bit of mould under your feet is not sweeter to you to eat than any other in this world, or in any world."

The other weapon with which he conquered all obstacles in science was patience. He knew how to sit immovable, a part of the rock he rested on, until the bird, the reptile, the fish, which had retired from him, should come back and resume its habits, nay, moved by curiosity, should come to him and watch him.

It was a pleasure and a privilege to walk with him. He knew the country like a fox or a bird, and passed through it as freely by paths of his own. He knew every track in the snow or on the ground, and what creature had taken this path before him. One must submit abjectly to such a guide, and the reward was great. Under his arm he carried an old music-book to press plants; in his pocket, his diary and pencil, a spy-glass for birds, microscope, jack-knife and twine. He wore a straw hat, stout shoes, strong gray trousers, to brave scrub-oaks and smilax, and to climb a tree for a hawk's or a squirrel's nest. He waded into the pool for the water-plants, and his strong legs were no insignificant part of his armor. On the day I speak of he looked for the Menyanthes, detected it across the wide pool, and, on examination of the florets, decided that it had been in flower five days. He drew out of his breast-pocket his diary, and read the names of all the plants that should bloom on this day, whereof he kept account as a banker when his notes fall due. The Cypripedium not due till to-morrow. He thought that, if waked up from a trance, in this swamp, he could tell by the plants what time of the year it was within two days. The redstart was flying about, and presently the fine grosbeaks, whose brilliant scarlet "makes the rash gazer wipe his eye," and whose fine clear note Thoreau compared to that of a tanager which has got rid of its hoarseness. Presently he heard a note which he called that of the night-warbler, a bird he had never identified, had been in search of twelve years, which always, when he saw it, was in the act of diving down into a tree or bush, and which it was vain to seek; the only bird which sings indifferently by night and by day. I told him he must beware of finding and booking it, lest life should have nothing more to show him. He said, "What you seek in vain for, half your life, one day you come full upon, all the family at dinner. You seek it like a dream, and as soon as you find it you become its prey."

His interest in the flower or the bird lay very deep in his mind, was connected with Nature,—and the meaning of Nature was never attempted to be defined by him. He would not offer a memoir of his observations to the Natural

History Society. "Why should I? To detach the description from its connections in my mind would make it no longer true or valuable to me: and they do not wish what belongs to it." His power of observation seemed to indicate additional senses. He saw as with a microscope, heard as with ear-trumpet, and his memory was a photographic register of all he saw and heard. And yet none knew better than he that it is not the fact that imports, but the impression or effect of the fact on your mind. Every fact lay in glory in his mind, a type of the order and beauty of the whole.

His determination on Natural History was organic. He confessed that he sometimes felt like a hound or a panther, and, if born among Indians, would have been a fell hunter. But, restrained by his Massachusetts culture, he played out the game in this mild form of botany and ichthyology. His intimacy with animals suggested what Thomas Fuller records of Butler the apiologist, that "either he had told the bees things or the bees had told him." Snakes coiled round his legs; the fishes swam into his hand, and he took them out of the water; he pulled the woodchuck out of its hole by the tail, and took the foxes under his protection from the hunters. Our naturalist had perfect magnanimity; he had no secrets: he would carry you to the heron's haunt, or even to his most prized botanical swamp,—possibly knowing that you could never find it again, yet willing to take his risks.

No college ever offered him a diploma, or a professor's chair; no academy made him its corresponding secretary, its discoverer or even its member. Perhaps these learned bodies feared the satire of his presence. Yet so much knowledge of Nature's secret and genius few others possessed; none in a more large and religious synthesis. For not a particle of respect had he to the opinions of any man or body of men, but homage solely to the truth itself; and as he discovered everywhere among doctors some leaning of courtesy, it discredited them. He grew to be revered and admired by his townsmen, who had at first known him only as an oddity. The farmers who employed him as a surveyor soon discovered his rare accuracy and skill, his knowledge of their lands, of trees, of birds, of Indian remains and the like, which enabled him to tell every farmer more than he knew before of his own farm; so that he began to feel a little as if Mr. Thoreau had better rights in his land than he. They felt, too, the superiority of character which addressed all men with a native authority.

Indian relics abound in Concord,—arrow-heads, stone chisels, pestles and fragments of pottery; and on the river-bank, large heaps of clam-shells and ashes mark spots which the savages frequented. These, and every circumstance touching the Indian, were important in his eyes. His visits to Maine were chiefly for love of the Indian. He had the satisfaction of seeing the manufacture of the bark canoe, as well as of trying his hand in its management on the rapids. He was inquisitive about the making of the stone arrow-head, and in his last days charged a youth setting out for the Rocky Mountains to find an Indian who could tell him that: "It was well worth a visit to California to learn it." Occasionally, a small party of Penobscot Indians would visit Concord, and pitch their tents for a few weeks in summer on the river-bank. He failed not to make acquaintance with the best of them; though he well knew that asking questions of Indians is like catechizing beavers and rabbits. In his last visit to Maine he had great satisfaction from Joseph Polis, an intelligent Indian of Oldtown, who was his guide for some weeks.

He was equally interested in every natural fact. The depth of his perception found likeness of law throughout Nature, and I know not any genius who so swiftly inferred universal law from the single fact. He was not pedant of a department. His eye was open to beauty, and his ear to music. He found these, not in rare conditions, but wheresoever he went. He thought the best of music was in single strains; and he found poetic suggestion in the humming of the telegraph-wire.

His poetry might be bad or good; he no doubt wanted a lyric facility and technical skill, but he had the source of poetry in his spiritual perception. He was good reader and critic, and his judgment on poetry was to the ground of it. He could not be deceived as to the presence or absence of the poetic element in any composition, and his thirst for this made him negligent and perhaps scornful of superficial graces. He would pass by many delicate rhythms, but he would have detected every live stanza or line in a volume and knew very well where to find an equal poetic charm in prose. He was so enamoured of the spiritual beauty that he held all actual written poems in very light esteem in the comparison. He admired Æschylus and Pindar; but when some one was commending them, he said that Æschylus and the Greeks, in describimng Apollo and Orpheus, had given no song, or no good one. "They ought not to have moved trees, but to have chanted to the gods such a hymn as would have sung all their old ideas out of their heads, and new ones in." His own verses are often rude and defective. The gold does not yet run pure, is drossy and crude. The thyme and marjoram are not yet honey. But if he want lyric fineness and technical merits, if he have not the poetic temperament, he never lacks the causal thought, showing that his genius was better than his talent. He knew the worth of the Imagination for the uplifting and consolation of human life, and liked to throw every thought into a symbol. The fact you tell is of no value, but only the impression. For this reason his presence was poetic, always piqued the curiosity to know more deeply the secrets of his mind. He had many reserves, an unwillingness to exhibit to profane eyes what was still sacred in his own, and knew well how to throw a poetic veil over his experience. All readers of "Walden" will remember his mythical record of his disappointments:—

> "I long ago lost a hound, a bay horse and a turtle-dove, and am still on their trail. Many are the travellers I have spoken concerning them, describing their tracks, and what calls they answered to. I have met one or two who have heard the hound, and the tramp of the horse, and even seen the dove disappear behind a cloud; and they seemed as anxious to recover them as if they had lost them themselves."

His riddles were worth the reading, and I confide that if at any time I do not understand the expression, it is yet just. Such was the wealth of his truth that it was not worth his while to use word in vain. His poem entitled "Sympathy" reveals the tenderness under that triple steel of stoicism, and the intellectual subtility it could animate. His classic poem on "Smoke" suggests Simonides, but is better than any poem of Simonides. His biography is in his verses. His habitual thought makes all his poetry a hymn to the cause of causes, the Spirit which vivifies and controls his own:—

> "I hearing get, who had but ears,
>   And sight, who had but eyes before;
>   I moments live, who lived but years,
>   And truth discern, who knew but learning's lore."

And still more in these religious lines:—

"Now chiefly is my natal hour,
And only now my prime of life;
I will not doubt the love untold,
Which not my worth nor want have bought,
Which wooed me young, and woos me old,
And to this evening hath me brought."

Whilst he used in his writings a certain petulance of remark in reference to churches or churchmen, he was a person of a rare, tender and absolute religion, a person incapable of any profanation, by act or by thought. Of course, the same isolation which belonged to his original thinking and living detached him from the social religious forms. This is neither to be censured nor regretted. Aristotle long ago explained it, when he said, "One who surpasses his fellow citizens in virtue is no longer a part of the city. Their law is not for him, since he is a law to himself."

Thoreau was sincerity itself, and might fortify the convictions of prophets in the ethical laws by his holy living. It was an affirmative experience which refused to be set aside. A truth-speaker he, capable of the most deep and strict conversation; a physician to the wounds of any soul; a friend, knowing not only the secret of friendship, but almost worshipped by those few persons who resorted to him as their confessor and prophet, and knew the deep value of his mind and great heart. He thought that without religion or devotion of some kind nothing great was ever accomplished: and he thought that the bigoted sectarian had better bear this in mind.

His virtues, of course, sometimes ran into extremes. It was easy to trace to the inexorable demand on all for exact truth that austerity which made this willing hermit more solitary even than he wished. Himself of a perfect probity, he required not less of others. He had a disgust at crime, and no worldly success could cover it. He detected paltering as readily in dignified and prosperous persons as in beggars, and with equal scorn. Such dangerous frankness was in his dealing that his admirers called him "that terrible Thoreau," as if he spoke when silent, and was still present when he had departed. I think the severity of his ideal interfered to deprive him of a healthy sufficiency of human society.

The habit of a realist to find things the reverse of their appearance inclined him to put every statement in a paradox. A certain habit of antagonism defaced his earlier writings,—a trick of rhetoric not quite outgrown in his later, of substituting for the obvious word and thought its diametrical opposite. He praised wild mountains and winter forests for their domestic air, in snow and ice he would find sultriness, and commended the wilderness for resembling Rome and Paris. "It was so dry, that you might call it wet."

The tendency to magnify the moment, to read all the laws of Nature in the one object or one combination under your eye, is of course comic to those who do not share the philosopher's perception of identity. To him there was no such thing as size. The pond was a small ocean; the Atlantic, a large Walden Pond. He referred every minute fact to cosmical laws. Though he meant to be just, he seemed haunted by a certain chronic assumption that the science of the day pretended completeness, and he had just found out that the *savans* had neglected to discriminate a particular botanical variety, had failed to describe the seeds or count the sepals. "That is to say," we replied, "the blockheads were not born in Concord; but who said they were? It was their unspeakable misfortune to be born in London, or Paris, or Rome; but, poor fellows, they did what they could, considering that they never saw Bateman's Pond, or Nine-Acre Corner, or Becky Stow's Swamp; besides, what were you sent into the world for, but to add this observation?"

Had his genius been only contemplative, he had been fitted to his life, but with his energy and practical ability he seemed born for great enterprise and for command; and I so much regret the loss of his rare powers of action, that I cannot help counting it a fault in him that he had no ambition. Wanting this, instead of engineering for all America, he was the captain of a huckleberry party. Pounding beans is good to the end of pounding empires one of these days; but if, at the end of years, it is still only beans!

But these foibles, real or apparent, were fast vanishing in the incessant growth of a spirit so robust and wise, and which effaced its defeats with new triumphs. His study of Nature was a perpetual ornament to him, and inspired his friends with curiosity to see the world through his eyes, and to hear his adventures. They possessed every kind of interest.

He had many elegancies of his own, whilst he scoffed at conventional elegance. Thus, he could not bear to hear the sound of his own steps, the grit of gravel; and therefore never willingly walked in the road, but in the grass, on mountains and in woods. His senses were acute, and he remarked that by night every dwelling-house gives out bad air, like a slaughter-house. He liked the pure fragrance of meliot. He honored certain plants with special regard, and, over all, the pond-lily,—then, the gentian, and the *Mikania scandens*, and "life-everlasting," and a bass-tree which he visited every year when it bloomed, in the middle of July. He thought the scent a more oracular inquisition than the sight,—more oracular and trustworthy. The scent, of course, reveals what is concealed from the other senses. By it he detected earthiness. He delighted in echoes, and said they were almost the only kind of kindred voices that he heard. He loved Nature so well, was so happy in her solitude, that he became very jealous of cities and the sad work which their refinements and artifices made with man and his dwelling. The axe was always destroying his forest. "Thank God," he said, "they cannot cut down the clouds!" "All kinds of figures are drawn on the blue ground with this fibrous white paint."

I subjoin a few sentences taken from his unpublished manuscripts, not only as records of his thought and feeling, but for their power of description and literary excellence:—

"Some circumstantial evidence is very strong, as when you find a trout in the milk."

"The chub is a soft fish, and tastes like boiled brown paper salted."

"The youth gets together his materials to build a bridge to the moon, or, perchance, a palace or temple on the earth, and, at length the middle-aged man concludes to build a wood-shed with them."

"The locust z-ing,"

"Devil's-needles zigzagging along the Nut-Meadow brook."

"Sugar is not so sweet to the palate as sound to the healthy ear."

"I put on some hemlock-boughs, and the rich salt crackling of their leaves was like mustard to the ear, the crackling of uncountable regiments. Dead trees love the fire."

"The bluebird carries the sky on his back."

"The tanager flies through the green foliage as if it would ignite the leaves."

"If I wish for a horse-hair for my compass-sight, I must go to the stable; but the hair-bird, with her sharp eyes, goes to the road."

"Immortal water, alive even to the superficies."

"Fire is the most tolerable third party."

"Nature made ferns for pure leaves, to show what she could do in that line."

"No tree has so fair a bole and so handsome an instep as the beech."

"How did these beautiful rainbow-tints get into the shell of the fresh-water clam, buried in the mud at the bottom of our dark river?"

"Hard are the times when the infant's shoes are second-foot."

"We are strictly confined to our men to whom we give liberty."

"Nothing is so much to be feared as fear. Atheism may comparatively be popular with God himself."

"Of what significance the things you can forget? A little thought is sexton to all the world."

"How can we expect a harvest of thought who have not had a seed-time of character?"

"Only he can be trusted with gifts who can present a face of bronze to expectations."

"I ask to be melted. You can only ask of the metals that they be tender to the fire that melts them. To nought else can they be tender."

There is a flower known to botanists, one of the same genus with our summer plant called "Life-Everlasting," a *Gnaphalium* like that, which grows on the most inaccessible cliffs of the Tyrolese mountains, where the chamois dare hardly venture, and which the hunter, tempted by its beauty, and by his love (for it is immensely valued by the Swiss maidens), climbs the cliffs to gather, and is sometimes found dead at the foot, with the flower in his hand. It is called by botanists the *Gnaphalium leontopodium*, but by the Swiss *Edelweiss*, which signifies *Noble Purity*. Thoreau seemed to me living in the hope to gather this plant, which belonged to him of right. The scale on which his studies proceeded was so large as to require longevity, and we were the less prepared for his sudden disappearance. The country knows not yet, or in the least part, how great a son it has lost. It seems an injury that he should leave in the midst his broken task which none else can finish, a kind of indignity to so noble a soul that he should depart out of Nature before yet he has been really shown to his peers for what he is. But he, at least, is content. His soul was made for the noblest society; he had in a short life exhausted the capabilities of this world; wherever there is knowledge, wherever there is virtue, wherever there is beauty, he will find a home.

Acknowledgments

A work like this could not have been made without the help of literally hundreds of people, known and unknown. Many are acknowledged below, but there are many who, I regret, have become anonymous, and for these omissions of credit I apologize. There is generosity and enthusiasm in the world for which I am appreciative, and it is rewarding to know that such dedication and passion exists.

I am indebted to the various Thoreau scholars who have donated their research to the collections of the Walden Woods Project, the Thoreau Society, and the Ralph Waldo Emerson Society. These collections, housed at the Thoreau Institute Library, Lincoln, Massachusetts, and managed by Walden Woods Project, are an invaluable and unparalleled resource, without which this book could not have been completed. And to Don Henley, founder and president of the Walden Woods Project, and to Kathi Anderson, its executive director, for their vision of a center for Thoreau studies, and for the opportunities it has offered, and the doors it has opened, thank you.

For the many chats—Tom Hersey, Whitney Retallic, and Richard Smith—colleagues who have become friends. And to the many students, scholars, and teachers I have met who have asked the questions that led me to write this book.

And my family—my daughters, Kazia and Zoë—and

my wife, Julia Berkley, my editor, my confidant, my love, my *friend*.

And to Jack Shoemaker for asking.

Grateful acknowledgment is made to the following institutions to quote from the following manuscript material:

Emerson, Ralph Waldo. Ralph Waldo Emerson Journals and Notebooks, 1820–1880, MS Am 1280H by permission of the Ralph Waldo Emerson Memorial Association and Houghton Library, Harvard University

Slack, Charles W. Ralph Waldo Emerson to Charles W. Slack, October 31, 1859, Charles W. Slack Papers, American Antiquarian Society

A Note on the Texts

Thoreau's and Emerson's texts have been minimally and silently emended in order to present the reader with a reliable reading text, unencumbered by obvious misspellings, dropped words ("Lyceum" for "the Lyceum"), and other minor slips of the pen. Punctuation, including the addition of terminal punctuation where missing from the manuscript text, or from a genetic text, has been added or emended for clarity, as has the spelling-out of abbreviations, symbols ("and" for &), and initials, or the adding of a forename or surname, for names. Stylistic policies of the various publishing houses, such as ligatures, the offsetting of quotations, periods following essay titles, have not been followed as a matter of course. For readers interested in scholarly and genetic texts of the authors' writings, please consult the editions listed in the bibliography.

Abbreviations Used in the Notes

CCE: *The Correspondence of Thomas Carlyle and Ralph Waldo Emerson, 1834–1872*. London: Chatto & Windus, 1883. 2 vols.

EJ: *Journals of Ralph Waldo Emerson: 1820–1872*. Edited by Edward Waldo Emerson and Waldo Emerson Forbes. Cambridge: Riverside Press, 1909–1914. 10 vols.

EJMN: The Journals and Miscellaneous Notebooks of Ralph Waldo Emerson. Edited by William H. Gilman et al. Cambridge: Harvard University Press, 1960–1982.

EL: *Letters of Ralph Waldo Emerson*. Edited by Ralph L. Rusk and Eleanor M. Tilton. New York: Columbia University Press, 1939, 1990–95. 10 vols.

ECW: *The Collected Works of Ralph Waldo Emerson*. Cambridge: Harvard University Press, 1971– .

ETE: Emerson, Ellen Tucker. *The Letters of Ellen Tucker Emerson*. Edited by Edith E. W. Gregg; foreword by Gay Wilson Allen. Kent, OH: Kent State University Press, 1982. 2 vols.

EW: *The Complete Works of Ralph Waldo Emerson*, with a biographical introduction and notes by Edward Waldo Emerson. Boston: Houghton, Mifflin and Company, 1903–04. 12 vols.

LJE: Emerson, Lidian Jackson. *The Selected Letters of Lidian Jackson Emerson*. Edited with an introduction by Delores Bird Carpenter. Columbia: University of Missouri Press, 1987.

TC: *The Correspondence of Henry David Thoreau.* Edited by Walter Harding and Carl Bode. New York: New York University Press, 1958.

TJ: *The Journal of Henry Thoreau.* Edited by Bradford Torrey and Francis H. Allen. Boston: Houghton Mifflin, 1906. 14 vols.

TPC: *The Correspondence of Henry D. Thoreau.* Edited by Robert N. Hudspeth. Princeton, NJ: Princeton University Press, 2013– .

TPJ: *Journal.* Edited by John C. Broderick et al. Princeton, NJ: Princeton University Press, 1981– .

TW: *The Writings of Henry D. Thoreau.* Boston: Houghton Mifflin, 1906.

Notes

Part I: Solid Seasons

1. Sanborn *Life* 128–129
2. Sanborn *Henry D. Thoreau* 59
3. Cameron *Transcendentalists* I:88
4. EW I:415
5. EW I:115
6. TJ I:37
7. EW I:89–90
8. Howard 18–19
9. Lowell *Fable* 30
10. Haskins 121–122
11. Sanborn "Unpublished Concord Journal" 834–835
12. "Thoreau's Lectures," *Worcester [Massachusetts] Daily Spy*, May 3, 1849, quoted in Dean, "Thoreau's Lectures Before Walden" 179
13. EJ VI:74
14. EL V:424
15. King 45
16. Smith, Elizabeth Oakes 140
17. EJMN V:409
18. TJ I:3
19. EJ IV:246
20. EJ III:246
21. TJ III:217
22. EJ VI:496—corrected "done" to "due" as in EJMN IX:77
23. Tilton 388
24. EJ IV:394–395
25. EJ IV:166
26. TJ I:14
27. TJ I:42–43
28. EJ V:36–37
29. EW IV:25
30. EJ IV:432

31. EJ V:208
32. EW II:76
33. EJ IV:397
34. EJ IV:406
35. EL II:182
36. Emerson *Early* III:92, 94
37. EJ V:128
38. EJ VIII:379–380
39. TJ XII:387
40. EJ V:128
41. EW I:298
42. TJ V:365
43. Alcott *Journals* 261
44. EJ IX:16
45. TJ III:250
46. TJ XI:119–120
47. EJ V:251—corrected "woodmen" to "wordmen" as in EJMN VII:238
48. EL II:225
49. EL II:243
50. EL II:225
51. EL III:75
52. EW II:213
53. EL II:283
54. EJ V:425–426
55. TJ I:153
56. TJ I:154
57. TJ I:155
58. TJ VI:363
59. TJ I:156
60. TJ I:205
61. EW IX:23–24
62. TJ I:235
63. TJ I:242
64. EL II:402
65. Shelburne 5
66. EL II:402
67. TJ I:253
68. EL II:394
69. Fuller *Letters* 2:210
70. CCE I:335
71. EL II:402

72. EL II:393

73. EL II:398

74. EL II:394

75. EL II:402

76. EJ V:558

77. LJE 92

78. EL II:447

79. EJ VI:74

80. MS Am 1280H by permission of the Ralph Waldo Emerson Memorial Association and Houghton Library, Harvard University

81. Thoreau *Collected Poems* 394

82. TW I:307

83. TW I:163

84. LJE 99. Only two contemporary sources mention the specific injury. Lidian Emerson's letter, the only account written in the immediacy of John's death, clearly states it was his thumb. The only other detailed account, a letter written a few weeks later by an anonymous correspondent to William Stevens Robinson, states it was his left-hand ring finger.

85. LJE 99

86. LJE 100

87. EL II:20

88. LJE 99

89. LJE 100

90. Myerson 371

91. LJE 99

92. Emerson, Edward *Henry Thoreau* 26

93. EL III:4

94. EL III:4

95. TJ I:321

96. LJE 105

97. TC 66

98. TPJ 1:447

99. CCE I:359

100. Alcott, Louisa May "Reminiscences of Ralph Waldo Emerson" 284

101. EJ VI:150–151

102. EJ V:115

103. EJ VI:153

104. EW II:126

105. EJMN VIII:365

106. EW IX:92
107. EJ VI:153–154
108. CCE I:359
109. EW III:48
110. Fuller *Letters* III:175
111. EL III:238
112. ECW VIII:ccxxv
113. LJE 108
114. TW VI:42
115. LJE 108
116. TC 64–65
117. TW V:270
118. TC 63–64
119. TJ I:339
120. EJ VI:436
121. TJ I:340–341
122. EL III:47
123. Lathrop 53
124. EW I:143
125. TPC 72
126. EW I:136
127. EW III:216
128. TC 52
129. LJE 118
130. TC 76
131. LJE 121–122
132. LJE 122
133. LJE 126–127
134. EL III:139
135. TC 81
136. EL III:129
137. LJE 128
138. TC 84
139. LJE 129
140. TC 86–87
141. TC 87
142. TC 91
143. LJE 130
144. TC 126
145. TW VI:102–103
146. TC 78
147. TC 89

148. EL III:158
149. EL III:172
150. Hawthorne, Nathaniel 371
151. EL III:172
152. Hawthorne, Nathaniel 369
153. EJ VI:371
154. EJ VI:371
155. EL III:172
156. EL VII:544
157. TC 103
158. TC 103
159. TC 107
160. TC 107
161. TC 125
162. EJ VI:440–441
163. TC 137
164. TC 515
165. TC 139
166. TC 111–112
167. EL VII:547
168. TC 110
169. TC 112
170. TW VI:87
171. TW VI:87–89
172. TC 137
173. TC 146
174. EL III:229
175. TC 136
176. TW IV:370
177. TJ I:361
178. TW II:94
179. TW II:3
180. TJ I:433
181. EL III:338
182. EW III:257
183. EW I:91
184. EW III:67
185. EW I:95
186. TJ I:418
187. EJ V:195
188. TW IV:377
189. TW IV:377–378

190. Although many biographers favor Thoreau's Aunt Maria as the anonymous taxpayer, there is no conclusive evidence as to who this person was.
191. EW X:612
192. Alcott *Journals* 183
193. EJ VII:219
194. EJ VII:221–222
195. EJ VII:223
196. EJ VII:222. There is an apocryphal exchange between Emerson and Thoreau that supposedly took place outside the jail, with Emerson asking, "Henry, what are you doing in there?" and Thoreau responding, "Waldo, what are you doing out there?" That dialog did not take place.
197. Alcott *Journals* 150–151, 179
198. EJ VI:412
199. Lane 16
200. *Herald of Freedom*, August 16, 1844, quoted in Petrulionis 44
201. EJ IX:507
202. EW I:220
203. TW III:37
204. Alcott *Journals* 179
205. Emerson, Edward *Emerson in Concord* 127–128
206. EJ VII:499
207. EL III:411
208. TPC 1:314–315
209. TPJ 2:355
210. TJ I:431–432
211. TJ I:432–433
212. EL III:376
213. EL III:377–378
214. EL III:384
215. *The Literary World* (March 27, 1847) 185
216. EW V:26
217. TW II:101
218. TW IV:370
219. TW II:355
220. TJ I:226
221. EW I:96
222. TW VI:320–321
223. EJ IX:425
224. Her name was sometimes spelled Foord.
225. TC 190–191

226. Harding 227
227. Lillie 131
228. TC 189
229. TC 191
230. TC 195
231. EL IV:151
232. *The Massachusetts Quarterly* (December 1849) 50
233. TPJ 3:26
234. TJ V:459
235. LJE 138
236. EL VIII:135–136
237. TC 199
238. TC 205
239. TW VI:150
240. TW I:290
241. TW VI:151
242. TC 207
243. LJE 145
244. EL VIII:164
245. TC 228
246. EW X:616–617
247. TPJ 3:54
248. TPJ 3:57
249. EL VIII:236
250. EL VIII:242
251. TC 262
252. TC 265
253. EJ VIII:122
254. TJ III:140
255. TJ IV:445
256. TJ IX:337
257. TJ X:235
258. TJ X:252
259. TJ III:142
260. TJ III:217
261. MS Am 1280H by permission of the Ralph Waldo Emerson Memorial Association and Houghton Library, Harvard University
262. MS Am 1280H by permission of the Ralph Waldo Emerson Memorial Association and Houghton Library, Harvard University
263. EJ VIII:228

264. TJ III:61–62
265. EJ VIII:260
266. TJ III:133
267. TJ III:146–147
268. TJ III:148–149
269. TJ III:167–168
270. TJ III:214
271. TJ III:181
272. TJ III:256
273. TJ III:262
274. TJ IV:314
275. EJ VIII:303
276. EJ VIII:352
277. EJ VIII:396–397
278. EJ VIII:415
279. EJ VIII:375
280. EJ VIII:352–353
281. EJ VIII:293
282. EJ VIII:424
283. TW IV:458
284. EJ VIII:425—"one" added as in EJMN XIII:270
285. EL IV:459–460
286. EJ VIII:567
287. EJ IX:34
288. EJ IX:15–16
289. EJ IX:91–92
290. EL V:95
291. Emerson, Edward Waldo "Personal Recollections" 88–89
292. EW VI:215
293. EJ XI:268
294. TW IV:433
295. Alcott *Journals* 316
296. Alcott *Journals* 316
297. TJ XII:417
298. TW IV:438
299. EW VII:427
300. Slack
301. Slack
302. Alcott *Journals* 322
303. Sanborn "Thoreau" 215
304. Sanborn "Thoreau" 215–216
305. Sanborn "Thoreau" 216; TJ XIII:3–4

306. Emerson *Selected Lectures* 253
307. EJ VII:303
308. MS Am 1280H by permission of the Ralph Waldo Emerson Memorial Association and Houghton Library, Harvard University
309. Dall 243
310. EL III:183
311. EL III:183
312. Slater 1
313. TJ III:116
314. TJ III:114
315. EW XI:628
316. EW XI:630
317. EL IV:230
318. EW XI:628
319. TW VI:198
320. EW XII:60
321. EJ VI:210
322. Pratt
323. ETE I:216–217
324. TC 609
325. Dedmond 289
326. Dedmond 295
327. EL IX:47
328. TW VI:383–384
329. Collyer 295
330. Conway I:335
331. Brown 3
332. TC 625
333. Lathrop 420
334. Dedmond 301
335. Dedmond 306
336. Alcott *Journals* 343
337. Dedmond 307
338. EJ IX:360–361
339. EJ IX:425
340. EJ IX:405
341. EJ IX:413—corrected "peace.'" to "peace." as in EJMN XV:246
342. EJ IX:413–414—corrected "old-established" to "old, established"—"reserve" to "reserved" as in EJMN XV:247
343. *Daniel Ricketson and His Friends* 143

344. Cameron *Emerson, Thoreau and Concord* 320
345. Alcott, Louisa May *Selected Letters* 74–75
346. Thoreau, Sophia
347. TJ I:321
348. EW X:460–461
349. Marble 179
350. *Daniel Ricketson and His Friends*, 143
351. Fields 70
352. Alcott, Louisa May *Selected Letters* 74
353. EW X:480
354. EW X:480
355. EW X:484–485
356. King 45
357. TW I:178
358. Alcott *Journals* 349
359. EL V:279
360. ETE I:274
361. EJ IX:430
362. ETE I:274
363. Davis 35
364. Davis 44
365. ETE I:330
366. EJ X:65
367. EL VI:298
368. EJ IX:522
369. EJ VIII:303
370. Alcott *Journals* 448
371. "The Contributor's Club" *The Atlantic Monthly* (June 1903) 858–859
372. ETE II:274
373. Gilchrist 245
374. Barrus 181–182

Part II: Thoreau
1. TW I:274–307
2. TW VI:12–13
3. TJ I:38–39
4. TJ I:42–43
5. TJ I:52
6. TJ I:107
7. TJ I:107

8. TJ I:108
9. TJ I:108
10. TJ I:108
11. TJ I:108
12. TJ I:108
13. TJ I:113
14. TJ I:113
15. TJ I:115
16. TJ I:121
17. TJ I:125
18. TJ I:153
19. TJ I:154
20. TJ I:155
21. TJ I:181–182
22. TJ I:189
23. TJ I:197
24. TJ I:204
25. TJ I:205
26. TJ I:218
27. TJ I:218
28. TJ I:223
29. TJ I:242
30. TJ I:246
31. TJ I:248–249
32. TJ I:327
33. TJ I:328
34. TJ I:339–341
35. TJ I:348
36. TJ I:352
37. TJ I:442
38. TJ I:456
39. TJ I:462
40. TC 103
41. TW V:154
42. TC 110
43. TW VI:87–89
44. TPJ 2:245
45. TW VI:164
46. TW I:80–81
47. TW I:315
48. TW I:387

49. TW IV:379
50. TPJ 3:17
51. TPJ 3:18–19
52. TPJ 3:20
53. TPJ 3:20
54. TPJ 3:21
55. TPJ 3:26–27
56. TPJ 3:29–30
57. TPJ 3:39
58. TPJ 3:40
59. TPJ 3:40–41
60. TPJ 3:43
61. TPJ 3:45–46
62. TPJ 3:46–48
63. TPJ 3:57
64. TPJ 3:52
65. TPJ 3:53
66. TPJ 3:54
67. TPJ 3:57
68. TPJ 3:58
69. TPJ 3:58
70. TPJ 3:58
71. TJ II:33
72. TJ II:48
73. TJ II:78
74. TJ II:98
75. TJ II:109–110
76. TJ II:130
77. TJ II:143
78. TJ II:161–162
79. TPJ 3:202
80. TJ II:181
81. TJ II:183–184
82. TJ II:266
83. TJ II:302
84. TJ II:315
85. TJ II:392
86. TJ II:402–403
87. TJ III:133
88. TJ III:139
89. TJ III:140–142

90. TJ III:146–147
91. TJ III:148–149
92. TJ III:150
93. TJ III:167–168
94. TJ III:172–173
95. TJ III:184–185
96. TJ III:187–188
97. TJ III:400
98. TPJ 4:436
99. TJ IV:163
100. TJ IV:348
101. TW VI:199–204
102. TJ IV:359
103. TW VI:206
104. TJ IV:397
105. TJ IV:467–468
106. TJ V:19
107. TJ V:86–87
108. TJ V:187
109. TJ VI:80
110. TJ VI:124
111. TW II:149–150
112. TW II:155
113. TW II:182
114. TW II:361
115. TJ VII:416–417
116. TJ VIII:199
117. TJ VIII:230–232
118. TJ VIII:348
119. TJ IX:151
120. TJ IX:249–250
121. TJ IX:272
122. TJ IX:276–278
123. TJ IX:279
124. TJ IX:400
125. TJ IX:479–481
126. TJ X:126–127
127. TJ X:172
128. TJ X:190
129. TJ X:235
130. TJ X:252

131. TJ XI:274–275
132. TJ XI:281–283
133. TW VI:344–345
134. TJ XI:438
135. TJ XI:439
136. TJ XI:445
137. TJ XI:451–452
138. *Reform Papers* 188
139. TW V:234
140. TJ I:253
141. TW VI:56–58
142. TPJ 1:459
143. TPJ 2:355
144. TJ I:431–432
145. TJ I:432–433
146. TJ I:433
147. TW VI:151–152
148. TJ II:48
149. TW VI:187–188
150. TJ III:61–62
151. TJ III:83
152. TJ III:134–135
153. TJ III:150
154. TJ III:214
155. TJ III:216–217—corrected "you thought" to "your thought" as in Thoreau, *I to Myself* 127
156. TJ III:218–219
157. TJ III:250
158. TJ III:256–260—corrected "——— [sic]" to "Emerson" as in TPJ 4:309
159. TJ III:262–265
160. TJ III:304
161. TJ III:389–390
162. TW VI:197
163. TJ IV:313–315—corrected "papillaceous feelers" to "papillary-feelers" as in Thoreau, *I to Myself* 164
164. TJ V:188
165. TJ V:365
166. TJ VI:15
167. TJ XI:77
168. TJ XI:119–120

Part III: Emerson

1. EW II:189–217
2. EJ III:100
3. EJ III:268
4. EJ III:311
5. EJ III:477
6. MS Am 1280H by permission of the Ralph Waldo Emerson Memorial Association and Houghton Library, Harvard University
7. EJ IV:3–4
8. EJ IV:39
9. EW I:46
10. EJ IV:62
11. EJ IV:67–68
12. CCE I:97
13. EJ IV:205
14. EJ IV:343
15. EJ IV:394
16. EJ V:32–33
17. EJ V:35
18. EJ V:80
19. EJ V:241
20. *Letters from Ralph Waldo Emerson to a Friend* 11–12
21. EJ V:320
22. *Topical Notebooks* III:176
23. *Letters from Ralph Waldo Emerson to a Friend* 16–17
24. EJ V:330
25. EJ V:342
26. EL II:242
27. CCE I:259
28. *Letters from Ralph Waldo Emerson to a Friend* 19–20
29. EW II:414
30. EJ V:417
31. EJ V:426
32. EJ V:430
33. EJ V:451–452 with additional material ("I must do nothing" to "farm in Illinois") from MS Am 1280H by permission of the Ralph Waldo Emerson Memorial Association and Houghton Library, Harvard University
34. EW II:307
35. EJ V:455

36. EW I:244
37. EL VII:447
38. EW X:390
39. EW II:145
40. EW II:160
41. EW II:125
42. EW IX:83
43. Emerson *Early Lectures* III:379
44. EW I:346
45. EW I:347
46. EJ VI:221
47. EJ VI:244
48. MS Am 1280H by permission of the Ralph Waldo Emerson Memorial Association and Houghton Library, Harvard University
49. *Letters from Ralph Waldo Emerson to a Friend* 48–49
50. EJ VI:348
51. EJ VI:348
52. EJ VI:436
53. EJ VI:364
54. EJ VI:411
55. EJ VI:367
56. *Topical Notebooks* III:147
57. *Topical Notebooks* III:147
58. EW III:56
59. EW III:102–103
60. EW III:111
61. EW III:112
62. EW III:113
63. EW III:164
64. EW III:189
65. EW III:244
66. EW IX:352
67. EW IX:352
68. EJ VII:30
69. MS Am 1280H by permission of the Ralph Waldo Emerson Memorial Association and Houghton Library, Harvard University
70. EJ VII:140
71. EJ VII:141
72. EW IX:78

73. EJ VII:246
74. EJ VII:346
75. EW V:310–311
76. EW IV:15
77. MS Am 1280H by permission of the Ralph Waldo Emerson Memorial Association and Houghton Library, Harvard University
78. EW VI:41
79. EW VI:124
80. EJ VIII:292–293
81. EJ VIII:447
82. CCE II:231
83. MS Am 1280H by permission of the Ralph Waldo Emerson Memorial Association and Houghton Library, Harvard University
84. EW XI:436
85. EW VIII:190
86. EW VII:128
87. EW VI:268
88. EW VI:73–74
89. EJ IX:272
90. EJ IX:273
91. EW X:141
92. EW VI:187
93. EW VI:192
94. EW VI:272
95. EW VI:273
96. EW VI:273
97. EJ IX:329
98. EJ IX:538
99. EJ IX:575
100. EJ IX:577
101. EJ X:11
102. EW VIII:89
103. EW VIII:92
104. EW VII:228
105. EW XI:480
106. EW XI:503
107. EW XII:176
108. EW IX:371
109. Sanborn *Henry D. Thoreau* 53–54

110. EJ IV:394–395
111. EJ IV:397
112. EJ IV:406
113. EJ IV:432
114. Sanborn *Henry D. Thoreau* 59
115. EJMN VIII:257, note 19
116. EL II:154
117. EJ V:36–37
118. EJ V:128–129
119. EL II:182
120. EJ V:208
121. EJ V:241
122. CCE I:256
123. EJ V:251—corrected "woodmen" to "wordmen" as in EJMN VII:238
124. EL II:225
125. EJ V:282
126. EL II:244
127. Scott 60
128. EJ V:339
129. EJ V:414
130. CCE I:335
131. EL II:402
132. EJ V:557–558
133. EJ VI:74
134. EL II:447
135. MS Am 1280H by permission of the Ralph Waldo Emerson Memorial Association and Houghton Library, Harvard University
136. EL III:75
137. EJ VI:152–153
138. EJ VI:199–200
139. EJ VI:298
140. EJ VI:304
141. EJ VI:371
142. EL III:172
143. EJ VI:440–441
144. EJ VI:467–468
145. MS Am 1280H by permission of the Ralph Waldo Emerson Memorial Association and Houghton Library, Harvard University

146. EJ VI:496—corrected "done" to "due" as in EJMN IX:77
147. EJ VI:515
148. EJ VI:515
149. EJ VII:17
150. MS Am 1280H by permission of the Ralph Waldo Emerson Memorial Association and Houghton Library, Harvard University
151. EJ VII:78
152. EJ VII:99
153. EJ VII:155
154. EJ VII:157—corrected "astronomy" to "astronomers" as in EJMN IX:366
155. EJ VII:184–185
156. EJ VII:209–210—corrected "excitement" to "excitant" as in EJMN IV:434
157. EJ VII:211
158. EL III:338
159. EJ VII:219
160. EJ VII:241
161. EL III:376
162. EL III:377–378
163. EJ VII:265
164. EL III:384
165. EJ VII:303
166. EJ VII:321
167. Furness 60–61
168. TC 205
169. EJ VII:386
170. EJ VII:405
171. EW X:616–617
172. EJ VII:498
173. EJ VII:499
174. EJ VII:526
175. EJ VII:521
176. EJ VII:551–552
177. EJ VII:557–558
178. MS Am 1280H by permission of the Ralph Waldo Emerson Memorial Association and Houghton Library, Harvard University
179. EJ VIII:62
180. EJ VIII:90

181. MS Am 1280H by permission of the Ralph Waldo Emerson Memorial Association and Houghton Library, Harvard University
182. EJ VIII:122
183. EJ VIII:131
184. EJ VIII:135–137
185. EJ VIII:178
186. EJ VIII:227–228
187. MS Am 1280H by permission of the Ralph Waldo Emerson Memorial Association and Houghton Library, Harvard University
188. EJ VIII:260
189. MS Am 1280H by permission of the Ralph Waldo Emerson Memorial Association and Houghton Library, Harvard University
190. EJ VIII:273
191. EJ VIII:292
192. EJ VIII:293
193. EJ VIII:294
194. EJ VIII:300
195. EJ VIII:303
196. EJ VIII:305–306
197. EJ VIII:307
198. MS Am 1280H by permission of the Ralph Waldo Emerson Memorial Association and Houghton Library, Harvard University
199. EJ VIII:339
200. EJ VIII:352—corrected "at home" to "is at home" as in EJMN XIII:128
201. EJ VIII:352–353
202. EJ VIII:375
203. EJ VIII:396–397
204. EJ VIII:379–380—corrected "the day" to "the boys" as in EJMN XIII:187
205. EJ VIII:414
206. EJ VIII:415
207. EL IV:388
208. EJ VIII:424–425—"one" added as in EJMN XIII:270
209. EJ VIII:450
210. EL VIII:399
211. EL IV:459–460

212. EJ VIII:467
213. EJ VIII:567
214. EJ VIII:569
215. EJ IX:15–16
216. EJ IX:34
217. EJ IX:43–45
218. EJ IX:47–48
219. EJ IX:49
220. EJ IX:59–60
221. EJ IX:18–19
222. EJMN XIV:125, note 22
223. EJ IX:91–92
224. EJ IX:96–97—corrected "sand" to "land" as in EJMN XIV:145
225. EJ IX:99
226. EJ IX:100
227. MS Am 1280H by permission of the Ralph Waldo Emerson Memorial Association and Houghton Library, Harvard University
228. EJ IX:113
229. EJ IX:117
230. EJ IX:123
231. EL V:95
232. EJ IX:143–144
233. EJ IX:144
234. EJ IX:152–154
235. EJ IX:247
236. Slack
237. EJ IX:270
238. EJ IX: 274–275
239. EJ IX:295–296
240. MS Am 1280H by permission of the Ralph Waldo Emerson Memorial Association and Houghton Library, Harvard University
241. EJ IX:306–307
242. EJ IX:304
243. EJ IX:341
244. EJ IX:360–361
245. EJ IX:401
246. EJ IX:401–402
247. EJ IX:404

248. EJ IX:404–405

249. EJ IX:413–414—corrected "'Never" to "Never"—"peace.'" to "peace.'"—"old-established" to "old, established"— "revered" to "reserved" as in EJMN XV:247

250. EJ IX:414–415

251. EJ IX:416

252. EJ IX:425

253. MS Am 1280H by permission of the Ralph Waldo Emerson Memorial Association and Houghton Library, Harvard University

254. MS Am 1280H by permission of the Ralph Waldo Emerson Memorial Association and Houghton Library, Harvard University

255. EJ IX:427—corrected "style of Henry" to "style" as in EJMN XV:264

256. EJ IX:427

257. MS Am 1280H by permission of the Ralph Waldo Emerson Memorial Association and Houghton Library, Harvard University

258. MS Am 1280H by permission of the Ralph Waldo Emerson Memorial Association and Houghton Library, Harvard University

259. EJ IX:430

260. Davis 44

261. EJ IX:507

262. EJ IX:522

263. EJ IX:524

264. EJ IX:531–532

265. EJ IX:551

266. EW VIII:290

267. MS Am 1280H by permission of the Ralph Waldo Emerson Memorial Association and Houghton Library, Harvard University

268. EJ X:59

269. EJ X:65

270. EL V:424

271. MS Am 1280H by permission of the Ralph Waldo Emerson Memorial Association and Houghton Library, Harvard University

272. EJ X:311–312

273. MS Am 1280H by permission of the Ralph Waldo

Emerson Memorial Association and Houghton Library, Harvard University

274. EJ X:340
275. EJ X:341–342
276. King 45–46
277. MS Am 1280H by permission of the Ralph Waldo Emerson Memorial Association and Houghton Library, Harvard University
278. EW XI:500
279. King 50
280. EL VI:298
281. "The Contributor's Club" *The Atlantic Monthly* (June 1903) 858–859; dating from EL VI:302
282. EW X:451–485

Bibliography

Albee, John. *Remembrances of Emerson*. New York: Robert G. Cooke, 1901.

Alcott, Bronson. *The Journals of Bronson Alcott*. Selected and edited by Odell Shepard. Boston: Little, Brown, 1938.

———. *The Letters of A. Bronson Alcott*. Edited by Richard L. Herrnstadt. Ames, IA: Iowa State University Press, 1969.

Alcott, Louisa May. "Reminiscences of Ralph Waldo Emerson" in *Some Noted Princes, Authors & Statesmen of Our Time*. Edited by James Parton. Norwich, CT: Henry Bell, 1886.

———. *The Selected Letters of Louisa May Alcott*. Edited by Joel Myerson and Daniel Shealy. Boston: Little, Brown, 1987.

Allen, Gay Wilson. *Waldo Emerson: A Biography*. New York: The Viking Press, 1981.

Barrus, Clara. *Whitman and Burroughs: Comrades*. Boston: Houghton Mifflin, 1931.

Borst, Raymond R. *The Thoreau Log: A Documentary Life of Henry David Thoreau, 1817–1862*. New York: G.K. Hall, 1992.

Brown, Simon. "Simon Brown's Journal." *Thoreau Society Bulletin* (Summer 1961).

Cameron, Kenneth Walter. *Emerson, Thoreau, and Concord in Early Newspapers: Biographical and Historical Lore for the Scholar and General Reader*. Hartford, CT: Transcendental Books, 1958.

———. "Thoreau and Emerson in Channing's Letters to the Watsons." *Emerson Society Quarterly*, XIV (1959).

———. *The Transcendentalists and Minerva*. Hartford, CT: Transcendental Books, 1958.

Carlyle, Thomas. *The Correspondence of Thomas Carlyle and Ralph Waldo Emerson, 1834–1872*. London: Chatto & Windus, 1883.

Channing, William Ellery II. *Thoreau, the Poet-Naturalist: With Memorial Verses*. New edition, enlarged and edited by F. B. Sanborn. Boston: C. E. Goodspeed, 1902.

Collyer, Robert. *Clear Grit: A Collection of Lectures, Addresses and Poems*. Boston: Beacon Press, 1913.

"The Contributor's Club." *The Atlantic Monthly* (June 1903).

Conway, Daniel Moncure. *Autobiographies, Memories and Experiences*. Boston: Houghton Mifflin, 1904.

Dall, Caroline. *Historical Pictures Retouched: A Volume of Miscellanies*. Boston: Walker, Wise, 1860.

Daniel Ricketson and His Friends: Letters, Poems, Sketches, etc. Edited by Anna and Walton Ricketson. Boston: Houghton, Mifflin, 1902.

Davis, Rebecca Harding. *Bits of Gossip*. Boston: Houghton Mifflin, 1904.

Dean, Bradley P., and Ronald Wesley Hoag. "Thoreau's Lectures After Walden: An Annotated Calendar." *Studies in the American Renaissance*, 1996.

———. "Thoreau's Lectures Before Walden: An Annotated Calendar." *Studies in the American Renaissance* (1995).

Dedmond, Francis B. "The Selected Letter of William Ellery Channing the Younger (Part Three)." *Studies in the American Renaissance* (1991).

The Dial: A Magazine for Literature, Philosophy, and Religion. Boston: Weeks, Jordan, 1840–1844; reprinted, New York: Russell and Russell, 1961.

Emerson, Edward Waldo. *Emerson in Concord: A Memoir*

Written for the "Social Circle" in Concord, Massachusetts.
Boston: Houghton Mifflin, 1889.

———. *Henry Thoreau as Remembered by a Young Friend.*
Boston: Houghton Mifflin, 1917.

———. "Personal Recollections," *The Bookman* (London),
June 1917, quoted as "A Different Drummer" in *Henry
David Thoreau: A Profile*. Edited by Walter Harding.
New York: Hill and Wang, 1971.

Emerson, Ellen Tucker. *The Letters of Ellen Tucker Emerson*. Edited by Edith E. W. Gregg; foreword by Gay
Wilson Allen. Kent, OH: Kent State University Press,
1982. 2 vols.

Emerson, Lidian Jackson. *The Selected Letters of Lidian Jackson Emerson*. Edited with an introduction by Delores
Bird Carpenter. Columbia: University of Missouri
Press, 1987.

Emerson, Ralph Waldo: *The Collected Works of Ralph Waldo
Emerson*. Cambridge: Harvard University Press, 1971– .

———. *The Complete Works of Ralph Waldo Emerson*. With a
biographical introduction and notes by Edward Waldo
Emerson. Boston: Houghton, Mifflin and Company,
1903–04. 12 vols.

———. *Early Lectures of Ralph Waldo Emerson*. Edited by
Stephen E. Whicher and Robert E. Spiller. Cambridge:
Harvard University Press, 1959–1972. 3 vols.

———. The Journals and Miscellaneous Notebooks of
Ralph Waldo Emerson. Edited by William H. Gilman et al. Cambridge: Harvard University Press,
1960–1982.

———. *Journals of Ralph Waldo Emerson: 1820–1872*. Edited by Edward Waldo Emerson and Waldo Emerson
Forbes. Cambridge: Riverside Press, 1909–1914. 10
vols.

———. *Letters from Ralph Waldo Emerson to a Friend,*

1838–1853. Edited by Charles Eliot Norton. Boston: Houghton, Mifflin, 1899.

———. *Letters of Ralph Waldo Emerson*. Edited by Ralph L. Rusk and Eleanor M. Tilton. New York: Columbia University Press, 1939, 1990–95. 10 vols.

———. *The Selected Lectures of Ralph Waldo Emerson*. Edited by Ronald A. Bosco and Joel Myerson. Athens: The University of Georgia Press, 2005.

———. *The Topical Notebooks of Ralph Waldo Emerson*. Edited by Susan Sutton Smith et al. Columbia: University of Missouri Press, 1990–1994. 3 vols.

Emerson in His Own Time: A Biographical Chronicle of His Life, Drawn from Recollections, Interviews, and Memoirs by Family, Friends, and Associates. Edited by Ronald A. Bosco and Joel Myerson. Iowa City: University of Iowa Press, 2003.

Fields, Annie. *Authors and Friends*. Boston: Houghton, Mifflin, 1897.

Fuller, Margaret. *The Letters of Margaret Fuller*. Edited by Robert N. Hudspeth. Ithaca, NY: Cornell University Press, 1983–1994. 6 vols.

———. *Memoirs of Margaret Fuller Ossoli*. Edited by R. W. Emerson, W. H. Channing, and J. F. Clarke. Boston: Phillips, Sampson, 1852. 2 vols.

Furness, William Henry. *Records of a Lifelong Friendship*. Boston: Houghton Mifflin, 1910.

Gilchrist, Anne Burrows. *Anne Gilchrist: Her Life and Writings*. Edited by Herbert Harlakendend Gilchrist. London: Fisher Unwin, 1887.

Harding, Walter. *The Days of Henry Thoreau*. New York: Knopf, 1965.

Haskins, David Greene. *Ralph Waldo Emerson: His Maternal Ancestors, with Some Reminiscences of Him*. Boston: Cupples, Upham, 1887.

348 ❧ BIBLIOGRAPHY

Hawthorne, Julian. *The Memoirs of Julian Hawthorne*. Edited by Edith Garrigues Hawthorne. New York: Macmillan, 1938.

Hawthorne, Nathaniel. *The American Note-Books*. Edited by Claude M. Simpson. Columbus: Ohio State University, 1972.

Howard, Leon. *Victorian Knight Errant*. Berkeley: University of California, 1952.

Howarth, William L. *The Literary Manuscripts of Henry David Thoreau*. Columbus: Ohio State University Press, 1974.

Johnson, Linck C. *Thoreau's Complex Weave: The Writing of A Week on the Concord and Merrimack Rivers, with the Text of the First Draft*. Charlottesville: Published for the Bibliographical Society of the University of Virginia, by the University Press of Virginia, 1986.

King, Pendleton. "Notes of Conversation with Emerson." *Lippincott's Magazine* (January 1884).

"Lake Philosophy," *Worcester [Massachusetts] Palladium* (May 2, 1849).

Lane, Charles. "State Slavery—Imprisonment of A. Bronson Alcott—Dawn of Liberty." *The Liberator* (January 27, 1843).

Lathrop, Rose Hawthorne. *Memories of Hawthorne*. Boston: Houghton Mifflin, 1897.

Lillie, B.C., and Arthur Wyman. *Elizabeth Buffum Chace*. Boston: W.B. Clarke, 1914.

The Literary World. New York: Osgood & Co., 1847–1853.

Lowell, James Russell. *A Fable for Critics*. New York: G.P. Putnam, 1848.

———. "A Week on the Concord and Merrimack Rivers." *The Massachusetts Quarterly* (December 1849).

Marble, Annie Russell. *Thoreau: His Home, Friends and Books*. New York: T. Y. Crowell, 1902.

Marshall, Megan. *Margaret Fuller: A New American Life*. Boston: Houghton Mifflin, 2013.

Matteson, John. *Eden's Outcasts: The Story of Louisa May Alcott and Her Father.* New York: W.W. Norton, 2007.

McAleer, John. *Ralph Waldo Emerson: Days of Encounter.* Boston: Little, Brown, 1984.

Myerson, Joel. "Barzillai Frost's Funeral Sermon on the Death of John Thoreau Jr." *The Huntington Library Quarterly* (1994).

Petrulionis, Sandra Harbert. *To Set This World Right: The Antislavery Movement in Thoreau's Concord.* Ithaca, NY: Cornell University Press, 2006.

Pratt, Anna (Alcott). *Anna Alcott Pratt Diary (1859–1862).* Transcribed and annotated by Ray Angelo. 2018. www.ray-a.com/AnnaAlcottPrattDiary.pdf.

Reynolds, David S. *John Brown, Abolitionist.* New York: Alfred A. Knopf, 2005.

Richardson, Robert D., Jr. *Emerson: The Mind on Fire.* Berkeley: University of California Press, 1995.

———. *Henry Thoreau: A Life of the Mind.* Berkeley: University of California Press, 1986.

Sanborn, Franklin Benjamin. *Henry D. Thoreau.* Boston: Houghton Mifflin, 1882.

———. *The Life of Henry David Thoreau: Including Many Essays Hitherto Unpublished, and Some Account of His Family and Friends.* Boston: Houghton Mifflin, 1917.

———. *Recollections of Seventy Years.* Boston: Gorham, 1909.

———. "Reminiscences of Hawthorne, Emerson, Thoreau and the Alcotts." Maine Library Association. *Papers and Proceedings* (1907).

———. "Thoreau." *Harvard Register* (April 1881).

———. "An Unpublished Concord Journal." *Century Magazine* (April 1922).

Scott, Leonora Cranch. *The Life and Letters of Christopher Pearse Cranch.* Boston: Houghton Mifflin, 1917.

Shelburne, Steven R. "A Reminiscence of Emerson and Thoreau." *The Thoreau Society Bulletin* (Autumn 1991).

Slack, Charles W. Ralph Waldo Emerson to Charles W. Slack, October 31, 1859, Charles W. Slack Papers, American Antiquarian Society.

Slater, Joseph. "Caroline Dall in Concord." *Thoreau Society Bulletin* (Winter 1958).

Smith, Elizabeth Oakes. *Selections from the Autobiography of Elizabeth Oakes Smith*. Edited by Mary Alice Wyman. Lewiston, ME: Lewiston Journal Co., 1924.

Smith, Harmon. *My Friend, My Friend: The Story of Thoreau's Relationship with Emerson*. Amherst, MA: University of Massachusetts Press, 1999.

Thoreau, Henry D. *Collected Poems of Henry Thoreau*. Enlarged edition. Edited by Carl Bode. Baltimore: The Johns Hopkins Press, 1965.

————. *The Correspondence of Henry D. Thoreau*. Edited by Robert N. Hudspeth. Princeton: Princeton University Press, 2013– .

————. *The Correspondence of Henry David Thoreau*. Edited by Walter Harding and Carl Bode. New York: New York University Press, 1958.

————. *Essays: A Fully Annotated Edition*. Edited by Jeffrey S. Cramer. New Haven: Yale University Press, 2013.

————. *The First and Last Journeys of Thoreau: Lately Discovered Among his Unpublished Journals and Manuscripts*. Edited by Franklin Benjamin Sanborn. Boston: The Bibliophile Society, 1905.

————. *I to Myself: An Annotated Selection from the Journal of Henry D. Thoreau*. Edited by Jeffrey S. Cramer. New Haven, CT: Yale University Press, 2007.

————. *Journal*. Edited by John C. Broderick et al. Princeton, NJ: Princeton University Press, 1981– .

————. *The Journal of Henry Thoreau*. Ed. Bradford Torrey

and Francis H. Allen. Boston: Houghton Mifflin, 1906. 14 vols.

———. *Reform Papers*. Edited by Wendell Glick. Princeton, NJ: Princeton University Press, 1973.

———. *Walden: A Fully Annotated Edition*. Edited by Jeffrey S. Cramer. New Haven: Yale University Press, 2004.

———. *The Writings of Henry D. Thoreau*. Boston: Houghton Mifflin, 1906.

Thoreau, Sophia. Sophia Thoreau to Mary Anne Dunbar, May 22, 1862 (The Thoreau Society Archives in the Thoreau Society Collections at the Walden Woods Project's Thoreau Institute Library).

Thoreau in His Own Time: A Biographical Chronicle of His Life, Drawn from Recollections, Interviews, and Memoirs by Family, Friends, and Associates. Edited by Sandra Harbert Petrulionis. Iowa City: University of Iowa Press, 2012.

Tilton, Eleanor. "Emerson's Lecture Schedule 1837–8 Revised." *Harvard Library Bulletin* 21 (October 1973).

Von Frank, Albert J. *An Emerson Chronology*. 2nd ed., revised and enlarged. Albuquerque: Studio Non Troppo, 2016.

Walls, Laura Dassow. *Henry David Thoreau: A Life*. Chicago: The University of Chicago Press, 2017.

JEFFREY S. CRAMER is the editor of *Walden: A Fully Annotated Edition*, winner of a 2004 National Outdoor Book Award, and *The Quotable Thoreau*, recipient of an Umhoefer Prize for Achievement in Humanities. In 2017, Cramer was the historical consultant for the Ken Burns–produced documentary *Walden*, created for the Walden Pond State Reservation during the Thoreau Bicentennial. Cramer is the curator of collections at Walden Woods Project's Thoreau Institute Library. He lives in Maynard, Massachusetts. Find out more at jeffreyscramer.com.